P9-CMS-085

SIXTH EDITION
INTERACTIONS
Reading

2

cause, and effect
problem - solution
comparison/contrast
opinion or argument
classification

coined
~~coni~~

Quotation marks " "

Parentheses ( )
  ↳ Parenthesis

Elaine Kirn

Pamela Hartmann

Lawrence J. Zwier
Contributor, Focus on Testing

156
204

Interactions 2 Reading, Sixth Edition

5 6 7 8 9 0 DOW/DOW 1 0 9 8 7 6 5

ISBN: 978-0-07-759510-4
MHID: 0-07-759510-6

Senior Vice President, Products & Markets: Kurt L. Strand
Vice President, General Manager, Products & Markets: Michael J. Ryan
Vice President, Content Production & Technology Services: Kimberly Meriwether David
Director of Development: Valerie Kelemen
Marketing Manager: Cambridge University Press
Lead Project Manager: Rick Hecker
Senior Buyer: Michael R. McCormick
Designer: Page2, LLC
Cover/Interior Designer: Page2, LLC
Senior Content Licensing Specialist: Keri Johnson
Manager, Digital Production: Janean A. Utley
Compositor: Page2, LLC
Printer: RR Donnelley

Cover photo: Rechitan Sorin/Shutterstock.com

All credits appearing on page iv or at the end of the book are considered to be an extension of the copyright page.

The Internet addresses listed in the text were accurate at the time of publication. The inclusion of a website does not indicate an endorsement by the authors or McGraw-Hill, and McGraw-Hill does not guarantee the accuracy of the information presented at these sites.

www.mhhe.com

www.elt.mcgraw-hill.com

A Special Thank You

The Interactions/Mosaic 6th edition team wishes to thank our extended team: teachers, students, administrators, and teacher trainers, all of whom contributed invaluably to the making of this edition.

Maiko Berger, **Ritsumeikan Asia Pacific University**, Oita, Japan • Aaron Martinson, **Sejong Cyber University**, Seoul, Korea • Aisha Osman, Egypt • Amy Stotts, **Chubu University**, Aichi, Japan • Charles Copeland, **Dankook University**, Yongin City, Korea • Christen Savage, **University of Houston**, Texas, USA • Daniel Fitzgerald, **Metropolitan Community College**, Kansas, USA • Deborah Bollinger, **Aoyama Gakuin University**, Tokyo, Japan • Duane Fitzhugh, **Northern Virginia Community College**, Virginia, USA • Gregory Strong, **Aoyama Gakuin University**, Tokyo, Japan • James Blackwell, **Ritsumeikan Asia Pacific University**, Oita, Japan • Janet Harclerode, **Santa Monica College**, California, USA • Jinyoung Hong, **Sogang University**, Seoul, Korea • Lakkana Chaisaklert, **Rajamangala University of Technology Krung Thep**, Bangkok, Thailand • Lee Wonhee, **Sogang University**, Seoul, Korea • Matthew Gross, **Konkuk University**, Seoul, Korea • Matthew Stivener, **Santa Monica College**, California, USA • Pawadee Srisang, **Burapha University**, Chantaburi, Thailand • Steven M. Rashba, **University of Bridgeport**, Connecticut, USA • Sudatip Prapunta, **Prince of Songkla University**, Trang, Thailand • Tony Carnerie, **University of California San Diego**, California, USA

Photo Credits

Text Credits

Table of Contents

A 21st-Century Course for the Modern Student

Interactions/Mosaic prepares students for university classes by fully integrating every aspect of student life. Based on 28 years of classroom-tested best practices, the new and revised content, fresh modern look, and new online component make this the perfect series for contemporary classrooms.

Proven Instruction that Ensures Academic Success

Modern Content:
From social networking to gender issues and from academic honesty to discussions of Skype, *Interactions/Mosaic* keeps students connected to learning by selecting topics that are interesting and relevant to modern students.

Digital Component:
The fully integrated online course offers a rich environment that expands students' learning and supports teachers' teaching with automatically graded practice, assessment, classroom presentation tools, online community, and more.

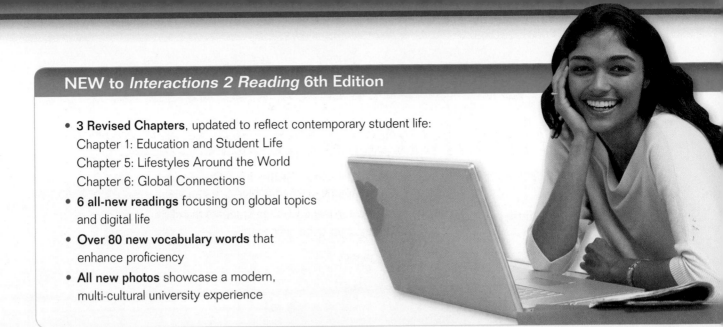

NEW to *Interactions 2 Reading* 6th Edition

- **3 Revised Chapters**, updated to reflect contemporary student life:
  Chapter 1: Education and Student Life
  Chapter 5: Lifestyles Around the World
  Chapter 6: Global Connections
- **6 all-new readings** focusing on global topics and digital life
- **Over 80 new vocabulary words** that enhance proficiency
- **All new photos** showcase a modern, multi-cultural university experience

Emphasis on Vocabulary:

Each chapter teaches vocabulary intensively and comprehensively. This focus on learning new words is informed by more than 28 years of classroom testing and provides students with the exact language they need to communicate confidently and fluently.

Practical Critical Thinking:

Students develop their ability to synthesize, analyze, and apply information from different sources in a variety of contexts: from comparing academic articles to negotiating informal conversations.

Highlights of *Interactions 2 Reading* 6th Edition

Part 1: Reading Skills and Strategies
Each chapter begins with a text on an engaging, academic topic and teaches students the skills that they need to be successful.

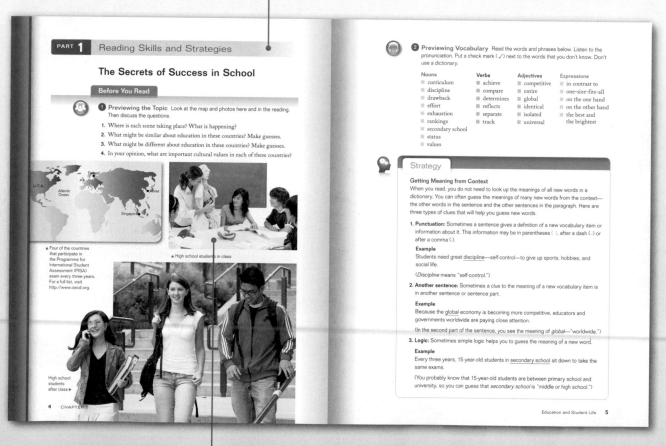

Communication for the Modern Student
A focus on real-life and academic communication based on engaging readings prepares students for success in school and in life.

Main Ideas and Details

Students are challenged by a second text and learn crucial reading skills like skimming for main ideas and finding supporting details.

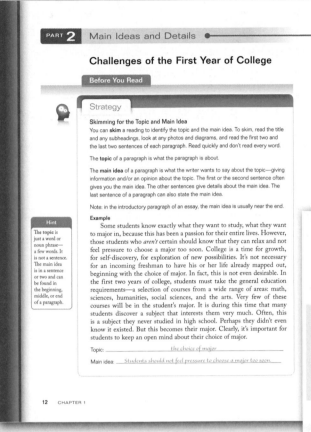

Topics for the Modern Student

Engaging social and academic topics draw the student in, making learning more engaging and more efficient.

Talk it Over

6 Beyond the Text: Interviewing Interview five people. Ask them their opinions about positive and negative aspects of the educational system in their country. Take notes on their answers. When you finish, report your findings to the class.

PART 3 Building Vocabulary and Study Skills

F☺CUS

The Academic Word List

There is a list of words that college students must know because these words occur frequently in academic English. This is called the "Academic Word List." In Part 3 of each chapter of this book, there is an activity to help you focus on these words. In the Self-Assessment Log at the end of each chapter, these words have an asterisk (*) next to them. For more information on the Academic Word List, see http://www.victoria.ac.nz/lals/resources/academicwordlist/.

1 Focusing on Words from the Academic Word List In this exercise, fill in the blanks with words from the Academic Word List in the box.

assignments	credits	obvious	resources
challenging	finally	required	schedule

Challenges of the First Year of College

B   Many students who are beginning college—even students who were very successful in high school—find that the classes are suddenly much more _____ than in high school and that much more studying
1
is _____. Educators usually agree on the solution to this
2
problem of too much work: you need to get organized. First, choose wisely the combination of classes you take in any one semester. Balance harder ones with easier ones. Also, limit the number of classes you take. Don't try to take more than a full-time load of _____ in the first
3

Education and Student Life   **17**

Part 3: Building Vocabulary and Study Skills   Extensive vocabulary exercises introduce language that is encountered in and out of the classroom.

---

semester. Second, keep a careful calendar of dates for all exams and when all _____ are due. Professors will hand out a page with these   10
4
dates on the first day of class; put them immediately on your master calendar and plan ahead. Third, _____ regular time and find a quiet
5
place in which to study so that you won't have to suddenly cram the day before an important exam. You might pass a test by cramming for it, but you won't remember much afterward—and this isn't true learning. Fourth, form   15
a study group with students in some of your classes, and meet with them once or twice a week. Also, take advantage of the _____ on
6
campus such as tutors or the writing center. Fifth, although this might seem _____, it's important to go to class. Some students believe they
7
can pass by simply doing the reading and taking exams, but this isn't true.   20
_____, it's essential to include breaks—short ones and longer
8
ones—to balance study time with time for fun. This will keep your mind fresh and clear.

2 Recognizing Word Meanings Match the words with their meanings. Write the letters on the lines, as in the example.

Column A	Column B
1. _e_ global	a. work or energy
2. _____ achieve	b. list of people or things in order
3. _____ reflect	c. courses and topics that students study
4. _____ effort	d. self-control
5. _____ drawback	e. worldwide
6. _____ status	f. whole
7. _____ discipline	g. decide on
8. _____ curriculum	h. show
9. _____ ranking	i. the same
10. _____ entire	j. get or reach (something) by working hard
11. _____ identical	k. disadvantage
12. _____ determine	l. social position

18   CHAPTER 1

Emphasis on Vocabulary

Each chapter presents, practices, and carefully recycles vocabulary-learning strategies and vocabulary words essential to the modern student.

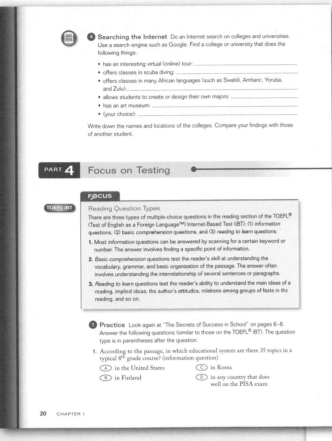

4 Searching the Internet Do an Internet search on colleges and universities. Use a search engine such as Google. Find a college or university that does the following things:

- has an interesting virtual (online) tour: _____
- offers classes in scuba diving: _____
- offers classes in many African languages (such as Swahili, Amharic, Yoruba, and Zulu): _____
- allows students to create or design their own majors: _____
- has an art museum: _____
- (your choice): _____

Write down the names and locations of the colleges. Compare your findings with those of another student.

PART 4 Focus on Testing

FOCUS

TOEFL® iBT

Reading Question Types
There are three types of multiple-choice questions in the reading section of the TOEFL® (Test of English as a Foreign Language™) Internet-Based Test (iBT): (1) *information* questions, (2) basic *comprehension* questions, and (3) *reading to learn* questions.

1. Most *information* questions can be answered by scanning for a certain keyword or number. The answer involves finding a specific point of information.

2. *Basic comprehension* questions test the reader's skill at understanding the vocabulary, grammar, and basic organization of the passage. The answer often involves understanding the interrelationship of several sentences or paragraphs.

3. *Reading to learn* questions test the reader's ability to understand the main ideas of a reading, implied ideas, the author's attitude, relations among groups of facts in the reading, and so on.

1 Practice Look again at "The Secrets of Success in School" on pages 6–8. Answer the following questions (similar to those on the TOEFL® iBT). The question type is in parentheses after the question.

1. According to the passage, in which educational system are there 35 topics in a typical 8th grade course? (information question)
   Ⓐ in the United States   Ⓒ in Korea
   Ⓑ in Finland   Ⓓ in any country that does well on the PISA exam

20   CHAPTER 1

2. Which of the following is closest in meaning to *exhaustion*, as it is used in Paragraph C? (basic comprehension question)
   Ⓐ success   Ⓒ tiredness
   Ⓑ self-c...   ...lack of friendship

...and are tired all th... ...s from reading Paragraph

3. W...
   Ⓑ Their classes are easy.   ...stress.
                                      ...t their

Self-Assessment Log

Read the lists below. Check (✓) the strategies and
this chapter. Look through the chapter or ask your i...
and words that you do not understand.

Reading and Vocabulary-Building Strategies
☐ Previewing vocabulary   ☐ Orga...
☐ Getting meaning from context   T-C...
☐ Identifying the main idea   ☐ S...
☐ Understanding reading structure ☐ ...sions

Target Vocabulary
■ di...   ...n contrast to ...one-size-fits-all
■ effort   ...on the one hand
■ exhaustion   ...obvious*   ...on the other hand
■ rankings   ■ reflect   ■ universal ...the best and the
■ resources*   ■ required*   brightest
■ secondary   ■ schedule*
  school   ■ separate
                     ■ track

* These words are from the Academic Word List. For more information on this list, see www.victoria.ac.nz/lals/resources/academicwordlist/.

Part 4: Focus on Testing

Students learn how to prepare for both typical college exams and international assessments.

Results for Students

A carefully structured program presents and practices academic skills and strategies purposefully, leading to strong student results and more independent learners.

Scope and Sequence

Chapter	Reading Selections	Reading Skills and Strategies
1 Education and Student Life p2 	*The Secrets of Success in School* *Challenges of the First Year of College*	Previewing the topic and vocabulary Identifying the main idea Understanding reading structure Skimming for the topic and main idea
2 City Life p22 	*A City That's Doing Something Right* *Sick-Building Syndrome*	Previewing the topic and vocabulary Identifying the main idea Identifying supporting details Predicting the content of a reading Skimming for the topic and the main ideas Scanning
3 Business and Money p46 	*Banking on Poor Women* *Consumerism and the Human Brain*	Previewing the topic and vocabulary Identifying the main idea and details Understanding conclusions Skimming for the topic and the main ideas Paying attention to phrases
4 Jobs and Professions p70 	*Changing Career Trends* *Looking for Work in the 21st Century*	Previewing the topic and vocabulary Getting meaning from context Previewing a reading Identifying the main idea Identifying important details Skimming for the topic and the main ideas

Critical-Thinking Skills	Vocabulary Building	Language Skills	Focus on Testing
Organizing information using a T-chart and Venn diagram Summarizing a paragraph Finding information about schools online	Getting meaning from context: punctuation, other sentences, logic Focusing on the Academic Word List Recognizing word meanings Identifying words and phrases that work together	Understanding pronoun reference Discussing educational systems in different cultures Writing a paragraph	**TOEFL® iBT** Focusing on question types
Organizing details using a graphic organizer Making inferences Summarizing a paragraph Understanding contrast	Getting meaning from context: examples, opposites, and connecting words Understanding the meaning of italics in readings Focusing on the Academic Word List Understanding and looking up parts of speech in a dictionary	Understanding pronoun reference Interviewing students about city life Discussing some problems and solutions in big cities Writing a paragraph	**TOEFL® iBT** Getting meaning of vocabulary from context
Identifying problems and solutions Organizing ideas using a Venn diagram Comparing and contrasting Making inferences Understanding irony Analyzing advertisements Summarizing a paragraph	Getting meaning from context (*e.g.* and *i.e.*) Using parts of speech to understand vocabulary Using suffixes to identify parts of speech Recognizing synonyms Focusing on the Academic Word List	Understanding pronoun reference Discussing social problems and solutions Analyzing advertisements Writing a paragraph	**TOEFL® iBT** Focusing on implications and inferences
Identifying cause and effect Organizing cause and effect using a graphic organizer Summarizing a paragraph Understanding proverbs and quotations	Using the prefix *over-* Focusing on the Academic Word List Understanding adjective and noun phrases Understanding and creating compound words	Understanding pronoun reference Discussing proverbs and quotations Identifying challenges and changes within today's work world Writing a paragraph	**TOEFL® iBT** Increasing reading speed: left-to-right eye movement

Scope and Sequence

Chapter	Reading Selections	Reading Skills and Strategies
5 Lifestyles Around the World p92 	*The Science of Happiness* *Happiness and the Home*	Previewing the topic and vocabulary Previewing the reading Identifying the main idea Identifying acronyms Getting meaning from context Marking text when you read
6 Global Connections p116 	*Globalization and Food* *Life in a Fishbowl: Globalization and Reality TV*	Previewing the topic and vocabulary Previewing the reading Identifying main ideas Skimming for main ideas
7 Language and Communication p140 	*If We Could Talk with Animals . . .* *"Parentese"*	Previewing the topic and vocabulary Previewing the reading Identifying the main ideas Identifying details Getting meaning from context Understanding italics and quotation marks Skimming for main ideas
8 Tastes and Preferences p168 	*The Silk Road: Art and Archaeology* *Fashion: The Art of the Body*	Previewing the topic and vocabulary Previewing the reading Getting meaning from context Recognizing summaries in a reading Identifying main ideas by analyzing details

Critical-Thinking Skills	Vocabulary Building	Language Skills	Focus on Testing
Interpreting source material from the Internet Studying for exams: organizing information Understanding italics Summarizing a paragraph	Focusing on the Academic Word List Analyzing prefixes and suffixes Understanding dictionary entries: words with single and multiple meanings	Discussing happiness and how it is measured Writing a paragraph	**TOEFL iBT** Focusing on vocabulary questions
Understanding the literal and figurative meanings of words Organizing information using an outline Summarizing in writing Understanding inferences	Understanding idioms and figurative language Focusing on the Academic Word List Focusing on expressions and idioms Using participles as adjectives	Stating and explaining opinions Writing a paragraph	**TOEFL iBT** Identifying inferences
Categorizing Interpreting a photograph Identifying details and analyzing material using graphic organizers Identifying inferences Distinguishing facts from assumptions Summarizing a paragraph	Understanding words with multiple meanings Focusing on the Academic Word List Working with prefixes and suffixes Understanding words in phrases Making a vocabulary log	Discussing the nature/ nurture question Writing a paragraph	**TOEFL iBT** Focusing on comprehension questions about details
Organizing information using an outline Identifying and making inferences Summarizing a paragraph	Recognizing words with similar meanings Understanding general and specific words Understanding connotations Focusing on the Academic Word List	Discussing ideas on art and beauty Writing a paragraph	**TOEFL iBT** Focusing on basic comprehension questions

Scope and Sequence

Chapter	Reading Selections	Reading Skills and Strategies
9 New Frontiers p196 	*The Human Brain— New Discoveries* *Personality: Nature or Nurture?*	Previewing the topic and vocabulary Previewing the reading Predicting the content of a reading Identifying the main ideas by analyzing details Skimming for main ideas
10 Ceremonies p218 	*Rites of Passage* *New Days, New Ways: Changing Rites of Passage*	Previewing the topic and vocabulary Previewing the reading Identifying the main ideas and writing summaries of each paragraph in a reading Understanding chronology: scanning for time words Understanding symbols

Critical-Thinking Skills	Vocabulary Building	Language Skills	Focus on Testing
Analyzing diagrams and photographs Distinguishing facts from assumptions Synthesizing and applying information from a reading Categorizing Making inferences Summarizing a paragraph	Matching words with similar meanings Putting words into categories Analyzing word roots and affixes Focusing on the Academic Word List	Expressing opinions based on facts Identifying similarities and differences among family members Writing a paragraph	**TOEFL® iBT** Getting meaning from context
Making inferences Comparing and contrasting Using a graphic organizer to organize and analyze information Distinguishing facts from opinions Summarizing a whole reading	Determining categories Analyzing word roots and affixes Focusing on the Academic Word List	Applying information in the reading to personal situations Conducting a survey on traditional and nontraditional weddings Writing a paragraph	**TOEFL® iBT** Identifying main idea patterns

1Education and Student Life

"An education isn't how much
you have committed to memory,
or even how much you know.
It's being able to differentiate
between what you do know and
what you don't."

Anatole France
French author

In this CHAPTER

In Part 1, you will read about how the educational systems in various countries contribute to the academic performance and lives of the students. In the rest of this chapter, you will read about, discuss, and explore challenges in adjusting to college life.

Connecting to the Topic

1. What do you see in the photo? What are the students waiting for?
2. What exams have you taken? How do you think these students feel?
3. What do you think is important in an education? What helps students to be successful?

The Secrets of Success in School

Before You Read

1 **Previewing the Topic**   Look at the map and photos here and in the reading. Then discuss the questions.

1. Where is each scene taking place? What is happening?
2. What might be similar about education in these countries? Make guesses.
3. What might be different about education in these countries? Make guesses.
4. In your opinion, what are important cultural values in each of these countries?

▲ Four of the countries that participate in the Programme for International Student Assessment (PISA) exam every three years. For a full list, visit http://www.oecd.org.

▲ High school students in class

High school students after class ▶

Preview → title   Pictures → caption
Subheadings   1st sentence of each paragraph

2 **Previewing Vocabulary** Read the words and phrases below. Listen to the pronunciation. Put a check mark (✓) next to the words that you don't know. Don't use a dictionary.

Nouns
- ☑ curriculum 课程
- ☑ discipline 学科
- ☐ drawback 退税
- ☐ effort 努力
- ☑ exhaustion 精疲力竭
- ☐ rankings 排名
- ☐ secondary school 特
- ☐ status 状态
- ☐ values 价值

Verbs
- ☐ achieve 实现
- ☐ compare
- ☑ determines
- ☑ reflects 反应
- ☐ separate 分离
- ☐ track 追踪

Adjectives 竞争的
- ☑ competitive
- ☑ entire 整個
- ☐ global
- ☐ identical
- ☑ isolated 孤立
- ☐ universal

Expressions
- ☐ in contrast to
- ☐ one-size-fits-all
- ☐ on the one hand
- ☐ on the other hand
- ☐ the best and the brightest

Strategy

Getting Meaning from Context

When you read, you do not need to look up the meanings of all new words in a dictionary. You can often guess the meanings of many new words from the context—the other words in the sentence and the other sentences in the paragraph. Here are three types of clues that will help you guess new words.

1. **Punctuation:** Sometimes a sentence gives a definition of a new vocabulary item or information about it. This information may be in parentheses ( ), after a dash (–) or after a comma (,).

   Example

   Students need great discipline—self-control—to give up sports, hobbies, and social life.

   (*Discipline* means "self-control.")

2. **Another sentence:** Sometimes a clue to the meaning of a new vocabulary item is in another sentence or sentence part.

   Example

   Because the global economy is becoming more competitive, educators and governments worldwide are paying close attention.

   (In the second part of the sentence, you see the meaning of *global*—"worldwide.")

3. **Logic:** Sometimes simple logic helps you to guess the meaning of a new word.

   Example

   Every three years, 15-year-old students in secondary school sit down to take the same exams.

   (You probably know that 15-year-old students are between primary school and university, so you can guess that *secondary school* is "middle or high school.")

③ Getting Meaning from Context This exercise will help you with vocabulary that you will find in the first reading selection. Read the sentences. Figure out the meanings of the underlined words from the context and write them on the lines.

1. <u>On the one hand</u>, there are many advantages to this system. <u>On the other hand</u>, there are also several disadvantages.

   on the one hand = _____*from one point of view*_____

   on the other hand = _____*from another point of view*_____

2. This is based on the belief that students are not born with <u>identical</u> ability. Because they are not <u>exactly the same</u>, some students will be bored, and others will have difficulty.

   identical = _____

3. Of course, one <u>drawback</u>, or <u>disadvantage</u>, is that students experience exhaustion and a great deal of stress.

   drawback = _____

4. In some countries, teachers have high <u>status</u>, or <u>social position</u>.

   status = _____

5. In the United States, each state <u>determines</u> its own curriculum. The fifty states <u>decide</u> on their own curricula.

   determine = _____

6. Each educational system is a <u>mirror</u> that <u>reflects</u> the values of its own culture.

   reflects = _____*show*_____

Read

④ Reading an Article As you read the following selection, think about the answer to this question: *What can we learn from countries with successful educational systems?* Read the selection. Do not use a dictionary. Then do the activities that follow the reading.

www.allnews/allday.com

The Secrets of Success in School

A   What leads to success in school? Every three years, 15-year-old students in **secondary school** sit down to take the same exams in reading, mathematics, and science. The PISA (Programme for International Student Assessment) collects and studies the results from sixty-four to seventy countries. Countries that usually do the best on these tests are Finland, Korea, and Singapore. Because the **global economy** is becoming more **competitive**, educators and governments worldwide are paying close attention to these tests to find how

5

their countries **compare**—and to learn how they can improve. What are these countries doing right? Should all countries follow their example? Is it *possible* to follow their example? 10

Tracking

B　　One **frequent** question is about the tracking of students. When schools **track** students, they place them in groups or classes according to their ability or need. This occurs in Singapore, for example—one of the most successful countries on the PISA tests. Tracking is based on the belief that students are not born with **identical** ability. Because they are not exactly the same, the 15 belief is that the best students will be bored, and weak students will have difficulty in the same class, with the same subjects. In Singapore, students in the "Special" group go on to the university. "Express" students become clerical workers. "Normal" students become sales people and road sweepers. However, in Finland, another of the most successful countries on the PISA 20 test, educators do *not* **separate** students into different groups or schools. Instead, different types of learners study together. Students who do well and **achieve** success serve as good examples for other students who aren't doing so well. Clearly, tracking works well in some countries but not others.

Hard Work

C　　How much **effort** is necessary for success in school? How hard do students 25 need to work? In Korea, typical high school students get up very early, spend all day in school, and spend many hours after school in private institutes or at night doing homework. Korean students need great **discipline**—self-control—to give up sports, hobbies, and social life. They do this in order to be successful both in school and on the important college entrance exams. 30

▲ How can students avoid exhaustion?

Their goal is to get into "the right university." A common belief among Korean students is that they can enter college if they get four hours of sleep each night—but not if they sleep five or more. Of course, one **drawback**, or disadvantage, is that 35 Korean students experience **exhaustion** and a great deal of stress. From this example, it seems that students from countries with high PISA scores have to work very hard. On the other hand, in Finland, children do not start school until they are seven years old. They don't have 40 to worry about grades because teachers don't give grades until high school. In high school, teachers give grades, but there are no lists with **rankings** of students from low to high. Perhaps most interesting, students have very little homework, and yet Finnish students still rank very high on the PISA exams. It appears that hard, competitive work is not the *only* road to success. 45

Educators

D　　Is there nothing that the top-ranking countries have in common? Is there no lesson we can learn from these countries? Well, actually, there is. The quality of teachers seems to be important to student success. In Singapore,

Korea, and Finland, teachers have high **status**, or social position. For this reason, the teaching profession attracts **the best and the brightest**. In Korea, people call them "nation builders." In Finland, getting into a teacher-training program is very competitive; only 10% of Finnish college graduates are accepted into teacher-training programs. All teachers must have master's degrees, which also gives them status. This is **in contrast to** many countries, such as the United States, where teachers generally do not have high status. The United States is not among the top PISA countries.

Curriculum

E   The PISA results also suggest the importance of **curriculum**. In countries such as Finland and Korea, there is a **universal** curriculum; students of the same age study the same subjects in the **entire** country. In the United States, each state **determines** its own curriculum. Perhaps because the fifty states decide on their own curricula*, some U.S. states rank very high on the PISA exams, and some rank low. The word *curriculum* refers not only to the courses that students take but also to all of the topics in each course. In countries that do well on the PISA exam, a typical 8th grade course focuses on 10–15 topics. In the United States, an 8th grade course typically includes *35* topics. Perhaps this is too many.

Conclusion

F   **On the one hand**, it seems that education is not a **"one-size-fits-all"** situation. There isn't one perfect educational system that is right for all countries. Each educational system is a mirror that **reflects** the **values** of its *own* culture. **On the other hand**, it seems clear that each country can improve. There is no magic solution, but in this global economy, no educational system is **isolated** from others, and each *can* learn from others.

curricula = plural of curriculum

After You Read

Strategy

Identifying the Main Idea

A reading passage may include many ideas, but there is one main idea, or point, of the reading. It is the main point, thought, or opinion that the author has about the topic. It is an "umbrella" that includes all of the more specific ideas and details. The main idea is usually stated in the introduction. Often, it is repeated in the conclusion.

5 **Identifying the Main Idea** Find one sentence in Paragraph A that seems to be the "umbrella" main idea of the entire reading passage. Then find another sentence in Paragraph F that seems to mean about the same. Write them here.

From Paragraph A: _The global economy is becoming more ... they can improve._

From Paragraph F: _There is no magic ... learn from others._

6 **Understanding Reading Structure** Paragraphs divide reading material into topics, or subjects. One paragraph is usually about one topic. Match the paragraphs from the reading on pages 6–8 with their topics below. Write the letters of the paragraphs on the lines.

1. __F__ Conclusion: The influence of educational systems on each other

2. __C__ The amount of time students in two countries spend studying

3. __E__ The courses that students take and the topics in each course

4. __B__ Two points of view on separation of students into groups

5. __D__ The importance of teachers

6. __A__ Introduction: Using the PISA exams in the global economy

7 **Checking Your Vocabulary** Check your understanding of vocabulary from the reading selection. Read the definitions below and write words and expressions that fit these definitions. The letters in parentheses refer to paragraphs in the reading.

1. a situation in which people or groups are trying to be more successful than others (A): _____ competitive _____

2. are similar to or different from (A): _____ compare _____

3. put students in groups or classes according to their ability or need (B): _____ track _____

4. to cause people or things *not* to be together (B): _____ separate _____

5. work or energy (C): _____ effort _____

6. lists of people or things in order of their ability or accomplishment (C): _____ ranking _____

7. people who are the most intelligent or who are the best at their profession (D): _the best and the brightest_

8. different from (D): _in contrast to_

9. done or experienced by everyone (E) _____ universal _____

10. whole (E): _____ entire _____

11. beliefs about what is right, what is important (F): _____ values _____

12. separate from others (F): _____ isolated _____
为名

Strategy

Organizing Information: Using a T-Chart and a Venn Diagram

Readings often present opposite views of a topic or positive and negative aspects of something (such as an educational system). Sometimes, you can find these because the writer uses words and expressions such as *advantages*, *disadvantages*, *on the one hand*, *on the other hand*, *but*, and *however*.

One effective study technique is to organize information on a graphic organizer. Here are two different types of graphic organizers:

- **T-chart** (called a T-chart because it is shaped like the letter *T*). This is good for contrasts or opposites.
- **Venn diagram**—two intersecting circles. This is useful when there are both differences and similarities (points that are the same).

8 **Organizing Information: Using Graphic Organizers** In the first T-chart below, fill in differences in the educational systems of Singapore and Finland from Paragraph B. In the second T-chart, fill in differences between Finland and Korea and the United States from Paragraph E. In the Venn diagram, fill in information from Paragraphs C and D. (Put two similarities in the center.) When you finish, compare your charts with other students' charts.

1. Paragraph B:

Singapore	Finland
special groub work together one of the most successful countries on the PISA test.	Different types of learns study together Success students serve as good examples for other students who aren't doing so well.

2. Paragraph E:

Finland and Korea	the United States
Same age students They take some subject and same class.	each state take curriculum They can determine Students have more topics than other countries in some grade.

3. Paragraphs C and D:

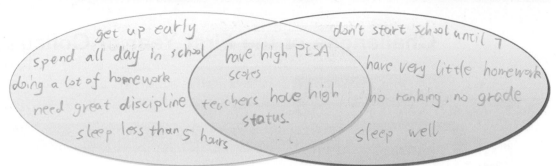

| Korea | Both | Finland |

Korea: get up early, spend all day in school, doing a lot of homework, need great discipline, sleep less than 5 hours

Both: have high PISA scores, teachers have high status.

Finland: don't start school until 7, have very little homework, no ranking, no grade, sleep well

---

Culture Note

What Do You Think?
Can the Finnish, Korean, or Singaporean system transfer to other countries?

You learned in the reading about three countries that do very well on the PISA exams. There is much discussion about how to improve education in countries that have poor or **average** (not good, not bad) results.

There is the question of homogeneity vs. heterogeneity. Some countries, such as Finland and Korea, are **homogeneous**: most of the population shares the same language, culture, and history. Other countries, such as the United States and Germany, which have only average scores on the PISA exams, are more **heterogeneous**. There is great **diversity** (a range of differences) in language and culture within the population because of generations of immigrants from many countries.

Is it more possible for homogeneous countries to have a successful educational system that is right for the entire population? If you think so, what about Singapore—a country with three major ethnic groups and four official languages? Some might say, "Singapore is a small country." Is it easier for a small country to organize an effective educational system? What do you think?

9 **Discussing the Reading** In small groups, talk about your answers to these questions about a country you know well.

1. Do you know how well this country does on the PISA exams?

2. Do the schools track students? If so, what kinds of groups are there? What is your opinion of tracking?

3. Do the students have a lot of homework? Do they go to private institutes after school? If so, what kind of institutes are these? What do the students study there?

4. Do the teachers have high status? How difficult is it to become a teacher there?

5. Is there a universal curriculum, or does each state or province have its own curriculum?

Challenges of the First Year of College

Before You Read

Strategy

Skimming for the Topic and Main Idea

You can **skim** a reading to identify the topic and the main idea. To skim, read the title and any subheadings, look at any photos and diagrams, and read the first two and the last two sentences of each paragraph. Read quickly and don't read every word.

The **topic** of a paragraph is what the paragraph is about.

The **main idea** of a paragraph is what the writer wants to say about the topic—giving information and/or an opinion about the topic. The first or the second sentence often gives you the main idea. The other sentences give details about the main idea. The last sentence of a paragraph can also state the main idea.

Note: in the introductory paragraph of an essay, the main idea is usually near the end.

Example

> Some students know exactly what they want to study, what they want to major in, because this has been a passion for their entire lives. However, those students who *aren't* certain should know that they can relax and not feel pressure to choose a major too soon. College is a time for growth, for self-discovery, for exploration of new possibilities. It's not necessary for an incoming freshman to have his or her life already mapped out, beginning with the choice of major. In fact, this is not even desirable. In the first two years of college, students must take the general education requirements—a selection of courses from a wide range of areas: math, sciences, humanities, social sciences, and the arts. Very few of these courses will be in the student's major. It is during this time that many students discover a subject that interests them very much. Often, this is a subject they never studied in high school. Perhaps they didn't even know it existed. But this becomes their major. Clearly, it's important for students to keep an open mind about their choice of major.

Topic: _____ *the choice of major* _____

Main idea: ___ *Students should not feel pressure to choose a major too soon.* ___

Hint

The **topic** is just a word or noun phrase—a few words. It is not a sentence. The main idea is in a sentence or two and can be found in the beginning, middle, or end of a paragraph.

1 **Skimming for the Topic and the Main Idea** Read the following paragraphs quickly. Do not use a dictionary, and don't worry about the details. When you finish, write the topic and main idea of each paragraph. You can copy the main idea directly from the sentence (or sentences), or use your own words to restate it.

6, 10   5, 23

Challenges of the First Year of College

A   Charles Dickens once famously referred to a specific period of history as "the best of times" and "the worst of times." This can also describe the college years of many students. College is a time of transition between high school and working life, between childhood and adulthood, between dependence on family and independence. Like any period of growth, the   5 college years can be both painful and exciting. Educators have some practical advice so that students can successfully deal with their problems and get the most out of their college experience.

Topic: _____

Main idea: _____

_____

B   Many students who are beginning college—even students who were very successful in high school—find that the classes are suddenly much more   10 challenging than in high school and that much more studying is required. Educators usually agree on the solution to this problem of too much work: you need to get organized. First, choose wisely the combination of classes you take in any one semester. Balance harder ones with easier ones. Also, limit the number of classes you take. Don't try to take more than a full-time   15 load of credits in the first semester. Second, keep a careful calendar of dates for all exams and when all assignments are due. Professors will hand out a page with these dates on the first day of class; put them immediately on your master calendar and plan ahead. Third, schedule regular time and find a quiet place in which to study so that you won't have to suddenly cram the   20 day before an important exam. You might pass a test by cramming for it, but you won't remember much afterward—and this isn't true learning. Fourth, form a study group with students in some of your classes, and meet with them once or twice a week. Also, take advantage of the resources on campus such as tutors or the writing center. Fifth, although this might seem obvious,   25 it's important to go to class. Some students believe they can pass by simply doing the reading and taking exams, but this isn't true. Finally, it's essential to include breaks—short ones and longer ones—to balance study time with time for fun. This will keep your mind fresh and clear.

Topic: _____

Main idea: _____

_____

C   Money is a problem for many college students. Every year, students drop   30
out because they simply can't afford to continue. Tuition costs are rising fast
at many colleges, and these fees for classes are not the only expense that
students have. There are also costs for housing (if the student lives away from
home), books, food, transportation, clothes, and entertainment. The solution
to the challenge of paying for a college education has several components.   35
It begins in the year *before* starting college. If possible, students need to
choose a college that's more affordable, even if it isn't their first choice. Then
they should explore the possibilities at the Financial Aid Office. Are there
scholarships? Are there student loans with a low rate of interest? Students
might need to get a job—on campus or off—and take fewer classes, even   40
if it means graduating later than they would like; this is often preferable to
having huge debt after graduation. One last component to dealing with the
challenge of money is to avoid credit cards. They are too easy to use, and
they get too many students into troublesome debt.

Topic: _____

Main idea: _____

_____

D   A problem for many college students is depression, usually as a result of   45
either loneliness or the pressure of their studies. The healthiest way to deal
with depression is to connect with other people on a regular basis. These can
be roommates, classmates, professors, and academic advisors. It's important,
too, to stay in touch with family and old friends. However, *serious* depression
probably requires the attention of a professional counselor. Most campuses   50
have free counseling services.

Topic: _____

Main idea: _____

_____

E   Problems with studies, money, and depression can make college "the worst of times." However, college is also where most students learn about themselves and learn about the world. This is where they make friends for life. With careful organization, planning, and attention to relationships with others, students can achieve a balance that can make college "the best of times," too.

Topic: _____

Main idea: _____

_____

After You Read

FOCUS

Understanding Pronoun Reference

As you know, pronouns take the place of nouns. When you read, it's important to understand the meaning of pronouns, to know which noun a pronoun refers to. To find the noun that a pronoun refers to, look back in the sentence or in the sentences that come before it.

Example

Educators have some practical advice so that students can successfully deal with the problems and get the most out of their college experience.

(The word *their* refers to students.)

2 **Understanding Pronoun Reference** Look back at the reading selection "Challenges of the First Year of College" to find the meanings of the following pronouns. What does each pronoun refer to?

1. them (Paragraph B, line 18) _____ these dates _____

2. it (Paragraph B, line 21) _____ test _____

3. this (Paragraph B, line 22) ___ Cram the day before an important exam ___ Cramming

4. them (Paragraph B, line 24) _____ Students _____

5. it (Paragraph C, line 36) _____ the Solution _____

6. they (Paragraph C, line 38) _____ students _____

7. they (Paragraph C, line 43 and 44) _____ credit cards _____

8. these (Paragraph D, line 47) _____ people _____

3 Discussing the Reading Discuss these questions. Think about a country you know well.

1. In that country, do college freshmen typically have difficulty with the amount of work and level of classes? Or are the high school years so difficult that college seems like a vacation, in comparison?

2. In that country, is college free, inexpensive, or expensive? How do college students typically pay for college tuition and textbooks? Do students take out loans? Do students get jobs? (If so, what kinds of jobs are typical?)

Responding in Writing

Strategy

Summarizing

In academic classes, the most common type of writing is *summary*. A summary is written in the student's own words. It includes the main idea and important details of another piece of writing (a paragraph, section, article, chapter, or book). It does not include less important details. Students who summarize well can prove to the instructor that they truly understand the reading material.

4 Summarizing Choose either Paragraph B or C from the reading in Part 2, pages 13–14. Write a summary of that paragraph. Because a summary is shorter than the original, try to write only two to four sentences. Follow these steps:

- Read the paragraph several times and make sure that you understand it well.
- Identify the topic, main idea, and important details.
- Put the original paragraph aside as you write. (If you look at it, the temptation is to copy from it.)
- Write the summary in your own words, including the important details. You can put some important details together in one sentence.
- Do not include the less important details.

When you finish writing, compare your summary with those of other students who summarized the same paragraph. Did you have the same main idea? Did you choose the same details?

5 Writing Your Own Ideas Choose one of the topics below to write a paragraph. Write your own thoughts. Try to use vocabulary from this chapter.

- the educational system in your country
- a comparison of the educational system in your country with the system in one other country from Part 1 (pages 6–8)
- what you know (or have heard) about ways that college students overcome problems

6 **Beyond the Text: Interviewing** Interview five people. Ask them their opinions about positive and negative aspects of the educational system in their country. Take notes on their answers. When you finish, report your findings to the class.

PART 3 **Building Vocabulary and Study Skills**

FOCUS

The Academic Word List

There is a list of words that college students must know because these words occur frequently in academic English. This is called the "Academic Word List." In Part 3 of each chapter of this book, there is an activity to help you focus on these words. In the Self-Assessment Log at the end of each chapter, these words have an asterisk (*) next to them. For more information on the Academic Word List, see http://www.victoria.ac.nz/lals/resources/academicwordlist/.

1 **Focusing on Words from the Academic Word List** In this exercise, fill in the blanks with words from the Academic Word List in the box.

assignments ✓	credits ✓	obvious ✓	resources ✓
challenging ✓	finally	required ✓	schedule ✓

Challenges of the First Year of College

B   Many students who are beginning college—even students who were very successful in high school—find that the classes are suddenly much more ___*challenging*___ than in high school and that much more studying
₁

is ___*required*___. Educators usually agree on the solution to this
₂

problem of too much work: you need to get organized. First, choose wisely   5

the combination of classes you take in any one semester. Balance harder

ones with easier ones. Also, limit the number of classes you take. Don't

try to take more than a full-time load of ___*credits*___ in the first
₃

semester. Second, keep a careful calendar of dates for all exams and when

all ___assignments___ are due. Professors will hand out a page with these   10
          4

dates on the first day of class; put them immediately on your master calendar

and plan ahead. Third, ___schedule___ regular time and find a quiet
                              5

place in which to study so that you won't have to suddenly cram the day

before an important exam. You might pass a test by cramming for it, but you

won't remember much afterward—and this isn't true learning. Fourth, form   15

a study group with students in some of your classes, and meet with them

once or twice a week. Also, take advantage of the ___resources___ on
                                                          6

campus such as tutors or the writing center. Fifth, although this might seem

___obvious___, it's important to go to class. Some students believe they
        7

can pass by simply doing the reading and taking exams, but this isn't true.   20

___Finally___, it's essential to include breaks—short ones and longer
      8

ones—to balance study time with time for fun. This will keep your mind

fresh and clear.

② Recognizing Word Meanings Match the words with their meanings. Write
the letters on the lines, as in the example.

Column A	Column B
1. __e__ global	a. work or energy
2. __j__ achieve	b. list of people or things in order
3. __h__ reflect	c. courses and topics that students study
4. __a__ effort 成就	d. self-control
5. __k__ drawback n. 缺点 连续	e. worldwide
6. __l__ status	f. whole
7. __d__ discipline n. 学科, 纪律 v. 训练	g. decide on
8. __c__ curriculum	h. show
9. __b__ ranking	i. the same
10. __f__ entire	j. get or reach (something) by working hard
11. __i__ identical adj. 完全相同	k. disadvantage
12. __g__ determine	l. social position

3 Words in Phrases As you read, it's important to begin noticing words that often go together. Go back to the paragraphs on pages 6–8. Find the words that complete the following phrases and write them in the blanks.

Paragraph A

1. leads _to_ success

Paragraph B

2. according _to_ their ability

3. do not separate students _into_ different groups

Paragraph C

4. need discipline to give _up_ sports, hobbies, and social life

5. worry _about_ grades

6. the only road _to_ success

Paragraph D

7. have (something) _in_ common _with sb._

8. _for_ this reason

9. _in_ contrast _to_ many countries

Paragraph E

10. focuses _on_ 10-15 topics

Using the Internet

Finding Information About Schools Online

Imagine you want to find a school that has certain features. Use a search engine such as Google. Type in the word "university" or "college" and add the words you are interested in to the search box

Example

Lars is interested in a US university that specializes in graphic design.

| US college + design | | Submit |

OR

| US colleges that offer graphic design | | Submit |

Your search results will look something like this:

Top 50 **Graphic Design Schools** and **Colleges** « Top Graphic Arts …
This ranking of **graphic design** schools began with the top…
www.graphic-design-schools.org

Graphic Design schools, Graphic Art schools **colleges** and…
Art **Schools**. Architecture Schools in **USA**… **Graphic Design Schools**, Graphic Art **Schools**, **Colleges** & Universities in **USA**… clickable Map of the **United States**…
www.a2zcolleges.com/arts/graphic_design/index.html

Best **Graphic Design** Programs | Top **Graphic Design Schools** | **US**…
Graphic designers

4 Searching the Internet Do an Internet search on colleges and universities. Use a search engine such as Google. Find a college or university that does the following things:

- has an interesting virtual (online) tour: _____
- offers classes in scuba diving: _____
- offers classes in many African languages (such as Swahili, Amharic, Yoruba, and Zulu):_____
- allows students to create or design their own majors: _____
- has an art museum: _____
- (your choice): _____

Write down the names and locations of the colleges. Compare your findings with those of another student.

PART 4 Focus on Testing

F⊕CUS

Reading Question Types

There are three types of multiple-choice questions in the reading section of the TOEFL® (Test of English as a Foreign Language™) Internet-Based Test (iBT): (1) *information* questions, (2) basic *comprehension* questions, and (3) *reading to learn* questions.

1. Most *information* questions can be answered by scanning for a certain keyword or number. The answer involves finding a specific point of information.

2. *Basic comprehension* questions test the reader's skill at understanding the vocabulary, grammar, and basic organization of the passage. The answer often involves understanding the interrelationship of several sentences or paragraphs.

3. *Reading to learn* questions test the reader's ability to understand the main ideas of a reading, implied ideas, the author's attitudes, relations among groups of facts in the reading, and so on.

1 Practice Look again at "The Secrets of Success in School" on pages 6–8. Answer the following questions (similar to those on the TOEFL® iBT). The question type is in parentheses after the question.

1. According to the passage, in which educational system are there 35 topics in a typical 8th grade course? (information question)

   (A) in the United States   (C) in Korea

   (B) in Finland   (D) in any country that does well on the PISA exam

2. Which of the following is closest in meaning to *exhaustion*, as it is used in Paragraph C? (basic comprehension question)

    (A) success   (C) tiredness

    (B) self-control   (D) lack of friendship

3. What can be inferred (guessed) about Finnish students from reading Paragraph C? (reading to learn question)

    (A) They don't get enough sleep and are tired all the time.   (C) They have a lot of stress.

    (B) Their classes are easy.   (D) They don't worry about their position in class.

Self-Assessment Log

Read the lists below. Check (✓) the strategies and vocabulary that you learned in this chapter. Look through the chapter or ask your instructor about the strategies and words that you do not understand.

Reading and Vocabulary-Building Strategies

☐ Previewing vocabulary
☐ Getting meaning from context
☐ Identifying the main idea
☐ Understanding reading structure

☐ Organizing information: Using a T-Chart and a Venn Diagram
☐ Skimming for the topic and main idea
☐ Understanding pronoun reference

Target Vocabulary

Nouns

☐ assignments*
☐ credits*
☐ curriculum
☐ discipline
☐ drawback
☐ effort
☐ exhaustion
☐ rankings
☐ resources*
☐ secondary school

☐ status*
☐ values

Verbs

☐ achieve*
☐ compare
☐ determine
☐ reflect
☐ required*
☐ schedule*
☐ separate
☐ track

Adjectives

☐ challenging*
☐ competitive
☐ entire
☐ global*
☐ identical*
☐ isolated*
☐ obvious*
☐ universal

Adverb

☐ finally*

Expressions

☐ in contrast to
☐ one-size-fits-all
☐ on the one hand
☐ on the other hand
☐ the best and the brightest

* These words are from the Academic Word List. For more information on this list, see www.victoria.ac.nz/lals/resources/academicwordlist/.

2 City Life

"When you look at a city, it's like reading the hopes, aspirations, and pride of everyone who built it."

Hugh Newell Jacobsen
U.S. Architect

In this **CHAPTER**
in Part 1, you will read about one city's creative solution for dealing with garbage collection, transportation, and other urban problems. In the rest of this chapter, you will read about, explore, and discuss different kinds of indoor and outdoor pollutants and solutions to a variety of environmental problems.

 Connecting to the Topic

1. Where are the people in the photo? What are they doing?

2. What are five advantages of living in a big city? What are five disadvantages?

3. Do you like living in a big or a small city? Do you like visiting a big or small city? Explain your answers.

A City That's Doing Something Right

Before You Read

1 Previewing the Topic Look at the photos and discuss the questions.

1. In what cities or countries do you think the photos were taken? What is it like to live there?

2. What adjectives can you think of to describe each photo? Make a list.

▲ Photo A

▲ Photo B

2 Thinking Ahead The first reading discusses some common problems in big cities and the solutions that one city has found. Before you read, think about the good and bad things about the city that you come from or the city that you live in now. Interview at least four students. Complete the chart below.

Student's Name and City	What are the three worst problems in your city?	What are the three best features of your city?
Kevin	Weather noise air pollution	food people near sea
Jana	hot weather noise	sea sky scrapers food
Dhari	Very hot street	people food

pròduce (n.)
prodúce (v.)

3 **Previewing Vocabulary** Read the words and phrases below. Listen to the pronunciation. Put a check mark (✓) next to the words that you don't know. Don't use a dictionary.

Nouns
- agricultural operation
- crops
- developing countries
- gridlock
- mass transit
- pedestrian zone

- pollution
- priorities
- produce *(n.)*
- recycling plant
- trash
- urban dwellers

Verbs
- commute
- crowd
- cultivate
- predict
- solve
- worsening

Adjectives
- affluent
- creative

Adverb
- efficiently

Strategy

Getting Meaning from Context

You do not need to look up the meanings of new words if you can guess them from the context. Here are three more types of clues that will help you guess new words.

1. The words *for example, for instance, such as,* and *among them* introduce examples that may help you. (Sometimes examples appear without these words, in parentheses, or between dashes.)

Example
Context: Almost four billion people will be living in cities in **developing countries** such as India and Nigeria.
Meaning: You can guess that developing countries are not rich.

2. Sometimes another word or group of words in a different part of the sentence or in another sentence has the opposite meaning from a new vocabulary word.

Example
Context: In some cities, instead of **worsening**, urban life is actually getting much better.
Meaning: You see that *worsening* is the opposite of *getting better.*

3. A definition or explanation follows the connecting words *that is* or *in other words*.

Example
Context: The downtown shopping area is now a **pedestrian zone**—in other words, an area for walkers only, not cars.
Meaning: A *pedestrian zone* is an area for walkers only.

4 Getting Meaning from Context This activity will help you with vocabulary in the first reading selection. Figure out the meanings of the underlined words and write them on the lines. Use punctuation, logic, examples, opposites, and connecting words to help you.

1. People who study population growth predict a nightmare by the year 2025: the global population will be more than eight billion, and almost four billion of these people will be living in cities in developing countries such as India and Nigeria.

   predict = _____ *say in advance that something will happen* _____

2. People spend hours in gridlock—that is, traffic so horrible that it simply doesn't move—when they commute daily from their homes to their work and back.

   gridlock = _____

   commute = _____

3. It might not be a surprise to find that life in affluent cities is improving, but what about cities that aren't rich?

   affluent = _____

4. Under his leadership, city planners established priorities—in other words, a list of what was most important.

   priorities = _____

5. In neighborhoods that garbage trucks can't reach, people bring bags of trash to special centers.

   trash = _____

6. They exchange the trash for fresh produce such as potatoes or oranges.

   produce = _____

7. At a recycling plant, workers separate glass bottles, plastic, and cans from other trash.

   recycling plant = _____

8. Curitiba needed a mass-transit system but couldn't afford an expensive subway. City planners began, instead, with an unusual system of buses.

   mass-transit = _____ *transportion* _____

9. There is an agricultural operation just outside Curitiba that looks like other farms but actually helps to solve a social problem, in addition to growing crops.

   agricultural operation = _____ *farm* _____

   crops = _____ *things grown at a farm* _____

10. They cultivate medicinal plants and then process them into herbal teas.

    cultivate = _____ *grow* _____

11. Curitiba provides the city people with 22 million square meters of parks and green areas; this is more than three times the amount that the World Health Organization recommends for urban dwellers.

    urban dwellers = _____ *city people* _____

5 Reading an Article As you read the following article, think about the answer to this question: *What is the city Curitiba, Brazil, doing right?* Then do the activities that follow the reading.

A City That's Doing Something Right

A   There's good news and bad news about life in modern cities—first, the bad. People who study population growth predict a nightmare by the year 2025: the global population will be more than eight billion, and almost four billion of these people will be living in cities in **developing countries** such as India and Nigeria. Population growth is already causing unbelievable 5 overcrowding. Due to this overcrowding, many cities have problems with air **pollution**, disease, and crime. People spend hours in gridlock—that is, traffic so horrible that it simply doesn't move—when they **commute** daily from their homes to their work and back. There isn't enough water, transportation, or housing. Many people don't have access to health services 10 or jobs. Now the good news: in some cities, instead of **worsening**, urban life is actually getting much better.

A City and Its Mayor

B   It might not be a surprise to find that life in **affluent** cities is improving. But what about cities that aren't rich? The city of Curitiba, Brazil, proves that it's possible for even a city in a developing country to offer a good life to 15 its residents. The former mayor of Curitiba for 25 years, Jaime Lerner, is an architect and a very practical person. Under his leadership, the city planners established a list of **priorities**—in other words, a list of what was most important to work on. They decided to focus on the environment and on the quality of life. With an average income of only about $2,000 per person per 20 year, Curitiba has the same problems as many cities. However, it also has some **creative** solutions.

Garbage Collection

C   One creative solution is the method of garbage collection—*Cambio Verde*, or Green Exchange. This does far more than clean the streets of **trash**. In neighborhoods that garbage trucks can't reach, poor people bring 25 bags of trash to special centers. At these centers, they exchange the trash for fresh **produce** such as potatoes and oranges. They receive one kilo of produce for every four kilos of trash that they bring in. At a **recycling plant**, workers separate glass bottles, plastic, and cans from other trash. *Two-thirds* of Curitiba's garbage is recycled, which is good for the environment. And the 30 plant gives jobs to the poorest people, which improves their lives.

Transportation

D Due to careful planning, Curitiba does not have the same traffic problems that most cities have. The statistics are surprising. The population has grown fast, to over two million people, but traffic has actually *decreased* 30 percent. Curitiba needed a **mass-transit** system but couldn't afford an expensive subway. City planners began, instead, with an unusual system of buses in the center lanes of five wide major streets. At each bus stop, there is a forty-foot-long glass tube. Passengers pay *before* they enter the tube. Then they get on the bus "subway style"—through wide doors. This allows people to get on and off the bus quickly and **efficiently**. People don't **crowd** onto the bus; loading and unloading takes only 30 seconds. This makes commuting more pleasant and also helps to **solve** the problem of air pollution.

▲ Passengers exit efficiently through the tube in Curitiba, Brazil.

A Creative Social Program

E There is an **agricultural operation** just outside Curitiba that looks like other farms but actually helps to solve a social problem, in addition to growing **crops**. At *Fazenda da Solidaridade* (Solidarity Farm), the workers are not experienced farmers. Instead, they are drug addicts and alcoholics who volunteer to spend up to nine months in a program called *Verde Saude* (Green Health). The program helps them in two ways. First, it gives them jobs. They **cultivate** medicinal plants and then process them into herbal teas, syrups, and other products that are sold in health food stores. Second, it helps them to get off drugs and alcohol and to turn their lives around. In exchange for their labor, they receive counseling, medical care, and job training.

▲ "There is little in the architecture of a city that is more beautifully designed than a tree," says Jaime Lerner.

The Environment

F   To make the environment both cleaner and more beautiful, Curitiba encourages green space. It has low taxes for companies that have green areas, 75 so several hundred major industries such as Pepsi and Volvo have offices in the city—since they are willing to incorporate green space in their plants in order to take advantage of the city's low tax rate. Bringing natural beauty into the city is a priority. For this reason, Curitiba gave 1.5 million young trees to neighborhoods to plant and take care of. And the downtown shopping area 80 is now a **pedestrian zone**—in other words, for walkers only, not cars—and is lined with gardens. Curitiba provides the city people with 22 million square meters of parks and green areas—more than three times the amount that the World Health Organization recommends for **urban dwellers**.

A Symbol of the Possible

G   Clearly, overcrowding in big cities worldwide is the cause 85 of serious problems. However, the example of Curitiba provides hope that careful planning and creative thinking can lead to solutions. Curitiba is truly, as Lewis Mumford once said of cities in general, a "symbol of the possible."

After You Read

Strategy

Identifying the Main Idea

As you read in Chapter 1, usually one or two sentences in an essay or article state the main idea of the whole passage (the "umbrella" idea). You can usually find the main idea near the beginning of an essay.

6 **Identifying the Main Idea** In the article that you just read, the main idea is in Paragraph B. Write the main idea below. Then find another sentence in the conclusion, Paragraph G, which seems to mean about the same.

From Paragraph B: _____

_____

From Paragraph G: _____

_____

Strategy

Identifying Supporting Details

Every paragraph includes a main idea and specific details (facts, ideas, and examples) that support and develop the main idea. You can organize the main ideas and details on different types of graphic organizers. One way to do this is to put the main idea in a box on the left and the details in boxes to the right. See the example below.

7 **Identifying Supporting Details** Complete this graphic organizer with information from Paragraphs C, D, and E in the reading to answer the questions. Follow the examples.

Main ideas:

Details:

How does this help the city?

> cleans the streets of trash

> poor people exchange the trash

Curitiba created a "Green Exchange" to help the city.

> garbage is recycled

> recycle plant gives jobs to poor people

What is good about this system?

> get on and off the bus quickly

Curitiba created an unusual mass-transit system to deal with traffic.

> makes commuting more pleasant

> solve the air pollution

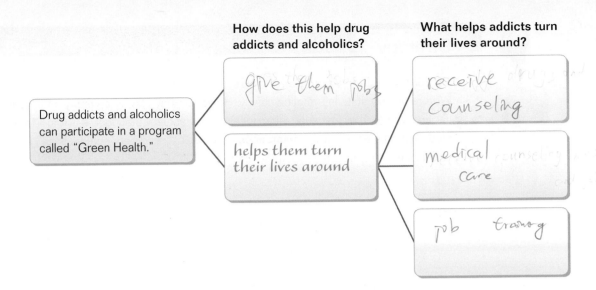

How does this help drug addicts and alcoholics?

What helps addicts turn their lives around?

Drug addicts and alcoholics can participate in a program called "Green Health."

give them jobs

helps them turn their lives around

receive drug counseling

medical care

job training

Understanding Italics

Writers use *italics* (slanted letters) for several reasons. Here are two:

1. Writers use italics for emphasis. The italics indicate that the word is important.

    Example
    Overcrowding is a *huge* problem in that city.

2. Italics indicate a foreign word in an English sentence.

    Example
    In open areas in Seoul, *kaenari* blooms everywhere in the spring.

---

8 **Understanding Italics** Find the words in italics in the reading on pages 27–29. Which are used for emphasis? Circle them. Read these sentences aloud, placing emphasis on the words in italics. Which words indicate a foreign word or term? Underline them.

Understanding Contrast

Sometimes writers use contrast to express an idea. In other words, they begin with the opposite of the point that they want to make.

---

9 **Understanding Contrast** The reading selection "A City That's Doing Something Right" can be divided into two parts. What is the first part? What is the second part? How do these parts show contrast? Discuss your answers with a classmate.

Strategy

Critical Thinking: Making Inferences

Writers usually state information clearly. However, they also often **imply** information. In other words, they just suggest an idea without actually stating it. It is important for students to be able to make **inferences**—that is, to "read between the lines" and understand information that is not clearly stated.

10 Making Inferences Below is information from the reading. Which information is stated in the reading? Write *S* on those lines. Which information is implied but not clearly stated? Write *I* on those lines. Look back at Paragraphs B, C, and D to decide.

1. __S__ Jaime Lerner was the mayor of Curitiba.
2. __I__ Jaime Lerner wanted the people of Curitiba to have a better quality of life.
3. __S__ Under his leadership, city planners established priorities.
4. __S__ Jaime Lerner was an architect.
5. __S__ Poor people receive fresh food when they bring bags of garbage to special centers.
6. __S__ Curitiba's mass-transit system consists of a system of buses.
7. __I__ Subways are more expensive than buses.
8. __S__ Subway-style doors allow passengers to get on and off the bus efficiently.

11 Discussing the Reading Talk about your answers to these questions.

1. What is the population of the major cities in your country? Is overcrowding a problem?
2. What are some problems in your city?
3. What kind of mass transit is available in your city? Is it clean and efficient?
4. Does your city have a recycling program? If so, tell your group about it. How does it work?
5. Are there homeless people in your city? If so, is there a program to help them?

PART 2 Main Ideas and Details

Sick-Building Syndrome

Before You Read

1 Making Predictions The next reading discusses a problem in big cities—indoor air pollution. Before you read, think about the causes of air pollution, both outdoors (outside) and indoors (inside buildings). Brainstorm as many causes as you can think of and write them in the chart on page 33. Look at the picture for help.

Causes of Outdoor Air Pollution	Causes of Indoor Air Pollution

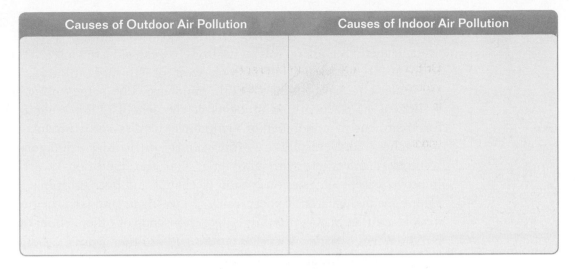

Reading Tip

As you learned in Chapter 1, a paragraph usually tells about one topic and gives a **main idea** or point about that topic. Often there is one sentence that tells the **main idea** of the paragraph.

▲ How many pollutants can you find?

Read

2 **Skimming for Main Ideas** Skim the next article. Do not use a dictionary, and don't worry about the details. When you finish each paragraph, write the topic and main idea of that paragraph. You can copy the main idea directly from the sentence or use your own words to restate the main idea.

Sick-Building Syndrome

A   Elizabeth Steinberg was a healthy 16-year-old student on the tennis team at St. Charles High School, west of Chicago, Illinois. But then she started to have strange health problems. The same thing happened to dozens of teachers and students at the school. They went to doctors for treatment of a number of symptoms such as sore throats, tiredness, 5 headaches, and respiratory (breathing) difficulties. Doctors treated respiratory infections with antibiotics, but the condition didn't seem to improve, except—mysteriously—on weekends and over vacations, when the symptoms disappeared. Experts came to investigate and find the cause. They discovered that St. Charles High, like thousands of other schools and office 10 buildings nationwide, is a "sick building"—in other words, a building that creates its own indoor air pollution.

Topic: _____

Main idea: _____

_____

B   People have worried about smog for many years, and the government has spent billions of dollars to try to clean up the air of big cities. But now we find that there is no escape from unhealthy air. Recent studies have shown 15 that air *inside* many homes, office buildings, and schools is full of pollutants: chemicals, mold, bacteria, smoke, and gases. These pollutants are causing a group of unpleasant and dangerous symptoms that experts call "sick-building syndrome." First discovered in 1982, sick-building syndrome most often includes symptoms similar to those of the flu (watering eyes, headaches, 20 and so on) and respiratory infections such as tonsillitis, bronchitis, and pneumonia.

Topic: _____

Main idea: _____

_____

C   Although most common in office buildings and schools, the indoor pollution that causes sick-building syndrome can also occur in houses. Imagine a typical home. The people who live there burn oil, wood, or gas for 25 cooking and heating. They might smoke cigarettes, pipes, or cigars. They use chemicals for cleaning. They use products made of particleboard, which is an inexpensive kind of board made of very small pieces of wood held together with a chemical. They use products such as computers, fax machines, and

copiers that are made of plastic. These products give off chemicals that we 30
can't see, but we do breathe them in. In some homes, carbon monoxide from
cars in the garage can enter the house. And in many areas, the ground under
the building might send a dangerous gas called radon into the home. The
people in the house are breathing in a "chemical soup."

Topic: _____

Main idea: _____

_____

D   Then what causes sick-building syndrome in an office building or school, 35
where people don't smoke or burn oil, wood, or gas? Experts have discovered
several sources of sick-building syndrome; among these are mold and
bacteria, synthetic products, and lack of ventilation—or the movement of
fresh air into and out of the building. In many buildings, rain has leaked in
and caused water damage to walls and carpets. This allows mold and bacteria 40
to grow. Air conditioning systems are another place where mold and bacteria
can grow. Synthetic (that is, man-made) products such as paint, carpeting,
and furniture can be found in all offices and schools. These products release
toxic (poisonous) chemicals into the air. Perhaps the most common cause of
sick-building syndrome, however, is lack of ventilation. Most modern office 45
buildings are tightly sealed; in other words, the windows don't open, so fresh
air doesn't enter the building. In a building with mold, bacteria, or toxic
chemicals, lack of ventilation makes the situation more serious.

Topic: _____

Main idea: _____

_____

E   There are several solutions to the problem of sick-building syndrome;
the most important of these is cleaning the building. First, of course, experts 50
must determine the specific cause in any one building. Then workers probably
need to take out carpets, wallpaper, and ceiling tiles in order to remove mold
and bacteria. Also, they need to clean out the air conditioning system and
completely rebuild the system of ventilation. They should remove synthetic
products and bring in natural products instead, if they are available. 55

Topic: _____

Main idea: _____

_____

F All of this sounds difficult and expensive. But there is another possible solution that is simple and inexpensive. NASA (the National Aeronautics and Space Administration) was trying to find ways to clean the air in space stations. One scientist with 60 NASA discovered that *houseplants* actually remove pollutants from the air. Certain plants seem to do this better than others. Spider plants, for example, appear to do the best 65 job. Even defoliated plants (without leaves) worked well! In another study, scientists found that the chemical interaction among soil, roots, and leaves works to remove pollutants. 70

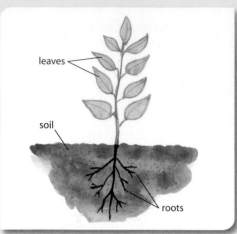

leaves

soil

roots

▲ Plants help clean the air.

Topic: _____

Main idea: _____

_____

G This seems like a good solution, but we don't know enough yet. There are many questions. For instance, which pollutants can plants remove? Which can't they remove? How many plants are necessary to clean the air in a room—one or two or a whole *forest* of plants? When we are able to answer these questions, we might find that plants offer an important pollution- 75 control system for the 21st century.

Topic: _____

Main idea: _____

_____

_____

After You Read

3 Checking Your Answers Compare your answers from Activity 2 with the answers of another student. Are they the same? Are they worded differently? Give reasons for your answers. It's okay if you want to change an answer after listening to your partner's ideas!

4 **Understanding Pronoun Reference** Look back at the reading selection "Sick-Building Syndrome" to find the meanings of the following pronouns. What does each pronoun refer to?

1. they (Paragraph A, line 4) _____

2. they (Paragraph C, line 26, twice) _____

3. them (Paragraph C, line 31) _____

4. these (Paragraph D, line 37) _____

5. these (Paragraph E, line 50) _____

6. they (Paragraph E, line 53) _____

7. they (Paragraph G, line 73) _____

Strategy

Scanning

You can scan a reading to find information quickly. Follow these steps to scan:

- Know the information that you want to find, or the question you want answered.
- Look for that information.
- Move your eyes quickly across the words until the information that you want "jumps out" at you.
- Don't read every word.

You will practice scanning throughout the book when you look for specific information and details.

5 **Scanning** Keep each of these questions in mind as you quickly scan the reading on pages 34-36. When you find each answer, underline it.

1. What are five pollutants?

2. What are several sources of sick-building syndrome?

6 **Discussing the Reading** Talk about your answers to these questions.

1. Is there a problem with smog in your city? When is it the worst? What are the causes?

2. Have you ever experienced sick-building syndrome? If so, what were your symptoms?

3. How many possible pollutants can you find in your home and classroom? Make a list.

4. In your country, do people usually have houseplants? Why or why not?

5. In your opinion, why wasn't sick-building syndrome a problem in the past?

7 **Summarizing** Choose one of the following paragraphs from the reading in Part 1, pages 27–28, to summarize.

- Garbage Collection (Paragraph C)
- Transportation (Paragraph D)
- A Creative Social Program (Paragraph E)

Because a summary is shorter than the original text, try to write only three or four sentences. To write this summary, follow these steps:

- Make sure that you understand the paragraph well.
- Identify the topic, the main idea, and important details.
- Choose two or three important details.
- Do not include less important details.

In order to summarize this in your own words, *don't look at the original paragraph as you write*. When you finish writing, compare your summary with those of other students who summarized the same paragraph. Is your main idea the same? Did you choose the same details?

8 **Writing Your Own Ideas** Choose one of the topics below to write a paragraph about. Write your own thoughts. Try to use vocabulary from this chapter.

- something you like (or don't like) about living in a city
- improving city life
- what you have learned about sick-building syndrome

What's the main idea of your paragraph? _____

Talk it Over

9 **Interviewing** Interview as many people as you can. Ask them the two questions below and take notes on their answers. Then compare your findings with those of other students.

1. Do you think that city life in the future will be better or worse than it is today? Give two reasons that explain why.
2. How will city life be different in the future from how it is today? Make three predictions.

1 **Focusing on Words from the Academic Word List** Fill in the blanks with words from the Academic Word List in the box.

access	established	global	priorities	transportation
environment	focus	predict	residents	

A City That's Doing Something Right

There's good news and bad news about life in modern cities—first, the bad. People who study population growth _____ a nightmare
1
by the year 2025: the _____ population will be more than
2
eight billion, and almost four billion of these people will be living in cities in developing countries such as India and Nigeria. Population growth is already   5
causing unbelievable overcrowding. Due to this overcrowding, many cities have problems with air pollution, disease, and crime. People spend hours in gridlock—that is, traffic so horrible that it simply doesn't move—when they commute daily from their homes to their work and back. There isn't enough water, _____, or housing. Many people don't   10
3
have _____ to health services or jobs. Now the good news: in
4
some cities, instead of worsening, urban life is actually getting much better.

A City and Its Mayor

It might not be a surprise to find that life in affluent cities is improving. But what about cities that *aren't* rich? The city of Curitiba, Brazil, proves that it's possible for even a city in a developing country to offer a good life   15
to its _____. The former mayor of Curitiba for 25 years, Jaime
5
Lerner, is an architect and a very practical person. Under his leadership, the city planners _____ a list of _____—in
6   7
other words, a list of what was most important to work on. They decided to
_____ on the _____ and on the quality of life.   20
8   9

Language Similarities: False Cognates

Some words in English might sound similar to words in your language. These are called cognates. Usually, cognates help your English vocabulary. However, sometimes the meaning is completely different. This can cause problems! Words in two languages with a similar sound but a different meaning are called **false cognates**. Do not try to translate them. Here are some examples.

- *Actualmente* (in Spanish) means "presently, now," so Spanish-speaking students think that *actually* (in English) means the same thing. But it doesn't. In English, actually means "really, truly" or "although this seems strange."

  Example The population has grown, but traffic has *actually* decreased 30 percent.

- *Manshon* (in Korean and Japanese) means "an expensive apartment building." However, in English, *mansion* means "a large expensive single-family house."

  Example If I win the lottery, I'll buy a *mansion* in Beverly Hills.

- *Magazi* (in Greek) means "store, shop." However, in English, a *magazine* is something to read.

  Example I read an interesting article yesterday in a news **magazine**.

- *Lunatik* (in Russian) means "a sleepwalker—a person who walks in his or her sleep." However, in English, *lunatic* means "a crazy person."

  Example Everyone thought he was a *lunatic* when he decided to quit school one month before graduation.

Are there any false cognates that give trouble to people who speak your language? If so, share them with the class.

Strategy

Understanding Parts of Speech

To figure out the meaning of a new word from the context, you may find it helpful to know its part of speech; that is, is the word a noun, a verb, an adjective, or an adverb? Many words are related to one another; they have the same stem (base word) but different endings for different parts of speech.

Example

Cities around the **globe** need to find solutions to similar problems, so city planners sometimes meet at a **global** conference. (*Globe* is a noun. *Global* is an adjective; it describes the noun *conference*.)

2 Understanding Parts of Speech Read the words below. Write the missing noun, verb, adjective, or adverb in the blank boxes. Then listen and check your answers. (The boxes with an X indicate that no word exists for that part of speech.)

Noun	Verb	Adjective	Adverb
beauty, beautification	beautify	*beautiful*	beautifully
creation	*creat*	creative	creative
crowd	*crowd*	crowded	
difference	*differ*	different	differently
difficulty		difficult	
efficiency		efficient	*efficiently*
pollution, pollutant	pollute	*polluted*	
prediction	predict	predictable	predictably
safety	save	*safe*	safely
solution	solve	solvable	
	worsen	worse	*worse*

Next, complete each sentence below and on the next page with words from the chart above. Use the correct form of the base word and write the part of speech in the parentheses after each blank—(n.) for noun, (v.) for verb, (adj.) for adjective, and (adv.) for adverb.

1. solve

   They are trying to find a _____*solution*_____ (*n.*) to the problem of overcrowding, but this is a difficult problem to _____*solve*_____ (*v.*).

2. pollute

   Most people know about air _____*pollution*_____ (*n.*) in big cities, but they're just beginning to learn about the many _____*pollutants*_____ (*n.*) that we have inside buildings.

3. crowd

   There are _____*crowds*_____ (*n.*) of people everywhere; the mass-transit system is especially _____*crowded*_____ (*adj.*).

4. save

   The city is not _____*safe*_____ (*adj.*) because of crime. People can't leave their homes _____*safely*_____ (*adv.*) at night, and the police can't provide for their _____*safety*_____ (*n.*).

5. beautify

   Many people bring plants into their homes because the plants are _____*beautiful*_____ (*adj.*). However, it's possible that these plants not only _____*beautify*_____ (*v.*) the environment but also clean the air.

6. predict, worsen

Some people _____ ( ) that urban life will get

_____ ( ); according to their _____ ( ),

conditions will _____ ( ) every year.

7. differ

The causes of indoor air pollution _____ ( ) from area to area.

One reason for the _____ ( ) is that people heat their homes

_____ ( ). People in some areas burn wood for heat; in

other areas, they use something _____ ( ).

8. efficient

The mass-transit system in our city is not very _____ ( ), so

we need to replace it with one that runs more _____ ( ).

F🔍CUS

Looking Up Parts of Speech

You learned in Chapter 1 that you don't need to look up every new word in a dictionary because you can often guess the meaning from the context. However, you may want to use a dictionary for other purposes. For instance, you might want to find out the part of speech of a word or learn related words. A dictionary will tell you the parts of speech a word can be, usually with these abbreviations:

n. = noun	adj. = adjective	prep. = preposition
v. = verb	adv. = adverb	conj. = conjunction

The abbreviation appears before the meanings of the word with that part of speech. The dictionary entry below shows that the word *access* can be a noun (with two meanings) or a verb (with one meaning). A related adjective is *accessible*.

---

ac·cess¹ / ˈæksɛs/ *n.* [U] **1** the right to enter a place, use something, see someone, etc.: *Anyone with* **access to** *the Internet can visit our website.* | *Many people living in developing countries do not* **have access to** *clean drinking water.* **2** the way you enter a building or get to a place, or how easy this is: *The only* **access to** *the building is through the parking lot.* | *The law requires businesses to improve* **access for** *disabled customers.* → **gain access** at GAIN¹ [ORIGIN 1300—1400 Old French *acces* "arrival," from Latin *accessus* "approach"]

access² *v.* [T] to find information, especially on a computer: *You can even access the Internet from this cell phone.*

ac·ces·si·ble /əkˈsɛsəbəl/ *adj.* **1** easy to reach or get into ANT **inaccessible**: *The park is not* **accessible by** *road.* **2** easy to obtain or use: *We want a low-cost health care system that is* **accessible to** *every citizen.* **3** easy to understand and enjoy: *We tried to make the play more accessible to a young audience by reducing it from its original three hours to ninety minutes.* | *I thought his last book was more accessible.* —**accessibility** /əkˌsɛsəˈbɪləţi /*n.* [U]

3 **Looking Up Parts of Speech** If possible, everyone in the class should use the same kind of dictionary for the following activity. Work quickly. The first student with the correct answers is the winner.

Find these words in your dictionary. Write the parts of speech on the lines before each word. (See page 42 for abbreviations.) Some words, in different contexts, can be more than one part of speech.

1. _adj._ terrible
2. _____ discipline
3. _____ value
4. _____ original
5. _____ pleasant

6. _____ water
7. _____ expert
8. _____ commute
9. _____ farm
10. _____ smog

11. _____ produce
12. _____ actually
13. _____ mystery
14. _____ individual
15. _____ trash

4 **Searching the Internet** Do an Internet search for English-language newspapers in one of the countries below (or choose any other country in which English is not the native language). Use a search engine such as Google.

Armenia	Egypt	Mexico	Senegal
Brazil	Greece	Russia	Taiwan
Costa Rica	Japan	Saudi Arabia	Thailand

What is happening in the capital city of that country today? Find an article online about this. Discuss your findings with another student.

PART 4 **Focus on Testing**

FOCUS

TOEFL® iBT

Getting Meaning of Vocabulary from Context

Some standardized exams test how well you can guess the meaning of a new word or phrase from the context. Often on such tests, one or more answers may be very close in meaning, but not correct. Another answer might have the correct part of speech, but the wrong meaning. Another might simply be wrong; perhaps it is the opposite of the correct answer or has the wrong part of speech. Always keep in mind that there is only one correct answer.

1 Practice Guess the meanings of the underlined words from the reading selection "Sick-Building Syndrome" on pages 34–36. Choose the correct answers.

1. They went to doctors for treatment of a number of <u>symptoms</u> such as tiredness, headaches, <u>sore</u> throats, and respiratory problems.

   symptoms:
   - (A) syndromes
   - (B) pains in the head
   - (C) signs of a sickness
   - (D) kinds of medicine
   - (E) kinds of tiredness

   sore:
   - (A) well
   - (B) painful
   - (C) difficult
   - (D) problem
   - (E) in the throat

2. These pollutants are causing a group of unpleasant and dangerous symptoms that experts call "sick-building <u>syndrome</u>."
   - (A) polluted
   - (B) problem with a large building
   - (C) symptom
   - (D) combination of symptoms
   - (E) danger

3. In many buildings, rain has <u>leaked in</u> and caused water damage to walls and carpets.
   - (A) escaped
   - (B) entered the ventilation system
   - (C) come in accidentally
   - (D) worsened
   - (E) fallen

4. The air was full of <u>pollutants</u>: chemicals, mold, bacteria, smoke, and gases.
   - (A) pollution
   - (B) chemicals
   - (C) smog inside a building
   - (D) things that pollute
   - (E) gases

Self-Assessment Log

Read the lists below. Check (✓) the strategies and vocabulary that you learned in this chapter. Look through the chapter or ask your instructor about the strategies and words that you do not understand.

Reading and Vocabulary-Building Strategies

☐ Getting meaning from context
☐ Recognizing the main idea
☐ Recognizing supporting details
☐ Understanding italics
☐ Making inferences
☐ Skimming for main ideas
☐ Understanding parts of speech
☐ Looking up parts of speech

Target Vocabulary

Nouns		Verbs	Adjectives
▪ access*	▪ pollution	▪ commute	▪ affluent
▪ agricultural operation	▪ priorities*	▪ crowd	▪ creative*
	▪ produce	▪ cultivate	▪ global*
▪ crops	▪ recycling plant	▪ established*	
▪ developing countries	▪ residents*	▪ focus*	**Adverb**
▪ environment*	▪ transportation*	▪ predict*	▪ efficiently
▪ gridlock	▪ trash	▪ solve	
▪ mass transit	▪ urban dwellers	▪ worsening	
▪ pedestrian zone			

* These words are from the Academic Word List. For more information on this list, see www.victoria.ac.nz/lals/resources/academicwordlist/.

3 Business and Money

> "Prosperity is a way of living and thinking, and not just money or things. Poverty is a way of living and thinking, and not just a lack of money or things."

Eric Butterworth
Author, scholar

In this **CHAPTER**

In Part 1, you will read about organizations that are helping people escape from poverty. In the rest of this chapter, you will read about, discuss, and explore why people buy things, advertising, and consumerism.

Connecting to the Topic

1 Describe the two businesses that you see in the picture. How are they similar? How are they different?

2 Name five things (products) that you shop for. Name five services that you shop for.

3 Name seven ways that a small or large business can advertise its products or services.

Banking on Poor Women

Before You Read

1 **Previewing the Topic** Look at the photos and discuss the questions.

1. Compare the social or economic classes of the people in the photos below. What are some words to describe their economic situations?

2. What might the businessmen with the laptop be discussing? Think of three possibilities.

3. What is necessary in order to get a business loan (to borrow money) from a bank?

▼ A woman weaving   ▼ A produce market

International business ▶

4. Is it possible for people to move up in their economic class? (If so, how?) Is there more possibility of this in some countries than in others?

5. Brainstorm about the problems of very poor people. Then brainstorm possible solutions to these problems. Write your ideas in the chart below.

Problems	Possible Solutions

2 **Thinking Ahead** Read these quotations. Can you state them in other words? Which one(s) do you like or agree with? Why? Discuss them in a group.

"From borrowing one gets poorer and from work one gets richer."
Isaac Bashevis Singer, Novelist (1904–1991)

"A bank is a place where they lend you an umbrella in fair weather and ask for it back when it begins to rain."
Robert Frost, Poet (1874–1963)

3 **Previewing Vocabulary** Read the words and phrases below. Listen to the pronunciation. Put a check mark (✓) next to the words that you don't know. Don't use a dictionary.

Nouns
- access
- capacity
- character
- collateral
- eradication
- fund
- grants
- literacy
- microlending
- poverty
- requirement

Verbs
- funding
- invest
- lift

Adjectives
- anonymous
- social
- subsidiary
- worthless

Expressions
- peer pressure
- took (take) the initiative

Strategy

Getting Meaning from Context: Understanding *e.g.* and *i.e.*
Sometimes certain abbreviations (shortened forms of words) help you understand a new word or phrase. Here are two.
e.g. = for example
i.e. = that is; in other words

4 **Getting Meaning from Context** Read the sentences below. Use a highlighter to mark the words that give clues to the meaning of the underlined word(s). Then answer the questions.

1. This is a group of <u>entrepreneurs</u>—i.e., people who own and run their own small businesses.

   What are entrepreneurs?

   _____

2. Instead of collateral, there is <u>peer pressure</u>; i.e., group members make sure that each person pays back his or her loan.

   What happens when there is peer pressure?

   _____

3. The Global Fund for Women helps find solutions to <u>social ills</u>—e.g., violence against women, lack of health care, and lack of education.

   What are examples of social ills?

   _____

Strategy

Recognizing Similar Meanings but Different Parts of Speech
Sometimes the context of a sentence has an explanation of the new vocabulary, but in order to think of a synonym, you need to change the part of speech.

Example
For many people, there seems to be no escape from **poverty**; in other words, they are **poor**, and they have no hope that this will change.

In this example, you see that *poverty* is close in meaning to *poor*, but the two words have different parts of speech. *Poverty* is a noun, and *poor* is an adjective. (*Poverty* is the condition of being poor.)

5 **Recognizing Synonyms** Highlight the words below that have the same or almost the same meaning as the underlined words. Then write your answers to the questions that follow.

If this woman wants to borrow money, she must show that she (1) is honest (has character), (2) is able to run her business (has capacity), and (3) owns a house or land or something valuable.

1. What part of speech is *character?* _____

2. What does *character* mean? _____

3. What part of speech is *capacity?* _____

4. What does *capacity* mean? _____

Strategy

Using Parts of Speech to Understand Vocabulary

Sometimes the context of a sentence does not give a clear definition or example of a new word. You can't be sure about the exact meaning, but you can still make an intelligent guess. First, figure out the part of speech of the new word. Then think about what other word might be logical in that place.

Example

Everyone in the group must **approve** the loan of every other group member, or Grameen Bank won't lend the money.

Part of speech: verb
Possible meanings: agree to; say OK about; sign

Some of your guesses might be wrong, but that's not a problem. If you see the word again in a different context, the meaning will become clearer.

6 **Using Parts of Speech to Understand Vocabulary** Make guesses about the underlined words below. Don't worry about being right or wrong. Just try to be logical. When you finish, compare your answers with a partner's.

1. A poor woman has an idea to lift herself and her family out of poverty.

Part of speech: _____ *V.* _____

Possible meanings: _____ *raise* _____

2. The primary goal of Grameen Bank and other similar programs is the eradication of poverty.

Part of speech: _____ n. _____

Possible meanings: _____ destruction; solution _____

3. As poverty has decreased, there have been some surprising secondary effects of microlending programs. Perhaps the main subsidiary effect has been a change in the social status of women.

Part of speech: _____ adj. _____

Possible meanings: _____ smaller   secondary _____

4. She began the Global Fund for Women. This fund has given $37 million to over 2,500 women's groups. It gives grants, not loans. The money is given, not lent.

fund

Part of speech: _____ n. _____

Possible meanings: _____ money   big pile of money _____

grants

Part of speech: _____ n, _____

Possible meanings: _____ gift _____

5. With careful planning and cooperation, most people use the money well and then invest both money and knowledge back into their communities.

Part of speech: _____ v _____

Possible meanings: _____ spend; award _____

Read

7 **Reading an Article** As you read the following article, think about the answer to this question: *How can banks help poor women change their lives?* Then do the activities that follow the reading.

Banking on Poor Women

A   For many people, there seems to be no escape from poverty; in other words, they are poor, and they have no hope that this will ever change. In addition, they have the social problems of poverty—among them, low social status, violence, poor health, and lack of education.

B   Imagine this situation: a poor woman has an idea for a small business 5 to lift herself and her family out of poverty. She needs a little money to begin this business. She goes to a bank to borrow the money, and the banker interviews her. At this bank, as at most banks, the borrower must meet three necessary conditions: **character, capacity,** and **collateral.** That is, if this woman wants to borrow money from the bank, she must show that she (1) is 10 honest (has character), (2) is able to run her business (has capacity), and (3) owns a house, land, or something valuable (has collateral) for the bank to take if she can't pay back the money. So what happens to the woman? The bank won't lend her the money because she doesn't have any collateral. In such a situation, there seems to be no way for the woman to break the cycle of poverty and the problems that are associated with it.

Microlending

One possible solution these days is **microlending**. This is a system of special banks and programs that are loaning money to "the poorest of the poor." The idea began in Bangladesh, with a man named Mohammad Yunus, who founded Grameen Bank. The bank lends small amounts of money to people who want to go into business. These are people who could never receive a loan from a "regular" bank. To receive a loan through Grameen Bank, people still must have character and capacity, but collateral is not necessary any longer. There is a different **requirement**: each borrower must join a "borrowing group." This small group meets regularly, follows a list of rules from the bank, and offers advice and support to members. Instead of collateral, there is **peer pressure**; i.e., group members make sure that each person pays back his or her loan. They want to keep their "good name" and continue doing business with the bank.

What Works, What Doesn't

Grameen Bank has had many successes and only a few failures. In a developing country such as Bangladesh, a person can buy a cow or a sewing machine and begin a small business with only $20 to $50. Today, there are 8.35 million borrowers in 81,379 villages in Bangladesh. The bank makes over $123 million in loans in a typical month, and the repayment rate is an amazing 96.67 percent. At first, the bank lent half of the money to men and half to women. Unfortunately, most of the Bangladeshi men spent the money on themselves, not the business. Now, 96 percent of the borrowers are women. In Bangladesh—and other countries that started similar microlending programs—the bankers soon learned that urban programs were not as successful as rural ones. Borrowers in cities did not always repay the loans. Because of the importance of peer pressure, microlending is more effective in small villages, where everyone knows and depends on everyone else, than in urban areas (where it's possible to be **anonymous**—unknown).

Subsidiary Effect

The primary goal of this and other similar programs is the **eradication** of poverty. However, as poverty has decreased, there have been some surprising secondary effects of microlending programs. Perhaps the main **subsidiary** effect has been a change in the **social** status of women. Traditionally, in some societies, people thought of women as **worthless**. But when a woman has **access** to money and is able to demonstrate her capacity for business, she often receives more respect than before from the male members of her family 50 and from the entire village.

Global Fund for Women

F In any country, women are the poorest of the poor. They produce more than 55 half of the world's food, but they own just one percent of the world's land. They are 51 percent of the 60 world's population, but very, very little money goes to programs to help them. In the late

▲ A woman in Benin travels to market

1980s, Anne Firth Murray **took the initiative** and began the Global Fund 65 for Women. Unlike microlending programs, this **fund** gives **grants**, not loans. The money is *given*, not *lent*. Another difference is that unlike Grameen Bank, which helps people begin businesses, the direct focus of the Global Fund for Women is to help find solutions to social ills—e.g., violence against women, lack of health care, and lack of education. Since 1987, the 70 fund has given $88 million to over 4,300 women's groups in 172 countries. For instance, the fund has helped the Petersburg Center for Women in St. Petersburg, Russia. This center cares for women who are the victims of violence and abuse from family members. In Kenya, the Global Fund supports a program that gives health care and education to women with 75 AIDS. In a village in southern India, it is **funding** a woman who has started a **literacy** program to teach poor women to read.

Breaking the Cycle

G Grameen Bank and the Global Fund for Women may use different methods, but they have the same goal—the eradication of poverty. They also have a lesson for banks around the world: it's good business to give a chance 80 to the poor. With careful planning, education, and cooperation, most people use the money well and then **invest** the money and knowledge back into their communities. There is hope that they can begin to break the cycle of poverty for themselves, their families, and society.

Strategy

Organizing Ideas: Focusing on Using a Venn Diagram

One way to show similarities and differences between two things is with a graphic organizer called a Venn diagram. This diagram has two connecting circles. In the center is anything that is true of *both* things. On the right and left are the differences between them.

Bananas	Bananas and Oranges	Oranges
• yellow color • long, curved shape	• fruit • sweet	• orange color • round shape

8 **Organizing Ideas Using a Venn Diagram** What is the goal of both Grameen Bank and the Global Fund for Women? How do they differ in the way they work? Fill in this graphic organizer with information about Grameen Bank and the Global Fund for Women to show that they share the same goal but work in different ways.

Grameen Bank   **Common Goals**   **Global Fund for Women**

How does it work?
loan small amount money to people who want to begin their business

grant
the eradication of poverty

How does it work?
give money to women to find the solutions to the social ills

9 **Checking Comprehension: Identifying Details** On a piece of paper, write your answers to these questions.

1. What is necessary in order to borrow from Grameen Bank? What *isn't* necessary?

2. Why does Grameen Bank lend mostly to women? Why does it not lend to people in urban areas?

3. What is a subsidiary effect of microlending programs?

4. What are some social problems that are often associated with poverty?

10 Critical Thinking: Making Inferences Read the excerpt below from Paragraph E. Answer this question: *What might be some specific ways in which a woman with her own business "receives more respect"?* In other words, make inferences about how this changes her life.

> Traditionally, in some societies, people thought of women as worthless. But when a woman has access to money and is able to demonstrate her capacity for business, she often receives more respect than before from the male members of her family and from the entire village.

11 Discussing the Reading Answer these questions based upon a country you know well. Discuss your answers in a group.

1. What kind of collateral do banks require before they loan money to someone?

2. Do people sometimes join a cooperative group to borrow money? If so, what are these groups called? How do they work?

3. What are some social problems? What are people doing to solve them?

12 Talk It Over: Understanding Irony *Irony* describes a situation that has the opposite result from what you might expect. Usually, this result is negative or bad. The following cartoon is ironic. What idea is the cartoonist expressing? Do you agree?

Consumerism and the Human Brain

Before You Read

Strategy

Previewing the Topic

It always helps to have ideas or questions in mind before you read. The more you think about and know about a topic before reading, the more you will understand the reading. The reading passage will confirm some of your ideas (tell you they are right), answer some of your questions, and correct some of your mistaken ideas.

1 **Previewing the Topic** Talk about your answers to the questions below.

1. Who are consumers? What do they do?

2. What are some reasons that people choose one brand of a product instead of a similar brand of the same product?

3. How does advertising influence people?

4. Look at the photo. Why might someone want to buy an SUV after seeing this?

▲ This could be yours!

Read

2 **Identifying the Topic and Main Idea** Read the following article. Do not use a dictionary and don't worry about the details. When you finish, write the topic and main idea of each paragraph. You can copy the main idea directly from the sentence, or use your own words to restate the main idea.

[handwritten margin notes, top left:]
Main Ideas of Paragraphs
① Topic sentence
② Summary at the end
③ Background info
(1~3 sentences)
destory adj.

[handwritten margin notes, top right:]
italics ① emphasis ② foreign words

Consumerism and the Human Brain

A   We are all consumers. We all buy and use products and services; that is, we consume. The word comes from the Latin *consumere*, which means "to use up, to waste or destroy." Most of us don't think of ourselves as wasteful or destructive, but the world economy is based on consumerism. Today, people worldwide have greater access than ever before to a huge variety of products and, often, to dozens of brands of the same product. What makes us decide to buy Brand A instead of Brand B, when the two items are really identical? Why do we buy things that we don't actually need? The answer lies in marketing—the advertising and selling of products. Successful marketers use their knowledge of psychology and, increasingly, of recent studies of the human brain, to persuade us to consume more and more.

5

10

Topic: _____

Main idea: _____

_____

B   A good understanding of human weakness is essential if a company wants to sell a product. One way that advertisers persuade us to buy a product is by targeting our dissatisfaction with ourselves, our fears. Consider for a moment a typical fear—fear of being offensive to other people. Advertisers persuade us, for example, that if we don't buy their mouthwash, we'll have bad breath and offend other people. Dentists tell us that mouthwash is actually unnecessary; they explain that we need only simple dental hygiene—regular, correct use of a soft toothbrush and of dental floss. But we continue to spend money on mouthwash, breath freshener, and breath mints. Our fear of offending people outweighs our dentists' logic.

15

20

Topic: _____

Main idea: _____

_____

C   In a similar way, advertisers also take advantage of our need for a good self-image, our desire to appear attractive, successful, and even exciting. Take the example of the Marlboro cowboy. For years, this famous image has appeared everywhere, in even the smallest rural villages. Many men see it and think that's the kind of person they would like to be—strong, handsome, and adventurous—a person with an exciting life. Although it's irrational—impossible to explain reasonably—they buy the cigarettes because they want to be like the Marlboro man. It's common knowledge that the original

25

model for these advertisements was a man addicted to smoking who died of lung cancer. However, this brand of cigarette remains very popular. Another example is the recent popularity in the United States of SUVs—sport utility vehicles. These vehicles are more expensive than most cars. They use more gas and create more pollution than most cars. They take up more space than most cars. But TV commercials show them climbing rocky mountain roads and crossing rivers, which seems exciting to many people. Most people who buy an SUV never get out of the city. They spend their morning commute in gridlock, not driving up and down mountains. Although it may seem irrational, advertisers persuade them that SUV owners are people with an exciting life.

▲ Is it worth it to have an SUV in the city?

Topic: _____

Main idea: _____

_____

D   With so many different (but almost identical) brands of the same product, what causes us to choose one brand instead of another? According to Dr. Alan Hirsch, our sense of smell actually influences our opinion of a product and our decision to buy it. A scientist at the Smell and Taste Treatment and Research Foundation in Chicago, Hirsch ran a careful, well-organized study. There were two identical rooms with an identical pair of Nike sneakers in each room. There was only one difference: he sprayed one of the rooms with a scent of flowers. Volunteers entered each room and

▲ Why is this person choosing one sneaker instead of another?

answered questions about the sneakers. The result was that 84 percent of the people preferred the sneakers in the room with the floral smell even though they were exactly the same as the ones in the other room! 70

Topic: _____

Main idea: _____

_____

fortune teller

E   There is also the effect of self-fulfilling prophecies. A self-fulfilling prophecy is a situation in which people cause a prediction to come true. (For example, a teacher tells a class that they are especially intelligent, and that semester the class does especially well on exams.) In marketing, a successful advertisement persuades consumers that a product works well; their belief 75 causes them to use the product in such a way that it does work well. For example, the ads for Brand X of a diet pill say, "Take this pill, and you will lose weight because you won't be hungry." So people buy Brand X. Because they believe it will cause weight loss, they begin to eat less. They establish a new habit of eating less. The result? They lose weight. Is this because of the 80 pill or because they are eating less?

Topic: _____

Main idea: _____

_____

F   Most of us like to think that we are reasonable, independent thinkers. We like to believe that we have a good reason for our choices. We don't want to buy products because of some strange compulsion—some irrational desire that we can't control. The truth is, however, that with their increasing 85 knowledge of what goes on in the human brain, marketers might have more power over us than we realize.

Topic: _____

Main idea: _____

_____

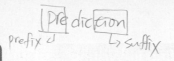
prefix **pre dic tion** ⤷ *suffix*

3 **Identifying the Topic and Main Idea** After you write the topic and main idea of each paragraph above, compare your answers with those of another student. Are your answers the same? Are they the same but perhaps worded differently? Give reasons for your answers. You can change an answer after listening to your partner's ideas.

4 **Understanding Pronoun Reference** Look back at the reading selection on pages 58–60 to find the meanings of the following pronouns. What does each pronoun refer to?

1. their (Paragraph A, line 10) _____ marketers _____
2. they (Paragraph B, line 18) _____ dentists _____
3. they (Paragraph C, line 28) _____ men _____
4. it (Paragraph D, line 52) _____ product _____
5. he (Paragraph D, line 64) _____ Hirsch / a scientist _____
6. their (Paragraph E, line 75) _____ consumers _____

Culture Note

Fighting Consumerism in Japan

In Japan, as in many other countries, advertising influences people to buy more and more. However, the Seikatsu Club is fighting against this. The Seikatsu Club is a **consumers'** cooperative group with over 400,000 members who don't like to call themselves **"consumers."** They are working to reduce the influence of marketing in their lives. They hold meetings at which they discuss the actual ingredients, value, and cost of various products. They do not buy any products (such as synthetic detergents) that harm the environment. They do not buy any food products that contain harmful or inessential chemicals. Most important, they are working to educate people to think for themselves. Are there organizations or movements similar to this in other countries?

5 **Discussing the Reading** Talk about your own buying habits. Follow these steps.

Step 1: Working alone, write a list of ten products that you buy regularly.
Step 2: Think about your answers to these questions:

- Do you always buy the same brand of each product?
- If so, can you give a reason for your choice?
- Does advertising influence your choice of products?

Step 3: In a group, share your list and answers.

6 **Summarizing** Choose one of the following paragraphs from the reading in Part 2, pages 58–59, to summarize.

- Paragraph B
- Paragraph C
- Paragraph D

Because a summary is shorter than the original text or paragraph, try to write only three or four sentences. To write this summary, follow these steps:

- Make sure that you understand the paragraph well.
- Identify the main idea.
- Choose two or three important details.
- Do not include less important details.

In order to summarize in your own words, *don't look at the original paragraph as you write.* When you finish writing, compare your summary with those of other students who summarized the same paragraph.

7 **Responding in Writing** Choose one of the topics below to write a paragraph about. Write your own thoughts. Try to use vocabulary from this chapter.

- your opinion of microlending
- your opinion of the Global Fund for Women
- your opinion of the Seikatsu Club
- something that you have learned about advertising

What's the main idea of your paragraph? _____

_____

Talk it Over

8 **Discussing Advertisements** In small groups, choose one of the following products: toothpaste, cars, laundry detergent, or a luxury vacation. Look online for advertisements for your product. Bring as many examples as you can to your group. Together, study them. What kind of psychology is the advertiser using? (Fear? Desire for a good self-image? Self-fulfilling prophecy?)

PART 3 Building Vocabulary and Study Skills

1 **Recognizing Word Meanings** Match the words with their meanings. Write the letters on the lines.

1. _____ literacy
2. _____ poverty
3. _____ requirement
4. _____ anonymous
5. _____ worthless

a. being poor
b. necessity
c. not valuable
d. ability to read
e. unknown

2 **Focusing on Words from the Academic Word List** Fill in the blanks with words from the Academic Word List in the box. This activity continues on the next page.

access	consumers	identical	logic
consume (used 2 times)	economy	items	targeting

Consumerism and the Human Brain

We are all _____. We all buy and use products and
                        1
services; that is, we _____. The word comes from the
                          2
Latin *consumere*, which means "to use up, to waste or destroy." Most
of us don't think of ourselves as wasteful or destructive, but the world
_____ is based on consumerism. Today, people worldwide have   5
            3
greater _____ than ever before to a huge variety of products,
              4
and, often, to dozens of brands of the same product. What makes us decide
to buy Brand A instead of Brand B, when the two _____ are
                                                      5
really _____? Why do we buy things that we don't actually
            6
need? The answer lies in marketing—the advertising and selling of products.   10
Successful marketers use their knowledge of psychology, and, increasingly,
of recent studies of the human brain, to persuade us to _____
                                                              7
more and more.

A good understanding of human weakness is essential if a company
wants to sell a product. One way that advertisers persuade us to buy a   15
product is by _____ our dissatisfaction with ourselves, our
                    8

fears. Consider for a moment a typical fear—fear of being offensive to other people. Advertisers persuade us, for example, that if we don't buy their mouthwash, we'll have bad breath and offend other people. Dentists tell us that mouthwash is actually unnecessary; they explain that we need only simple dental hygiene—regular, correct use of a soft toothbrush and of dental floss. But we continue to spend money on mouthwash, breath freshener, and breath mints. Our fear of offending people outweighs our dentists' _____.

₉

FOCUS

Understanding Parts of Speech: Suffixes

Remember that in order to guess the meaning of a new word from the context, you might find it helpful to know its part of speech. Sometimes you can tell the part of speech from the suffix (the word ending). Here are some common suffixes, listed by the parts of speech that they usually indicate.

Nouns		Adjectives	
-er/-or	-ee	-ive	-ful
-ist	-(i)ty	-able/-ible	-ant/-ent
-sion/-tion	-ance/-ence	-(u)al	-ous
-ment	-ure	-ic(al)	-ar(y)
-acy		-ate	

---

3 **Understanding Parts of Speech: Suffixes** Are the following words nouns or adjectives? The suffixes will tell you. On the lines, write *n.* or *adj.* as in the examples.

1. *adj.* compulsive
2. *n.* spender
3. *adj.* successful
4. *n.* marketer
5. *n.* psychologist
6. *n.* literacy
7. *adj.* identical
8. *adj.* violent
9. *n.* influence
10. *n.* information
11. *adj.* offensive

12. *adj.* influential
13. *n.* compulsion
14. *n.* violence
15. *n.* computer
16. *adj.* pressure
17. *n.* society
18. *n.* addition
19. *adj.* expensive
20. *adj.* different
21. *n.* poverty
22. *n.* requirement

23. *adj.* pleasure
24. *adj.* enormous
25. *n.* scientist
26. *adj.* basic
27. *adj.* failure
28. *adj.* special
29. *n.* consumer
30. *adj.* public (*n.*)
31. *adj.* floral
32. *adj.* logical
33. *n.* culture

4 **Understanding Parts of Speech: Changing the Suffix** Complete each sentence with a word related to the underlined word. Then look back at the list of suffixes to check your answers. The first one is done as an example.

1. _____Marketers_____ use their knowledge of psychology to <u>market</u> their products. They hope that ___Consumer___ will buy their goods, <u>consume</u> them, and soon feel the need to buy more.

2. That ___Violence___ TV commercial was ___offensive___ to many people. They were <u>offended</u> by its <u>violence</u> and didn't see the need for it.

3. Advertising is a kind of ___Influenced___ that has a strong ___Information___ on consumers; it should not only <u>influence</u> people to buy products, but also <u>inform</u> them.

4. This organization has been ___socially___ in solving some serious <u>social</u> problems in that ___successful___. Their <u>success</u> is due to hard work and the cooperation of many people.

Strategy

Paying Attention to Phrases

In recent years, linguists (experts on language) have been emphasizing the importance of learning new words in *phrases* instead of individually. Learning phrases instead of single words will help you to know how to use each new word as you learn it.

Certain words belong together in phrases. For example, a *noun phrase* can include adjectives and other words before or after the noun. A *verb phrase* may include noun objects or adverbs. A *prepositional phrase* begins with a preposition. An *infinitive phrase* begins with an infinitive and includes an object after the verb.
Examples include the following:

Noun Phrases
greater access
access to information

Verb Phrases
spend money
educate people to spend wisely

Prepositional Phrases
in a similar way
with exciting lives

Infinitive Phrases
to save money
to buy Brand X

When you read, it is important to begin to notice words in phrases. Look just before and just after a word to see if it is part of a phrase. What kind of phrase is it a part of? For example, if the word is a verb, is it followed by an object or by a preposition? If it is followed by a preposition, which one?

5 Paying Attention to Phrases Read the following paragraph from Part 1. Notice the underlined phrases. (There are more phrases than the ones underlined, but don't worry about those.) When you finish reading, decide what type of phrase each one is: *noun, verb, prepositional,* or *infinitive.*
Write your answers in your notebook.

<u>For many people</u>, there seems to be no <u>escape from poverty</u>; <u>in</u>
        1   <u>other words</u>, they are poor, and they <u>have no hope</u> that this will ever
        3   4
change. <u>In addition</u>, they have the <u>social problems</u> of poverty. <u>Imagine</u>
                    5   6   7
<u>this situation</u>: <u>a poor woman</u> <u>has an idea</u> for a <u>small business</u> to lift
                        8   9   10
herself and her family <u>out of poverty</u>. She needs <u>a little money</u> to begin
this business. She <u>goes to a bank</u> <u>to borrow the money</u>, and the banker
                        11   12   13
interviews her. At this bank, as <u>at most banks</u>, the borrower must <u>meet</u>
                        14   15
<u>three necessary conditions</u>: character, capacity, and collateral. That is,
                16   17
if this woman wants <u>to borrow money</u> <u>from the bank</u>, she must show
                        18   19
that she (1) is honest (<u>has character</u>), (2) is able <u>to run her business</u>
                                20   21
(has capacity), and (3) <u>owns a house</u>, land, or something valuable (has
                        22
collateral) for the bank to take if she can't <u>pay back the money</u>. So what
                                                        23
happens to the woman? The bank won't <u>lend her the money</u> because she
                                                        24
doesn't have any collateral. <u>In such a situation</u>, there seems to be no way
                                                25
for the woman <u>to break the cycle</u> of poverty.
                        26

collocations

6 Noticing Words in Phrases Fill in the blanks with words that complete the phrases. If you need help (or to check your answers), you can scan each paragraph that follows the set of phrases. These paragraphs are from the reading in Part 2, "Consumerism and the Human Brain."

1. persuade us _____ *to* _____ buy a product

2. dissatisfaction _____ *With* _____ ourselves

3. fear of being offensive _____ *to* _____ other people

4. _____ *dental* _____ hygiene

5. _____ *dental* _____ floss

6. our fear _____ *of* _____ offending people

A   A good understanding of human weakness is essential if a company wants to sell a product. One way that advertisers persuade us to buy a product is by targeting our dissatisfaction with ourselves, our fears. Consider for a moment a typical fear—fear of being offensive to other people. Advertisers persuade us, for example, that if we don't buy their mouthwash, we'll have bad breath and offend other people. Dentists tell us that mouthwash is actually unnecessary; they explain that we need only simple dental hygiene—regular, correct use of a soft toothbrush and of dental floss. But we continue to spend money on mouthwash, breath freshener, and breath mints. Our fear of offending people outweighs our dentists' logic.

7. _____In_____ a similar way
8. Advertisers _____take_____ advantage _____of_____ our need for a good self-image
9. _____Common_____ knowledge
10. addicted _____to_____ smoking
11. died _____of_____ lung cancer

B   In a similar way, advertisers also take advantage of our need for a good self-image, our desire to appear attractive, successful, and even exciting. Take the example of the Marlboro cowboy. For years, this famous image has appeared everywhere, in even the smallest rural villages. Many men see it and think that's the kind of person they would like to be—strong, handsome, and adventurous—a person with an exciting life. Although it's irrational— impossible to explain reasonably—they buy the cigarettes because they want to be like the Marlboro man. It's common knowledge that the original model for these advertisements was a man addicted to smoking who died of lung cancer. However, this brand of cigarette remains very popular.

12. sport _____utility_____ vehicles
13. take _____up_____ more space
14. get _____out_____ _____of_____ the city

C   Another example is the recent popularity in the United States of SUVs— sport utility vehicles. These vehicles are more expensive than most cars. They use more gas and create more pollution than most cars. They take up more space than most cars. But TV commercials show them climbing rocky mountain roads and crossing rivers, which seems exciting to many people. Most people who buy an SUV never get out of the city. They spend their morning commute in gridlock, not driving up and down mountains. Although it may seem irrational, advertisers persuade them that SUV owners are people with an exciting life.

 7 Searching the Internet Do an Internet search on the home page of one of the organizations in the chart on the next page. Find the answer to the question, write it in the chart, and share it with two other students.

Organization	Question	Answer
Grameen Bank	What types of businesses do Grameen borrowers have?	
Global Fund for Women	What is one program that the Global Fund is currently supporting?	
Seikatsu Club	What are some of the club's principles on safety, health, and the environment?	

PART 4

Focus on Testing

FOCUS

TOEFL® iBT

Implications and Inferences

In this chapter and others, you have learned about implications and inferences. In the Focus on Testing section in Chapter 1, you also saw an example of how an inference question on the TOEFL® Internet-Based Test might be worded: *What can be inferred about Finnish students from reading Paragraph C?*

After every passage in the reading section of the TOEFL® iBT, there will be at least one question about inferences or implications. Here is a summary of the differences between *imply* and *infer.*

About the verb *imply*:

- It means "communicate a meaning without directly saying it."
- Its subject is a person or thing that can communicate meanings. For example, "I implied that… "; "The author implies that… "; "Paragraph 4 implies that… "

About the verb *infer*:

- It means "understand a meaning even though it is not stated directly."
- Its subject must be a human or group of humans. For example, "I inferred that… "; "Readers might infer that… "; "The police inferred that… "

1 **Practice** Look again at the reading "Consumerism and the Human Brain" on pages 58–60. Read it. Then read the statements below and put a checkmark (✓) next to any statement that is both true according to the reading and grammatically correct. (Three sentences use *imply* and *infer* incorrectly—don't check those; underline them.) Write *F* next to the sentences that are false.

1. _____ Paragraph A implies that people are more wasteful than they think they are.

2. _____ Paragraph A infers that successful marketers are in favor of more consumption.

3. _____ We can infer from Paragraph B that good tooth care stops bad breath.

4. _____ In Paragraph C, the author implies that SUV owners live an exciting life.

5. _____ In Paragraph C, the author infers that SUV owners do not use their vehicles for exciting trips.

6. _____ Dr. Hirsh's research implies that a product could sell better if it smells better.

7. _____ Paragraph E implies that diet pills really do reduce a person's weight.

8. _____ Paragraph E implies that people believe diet pills work better than they actually do.

9. _____ The author implies throughout the reading that advertisers try to manipulate consumers' thoughts.

10. _____ Most readers will imply that this article takes a negative view of advertisers.

Self-Assessment Log

Read the lists below. Check (✓) the strategies and vocabulary that you learned in this chapter. Look through the chapter or ask your instructor about the strategies and words that you do not understand.

Reading and Vocabulary-Building Strategies

- ☐ Getting meaning from context: understanding *e.g.* and *i.e.*
- ☐ Recognizing synonyms
- ☐ Using parts of speech to understand vocabulary
- ☐ Organizing ideas: using a Venn diagram
- ☐ Understanding irony
- ☐ Skimming for the topic and main idea
- ☐ Understanding pronoun reference
- ☐ Understanding parts of speech: suffixes
- ☐ Paying attention to phrases

Target Vocabulary

Nouns
- access*
- capacity*
- character
- collateral
- common knowledge
- consumer*
- economy*
- eradication
- fund*
- grants*
- items*
- literacy
- logic*
- microlending
- poverty
- requirement*

Verbs
- consume*
- invest*
- target*

Adjectives
- anonymous
- identical*
- social
- subsidiary*
- worthless

Expressions
- peer pressure
- took (take) the initiative

* These words are from the Academic Word List. For more information on this list, see www.victoria.ac.nz/lals/resources/academicwordlist/.

4 Jobs and Professions

> Every job is a self-portrait of the person who does it. "

Unknown

In this **CHAPTER**

In Part 1, you will read about how the world of work is changing due to globalization and technology. In the rest of the chapter, you will explore and discuss the workplace and different ways of finding a job.

 Connecting to the Topic

1. Describe everything you see in this photo. Who are these people?

2. What business do you think these people are involved in? Why?

3. Does this look like a company you would like to work for? Why or why not?

Changing Career Trends

Before You Read

1 **Previewing the Topic** Look at the photos and discuss the questions.

1. Where are the people in each photo? What are they doing?

2. What are five advantages of working from home? What are five disadvantages?

3. Can you think of some ways in which work has changed in the past decade (10 years)? How about changes in the last 50 years?

4. Are the situations in the photos similar to work situations around the world?

▲ Working from home

▲ Working in cubicles

2 **Previewing Vocabulary** Read the words and phrases below. Listen to the pronunciation. Put a check mark (✓) next to the words that you don't know. Don't use a dictionary.

Nouns

career counselors	manufacturing jobs
cell phones	outsourcing
construction	pleasure
drawback	posts
globalization	self-confidence
identity	stress
job hopping	telecommuting
job security	workaholism
livelihood	workforce

Verbs

distract	passionate
keep up with	rigid
overwork	secure
upgrade	temporary
varies (vary)	worldwide

Adjectives

flexible

leisure

Expression

on the move

3 Getting Meaning from Context Use both specific clues in these sentences and your own logic to determine the meanings of the underlined words and expressions. Then write your guess about the meaning. Compare your answers with those of a partner.

1. Twenty years ago, in many countries, people could choose their <u>livelihood</u>, but they couldn't usually choose to change from one <u>profession</u> to another.

   job

2. Many people with temporary <u>jobs</u> would prefer more permanent <u>posts</u>.

   _____

3. Even in Japan, where people traditionally had a very <u>secure</u> job for life, there is now no promise of a <u>lifetime job</u> with the same company.

   _____

4. When they lose their job, they also lose their <u>self-confidence</u>, or <u>belief in their own ability</u>.

   _____

5. They usually need to <u>upgrade</u> their skills to find a new, <u>better job</u>.

   _____

6. Because technology <u>changes fast</u>, workers need <u>continuing</u> education if they want to <u>keep up with</u> the field.

   learn about the changes

7. In many professions, <u>telecommuting</u> is now possible. People can <u>work at home</u> for some—or all—of the week and communicate by e-mail, cell phone, and video chat.

   _____

8. It's difficult for some people to <u>focus</u> on work when they are at home. The refrigerator, TV, and their children often <u>distract</u> them.

   things that make you lose focus

9. There is an <u>advantage</u> to technology: customers and clients have access to businesspeople at any time and anywhere. However, there is also a <u>drawback</u>: many businesspeople don't *want* to be available day and night.

   disadvantage

10. Many people don't have time for their family, friends, or <u>leisure</u> activities such as hobbies, sports, or movies.

    time , free time

11. Though <u>globalization</u> has its advantages and disadvantages, we are all affected by the increase in the international exchange of money and ideas.

    _____

12. Some people are <u>flexible</u> and can adjust well to change, but others are more <u>rigid</u>.

flexible: _____

rigid: _____ Can't _____

13. Many people in society suffer from alcoholism, an <u>addiction</u> to alcohol. <u>Workaholism</u> is another common problem in the 21st century.

_____ addition to work. _____

 4 **Comparing Answers** Compare your answers in the previous activity with those of other students. Were your answers similar to different from theirs?

 ## Strategy

Previewing a Reading

It helps to preview a chapter or passage before you read it so you can get an idea of what the article is about. In other words, look it over quickly to see what you can expect. Specifically, look at

- headings (the "titles" of the paragraphs), which indicate main topics
- pictures
- charts, figures, or diagrams

5 **Previewing a Reading** Look over the reading on pages 75–77, "Changing Career Trends." Answer the questions below.

1. What is the main topic? (Look at the title.) What are the five subtopics? (Look at the headings in bold.)

2. What do the pictures tell you about the article?

3. Write at least two questions you have about the topic after previewing the article.

Read

 6 **Reading an Article** As you read the following article, think about the answer to this question: *What are some ways in which work is changing?* Read the selection. Do not use a dictionary. Then do the exercises that follow the reading.

Changing Career Trends

A   A hundred years ago in most of the world, people didn't have much choice about the work that they would do, where they would do it, or how they would do it. If their parents were farmers, they became farmers. The society—and tradition—determined their profession. Twenty years ago in many countries, people could choose their **livelihood**. They also had the   5 certainty of a job for life, but they usually couldn't choose to change from one employer to another or from one profession to another. Today, this is not always the case. **Career counselors** tell us that the world of work is changing at great speed and will change dramatically in the next 25 years.

adv. a lot

Job Security

B   The situation **varies** from country to country, but in today's economy,   10 there is generally less job security **worldwide**. Even in Japan, where people traditionally had a very **secure** job for life, there is now no promise of a lifetime job with the same company.   15 One reason for the lack of **job security** is the worldwide decrease in **manufacturing jobs**. Another reason is employers' need to hold down   20 costs. This has resulted in two enormous changes for the **workforce**. First, employers are creating more and more **temporary** jobs because they   25 don't need to pay health insurance or other benefits to employees in these positions, as they would to people in **permanent posts**. Second,   30 more and more companies are **outsourcing**. In other words, they are closing offices and factories and sending work to other areas of the country or   35 to other countries where labor is cheaper. This happens with factory work and computer programming. Also, the call center industry is **on the move**   40

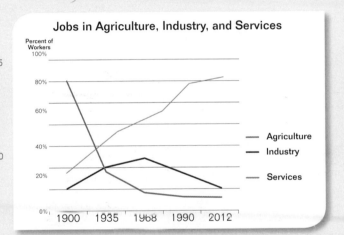

Jobs in Agriculture, Industry, and Services

▲ A busy call center in India

—mostly to India. Increasingly, when customers in Canada, the United States, England, and Australia call a company to order a product or ask for help with their computer, they actually speak with someone in India, although they might not know it. India is popular with companies because there is a well-educated workforce, salaries are much lower than in other countries, and educated people are already fluent in English. New call center employees in India spend months in training. They learn to use the accent of their customers—Australian or American, for example.

The Effect of Insecurity

C   On the surface, it may seem that lack of job security is something undesirable. Indeed, pessimists point out that it is certainly a cause of **stress**. Many people find an **identity**—a sense of self—through their work. When they lose their job (or are afraid of losing it), they also lose their **self-confidence**, or belief in their own ability. This causes worry and depression. In Japan, for example, the daily newspaper *Asahi* reports a sudden rise in the number of businessmen who need psychological help for their clinical depression. However, this decrease in job security may not necessarily be something bad. It is true that these days, workers must be more **flexible**—able to change to fit new situations. But optimists claim that flexible people are essentially happier, more creative, and more energetic than people who are **rigid**.

▲ Japanese workers have far less job security than in the past.

Job Hopping

D   Jumping from job to job (or "**job hopping**") has always been more common in some professions, such as building **construction**, and not very common in other professions like medicine and teaching. Today, job hopping is increasingly common in many fields because of **globalization**, technology, and a movement from **manufacturing** to services in developed countries. For example, people with factory jobs in industrial nations lose their jobs when factories move to countries where the pay is lower. The workers then need to **upgrade** their skills to find a new job. This is stressful, but the new job is usually better than the old one. Because technology changes fast, workers need continuing education if they want to **keep up with** the field. Clearly, technology provides both challenges and opportunities.

Telecommuting

E In many ways, technology is changing the way people work. There are advantages and disadvantages to this. In some professions, for instance, **telecommuting** is now possible. People can work at home for some—or all—of the week and communicate by e-mail, cell phone, and video chat. An advantage of this is that it saves them from the stress of commuting to the workplace. It also allows them to plan their own time. On the other hand, it is difficult for some people to focus on work when they are at home. The refrigerator, TV, and their children often **distract** them. Telecommuters must have enormous discipline and organizational skills.

▲ Do cell phones make life easier or more stressful?

Technology is changing the way people work in another way—in the use of **cell phones**. There is an advantage: customers and clients have access to businesspeople at any time, anywhere. However, there is also a **drawback**: many businesspeople don't *want* to be available day and night. They prefer to have a break from their work life.

Workaholism

F In the 21st century, **workaholism** will continue to be a fact of life for many workers. Workaholics are as addicted to their work as other people are to drugs or alcohol. This sounds like a problem, but it isn't always. Some people **overwork** but don't enjoy their work. They don't have time for their family, friends, or **leisure** activities such as hobbies, sports, and movies. These people become tired, angry, and depressed. The tension and stress often cause physical **symptoms** such as headaches. However, other people love their work and receive great **pleasure** from it. These people appear to be overworking but are actually very happy. Psychologists tell us that the most successful people in the changing world of work are flexible, creative, disciplined, and **passionate** about their work. But they are also people who make time for relaxing activities and for other people. They enjoy their work and enjoy time away from it, too.

85

90

95

100

105

110

115

120

7 Finding the Main Idea Read the sentences below and select the one main idea of the whole reading selection.

A Workaholism can lead to serious problems, but it can also create a happy life.

B Job hopping is a new trend that causes stress but can also lead people into good work experiences if they learn new job skills.

C It is important for people to be flexible in this changing world of work and to continue their education because they may need to change jobs several times in their lifetime.

D The world economy, globalization, and technology are causing many changes in the way people work today.

E In the workplace today, new technology is making it possible for people to work in different locations, even from home.

8 Comprehension Check: Finding Important Details Which statements are true about work today, according to the reading? Check (✓) them.

1. ✓ People probably need to be prepared to change jobs several times in their lifetimes.

2. ✓ Decreasing manufacturing jobs and increasing use of outsourcing are leading to less job security today than in the past.

3. _____ Lack of job security is always a bad thing.

4. ✓ People who can change to fit a new situation are usually happier than people who can't.

5. ✓ Many people find a sense of self through their work.

6. ✓ People in some professions move from job to job more often than people in other professions.

7. _____ Technology is making work life better for everyone.

8. ✓ Telecommuters don't need to drive to the office every day.

9. _____ All workaholics have problems with stress.

10. _____ The most successful people are workaholics.

9 Checking Vocabulary Find a word or expression in the reading for each definition below.

1. people who give advice about professions and careers = _career councelor_

2. the feeling that a worker will never lose his or her job = _job security_

3. the movement of jobs to places with lower salaries = _outsourcing_

4. changing from one job to another = _on the time_

5. disadvantage = _drawback_

Strategy

Critical Thinking: Recognizing Cause and Effect
In Chapters 1, 2, and 3 you saw three types of graphic organizers. Another use of a graphic organizer is to show causes (or reasons) and effects (or results). This graphic organizer shows the relationship between different actions such as why something happens or the result of an action.

10 **Critical Thinking: Recognizing Cause and Effect** Paragraph B of the reading presents several causes and effects. Look back at Paragraph B and find information to complete this graphic organizer.

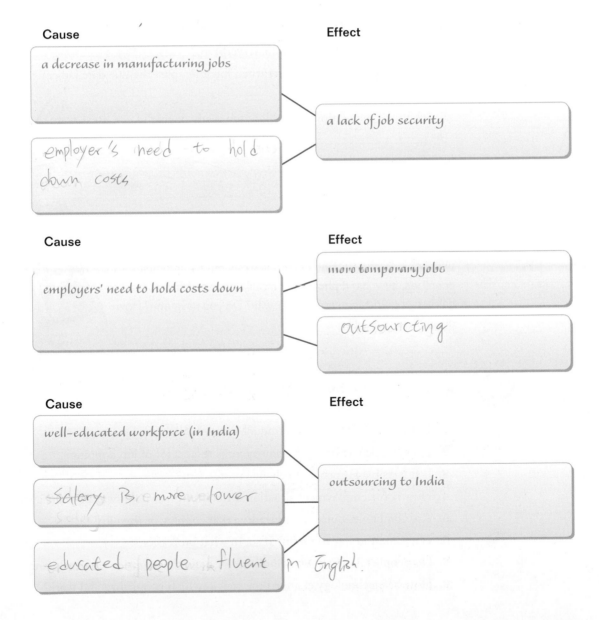

Cause

a decrease in manufacturing jobs

employer's need to hold down costs

Effect

a lack of job security

Cause

employers' need to hold costs down

Effect

more temporary jobs

outsourcting

Cause

well-educated workforce (in India)

Salary is more lower

educated people fluent in English.

Effect

outsourcing to India

Using The Prefix *Over-*

The prefix *over-* can appear as part of a noun, verb, or adjective. In some words, it indicates that there is too much of something or that someone is doing too much of a certain action.

Example Some people **overwork** and don't enjoy their work.

    overwork (verb) = work too much

11 Using the Prefix *Over-* Read the definitions below. Write the words being defined. They begin with over. Then compare your answers with another student's.

1. do something too much (verb) = _____*overdo*_____

2. a place with too many people or things; a crowded place (adjective) =

    _____

3. give an estimate that is too high (verb) = _____

4. left unpaid, undone, or unreturned too long, past the due date (adjective) =

    _____

5. when the population is too high; too many people in one area (noun) =

    _____

Culture Note

What Do You Call It?

In various countries, people have different terms for a portable telephone. In some countries, this is a **cell phone**. In other countries, it's a **hand phone** or a **mobile phone**. What do people call it in countries you are familiar with? Do you have one? How often do you use it?

◀ "Hello?"

12 Discussing the Reading Answer these questions about a country you know well. Discuss your answers in a group.

1. Is it difficult for people to find jobs there? Why or why not?
2. Do most people have job security, or is there a lot of job hopping?
3. Is it possible for people to change professions?
4. How is the employment situation different from what it was 20 years ago?
5. Are companies outsourcing work *to* that country or *from* it?
6. Is telecommuting common? If so, in what professions?
7. Do people talk about workaholism? If so, do they consider it a problem?
8. How has technology changed the way in which people live and work?

Looking for Work in the 21st Century

Before You Read

1 **Thinking Ahead** Discuss your answers to these questions.

1. Where do people usually find out about job openings? Make a list of the places.

2. How do people prepare for a career? What steps do they need to take?

2 **Skimming for the Topic and the Main Idea** Read these paragraphs quickly. Don't worry about the details. When you finish, write the topic and main idea of each paragraph.

Looking for Work in the 21st Century

A   Not very long ago, when people needed to find a job, there were several possible steps. They might begin with a look through the classified ads in the newspaper. They could go to the personnel office at various companies and fill out an application, or they could go to an employment agency. They could even find out about a job opening through word-of-mouth—from   5
another person who had heard about it.

JOBS OFFERED

Jobs Domestic	8200

AUPAIR L/I 2 kids 8 & 9 House-keeping & driving. H-(818) 555-1890

ACCOUNTING MANAGER Mountain Plumbing Contractor looking for an Asst to Controller. Ideal Candidate will have 3-5 Yrs. Const. Acctng/Job Costing Exp. Handling Revenues $5MM & greater. Proficiency in Windows based-computer environment w/Exp. in Excel/Word a must. Fax Resume to 714-555-5870 Attn: Oscar

ACTORS Comedians and great personalities to teach fun traffic school 16-24hrs/wk. $12/hr. 800-555-6463

ADMINISTRATIVE ASSISTANT City office of nat'l org dedicated to helping low-income communities find creative solutions to financial problems. Fax Resume to 818-555-1020 Attn: Irene

CHEF Sushi - Select, clean, carve, & prepare traditional Japanese sushi & sashimi incl. tuna, yellowtail, salmon, albacore, octopus, snapper, mackerel, eel, shimp, squid, scallops, sea urchin, smelt roe, lobster, rice, seaweed, & vegetables. Requires 2 yrs exp. in job offered. $4200/mo. 11a-2p & 5-10p Wed-Sun. Interview &

▲ Classified Ads

Topic: _____

Main idea: _____

B   These days, job hunting is more complicated. The first step is to determine what kind of job you want (which sounds easier than it is) and make sure that you have the right education for it. Rapid changes in technology and science are creating many professions that never existed until 10 recently. It is important to learn about them because one might be the perfect profession for you. The fastest-growing areas for new jobs are in computer technology and health services. Jobs in these fields usually require specific skills, but you need to find out exactly which skills and which degrees are necessary. For example, it may be surprising to learn that in the sciences, an 15 M.S. is more marketable than a PhD! In other words, there are more jobs available for people with a Master of Science degree than for people with a doctorate. (However, people who want to do research still need a PhD).

Topic: _____

Main idea: _____

_____

C   How do people learn about "hot" new professions? How do they discover their "dream job"? Many people these days go to a career counselor. In some 20 countries, job hopping has become so common that career counseling is now "big business." People sometimes spend large amounts of money for this advice. In Canada and the United States, high school and college students often have access to free vocational counseling services on campus. There is even a career organization, the Five O'Clock Club, which helps members to 25 set goals. Members focus on this question: What sort of person do you want to be years from now? The members then plan their careers around that goal. All career counselors—private or public—agree on one basic point: It is important for people to find a career that they love. Everyone should be able to think, "I'm having such a good time. I can't believe they're paying me to 30 do this."

Topic: _____

Main idea: _____

_____

D   After people have determined what their dream job is, they need to find it. The biggest change in job hunting these days is the use of the Internet. More and more employers are advertising job openings on their computer websites. More and more job hunters are applying for jobs online. There are also 35 several thousand job boards, among them HotJobs.com, Jobsjobsjobs.com, and Monster.com. Some people think that online job hunting is only for people in technology fields, but this isn't true. Over 65 percent of online job seekers are from nontechnical fields. Even truck drivers now find jobs on the Internet!

Topic: _____

Main idea: _____

_____

E   So how does this 40 work? A job seeker can reply to a "Help Wanted" notice on a company's website. This person can also 45 post his or her résumé (page with information about education and work experience) on one—or many— of 50 the online job boards. If a company is interested, the person still has to take the next step the old-fashioned way—actually go to the job interview and perhaps take a skills test. However, even this has changed. Now, companies are able to give skills tests and do background checks online. But what about the interview? Companies 55 are now able to interview the person by video chat, so people can interview for jobs in other cities—or even other countries— without leaving home. Clearly, job hunting is not what it used to be.

▲ How does the Internet help employers and employees?

Topic: _____

Main idea: _____

_____

After You Read

3 Checking Your Answers After you write the topic and main idea of each paragraph, exchange answers with another student. Do you agree about the topics? Do you agree about the main ideas? If you don't agree, give reasons for your answers. One of you might want to change an answer!

4 **Understanding Pronoun Reference** Look back at the reading selection "Looking for Work in the 21st Century" to find the meaning of the following pronouns. What does each pronoun refer to?

1. they (Paragraph A, line 2) _____

2. them (Paragraph B, line 11) _____

3. it (Paragraph D, line 32) _____

4. them (Paragraph D, line 36) _____

5. this (Paragraph E, line 45) _____

6. this (Paragraph E, line 54) _____

5 **Discussing the Reading** Talk about your answers to these questions.

1. Have you ever gone job hunting? If so, what steps did you take?

2. Do you already know what your "dream job" is? If so, what will you need to do to get it?

3. Do people in most countries usually go to career counselors? Are there vocational counseling services in high schools and colleges? Have you ever gone to a career counselor for advice?

4. Have you ever visited an online job board? If so, tell your group about it.

Culture Note

Globalization

There are 196 countries in the world. Which five do you think are the most **globalized**? These are the five countries with the most cell phones, computers, political involvement, and free movement of international visitors. Each also has a vibrant economy. Write your guesses here and check your answers at the end of this chapter on page 91.

_____

_____

Responding in Writing

6 **Summarizing** Choose one of the following topics from the reading in Part 1, pages 75–77, to summarize.

- advantages and disadvantages of less job security (Paragraph C)
- telecommuting (Paragraph E)
- workaholism (Paragraph F)

Because a summary is shorter than the original, try to write only three or four sentences. To write this summary, follow these steps:

- Make sure that you understand the paragraph well.
- Identify the topic, main idea, and important details.
- Choose two or three important details.
- Do not include less important details.

In order to summarize in your own words, *don't look at the original paragraph as you write*. When you finish writing, compare your summary with those of other students who summarized the same paragraph. Did you include the same main idea? The same details?

7 **Writing Your Own Ideas** Choose one of the topics below to write an opinion paragraph about. Write your own thoughts. Try to use vocabulary from this chapter.

- workaholism
- telecommuting
- job hunting online
- your idea of a "dream job"

What is the main idea of your paragraph?

_____

_____

Talk it Over

8 **Discussing Proverbs and Quotations** Below are proverbs and quotations about work. Read them and then in small groups, discuss your answers to the questions that follow.

Proverbs and Quotations

"Ninety percent of inspiration is perspiration."   proverb

"Work expands to fill the time available."   C. Northcote Parkinson

"Laziness travels so slowly that poverty soon overtakes him."   Benjamin Franklin

"It is neither wealth nor splendor, but tranquility and occupation, which give happiness."
Thomas Jefferson

Questions

1. What does each proverb (or quotation) mean? (You might need to use a dictionary for a few words.)

2. Do you agree with each one?

3. What are some proverbs about work in your language? Translate them into English and explain them.

1 **Focusing on Words from the Academic Word List** Fill in the blanks with words from the Academic Word List in the box. The first one has been done for you as an example. When you finish, turn back to page 75, Paragraph B, and check your answers.

areas	creating ✔	job ✔	labor	traditionally ✔
benefits ✔	economy ✔	job security ✔	secure ✔	~~varies~~
computer	enormous ✔	jobs ✔	temporary ✔	

The situation ____varies____ from country to country, but in today's
____economy____, there is generally less job security worldwide. Even in
Japan, where people ____traditionally____ had a very ____secure____
job for life, there is now no promise of a lifetime ____job____
with the same company. One reason for the lack of ____job____ ____security____ is
the worldwide decrease in manufacturing ____jobs____. Another
reason is employers' need to hold down costs. This has resulted in two
____enormous____ changes for the workforce. First, employers are
____creating____ more and more ____temporary____ jobs because they
don't need to pay health insurance or other ____benefits____ to employees
in these positions, as they would to people in permanent posts. Second, more
and more companies are outsourcing. In other words, they are closing offices
and factories and sending work to other ____areas____ of the country
or to other countries where ____labor____ is cheaper. This happens
with factory work and ____computer____ programming. Also, the call
center industry is on the move—mostly to India.

Understanding Adjective and Noun Phrases

Some words often appear together in phrases. In some phrases, there is a hyphen (-). If you have a question about whether to use a hyphen, look up the word in a dictionary.

Example

Many people have to accept **part-time** jobs.

The last word of a phrase is usually a noun or an adjective. The first word may be a noun, an adjective, or an adverb.

Example

city life (noun + noun)
social sciences (adjective + noun)
especially interesting (adverb + adjective)

2 **Understanding Adjective and Noun Phrases** In each sentence below, add a word to complete the adjective or noun phrase. The first one has been done for you as an example. Choose from the following words:

career ✓	computer ✓	mass ✓	self ✓	traffic ✓
city ✓	dream ✓	part ✓	shopping ✓	unemployment ✓
classified	job ✓	personnel		

1. He looked through the _____classified_____ ads and hoped to find his _____dream_____ job.

2. In that country, the _____unemployment_____ rate is very high, and many people have to accept _____part_____-time jobs temporarily. This sometimes causes depression and loss of _____self_____-confidence.

3. Some advantages of _____city_____ life are the _____shopping_____ centers and _____mass_____-transit systems. A disadvantage, though, is the problem of _____traffic_____ jams.

4. Because she likes technology, her _____career_____ counselor told her about the many possible jobs in _____computer_____ science.

5. When I began _____job_____ hunting last year, I put in my application at the _____personnel_____ office of many companies.

3 Creating Adjective and Noun Phrases Match a word on the left with a word on the right to create a new phrase. The first one has been done for you as an example.

1. old- _fashioned_
2. dream _job_
3. cell _phone_
4. technology _field_
5. job _agency_
6. career _counseling_
7. employment _opening_
8. self- _confidence_

a. job ✓
b. opening
c. agency ✓
d. fashioned
e. field 完成
f. confidence ✓
g. counseling ✓
h. phone ✓

FOCUS

Understanding Compound Words
Some words belong together in "compounds" (long words that consist of smaller words).
Example
I talked to a **salesclerk** at the **supermarket**.

---

4 Understanding Compound Words Read the compound words in Column A below. Draw a line between the two words of each compound word. Then match the compound words with the definitions in Column B. The first one has been done for you as an example.

Column A

1. _h_ over/seas
2. _e_ drawback
3. _j_ overcrowding
4. _a_ gridlock
5. _i_ worldwide
6. _b_ overworked
7. _c_ workforce
8. _f_ upgrade
9. _d_ online
10. _g_ background

Column B

a. terrible traffic jam
b. given too much work
c. people who are working
d. using the Internet
e. disadvantage
f. improve
g. one's experience and education
h. in another country across an ocean
i. everywhere in the world
j. too many people in one place

5 Creating Compound Words and Phrases How many compound words or phrases can you make from the words below? Work as fast as you can for five minutes and write the words on the lines. The group with the most *correct* words or phrases is the winner.

high	work	network
lab	exam	security
office	public	market
college	interview	department 部门
self	tuition 学费	confidence
science	school	job
social	service	computer
life	city	planning

city life   _school_ _~~city~~_ _life_
social life
job security
self-confidence
high school
computer science

6 Searching the Internet Look at some online job boards. Find one that looks interesting. How can that website help you with work-related questions? What can you do on that site? Tell the class about the site and list at least five helpful things people can do on that site.

Website: _____

Useful job-related information:

1. _____
   _____

2. _____
   _____

3. _____
   _____

4. _____
   _____

5. _____
   _____

FOCUS

Faster Reading Speed—Left-To-Right Eye Movement

Slow readers look at the same words several times. Their eyes move back and forth over each sentence. Fast readers usually move their eyes from left to right one time for each line. They don't look back very often. A fast left-to-right eye movement increases reading speed. If you can read quickly, you may feel less nervous during tests.

There are exercises to help you improve reading speed. You will practice one below. This exercise is timed. It shows an underlined word in the first column of each section. You will be asked to read across each line and underline the words in that line that are the same as the underlined word on the left.

Example

globe	globalize	globalization	globe	glide	global
workforce	work	workforce	workplace	workforce	worked
stress	stress	stressful	address	stressed	stress

1 **Practice** Your teacher will tell you when to begin each section. Quickly underline each word that is the same as the underlined word. At the end of each section, write down how long it took you to do that section.

Section 1

banking	banks	banking	bank	banking	banking
challenge	challenges	challenging	challenge	challenge	challenged
savings	savings	save	savings	saving	saver
benefit	benefits	beneficial	benefited	benefit	benefit
employer	employ	employment	employee	employer	employed

Time: _____

Section 2

experience	experience	experienced	expertise	experience	expert
opening	opening	opening	opened	open	opened
excellent	excel	excelled	excellent	excellent	excellent
identity	indent	identity	identify	identity	indent
account	account	accounting	account	accounts	account

Time: _____

Section 3

part-time	part-time	partly	party	part-time
position	possible	position	positive	position
public	public	publicity	public	publicize
appointment	appoint	appointed	appoints	appointment
personnel	person	personal	personnel	personable

Time: _____

Section 4

<u>salary</u>	salary	celery	salaries	salaried	sales
<u>apply</u>	applied	apply	apply	apply	application
<u>pleasure</u>	pleasure	pleasant	pleasurable	pleased	pleasant
<u>skills</u>	skilled	skill	skills	skills	skillful
<u>ability</u>	ability	able	capable	ability	capability

Time: _____

Self-Assessment Log

Read the lists below. Check (✓) the strategies and vocabulary that you learned in this chapter. Look through the chapter or ask your instructor about the strategies and words that you do not understand.

Reading and Vocabulary-Building Strategies

☐ Getting meaning from context
☐ Previewing a reading
☐ Finding the main idea
☐ Finding important details
☐ Recognizing cause and effect

☐ Using the prefix *over-*
☐ Skimming for topics and main ideas
☐ Understanding pronoun reference
☐ Understanding adjective and noun phrases
☐ Understanding compound words

Target Vocabulary

Nouns
- areas*
- benefits*
- career counselors
- cell phones
- computer*
- construction
- drawback
- dream job
- economy*
- employment agency
- globalization*
- identity*
- job hopping
- job security
- labor*
- livelihood
- manufacturing jobs
- outsourcing
- pleasure
- posts
- self-confidence
- stress*
- telecommuting
- workaholism
- workforce

Verbs
- create*
- distract
- keep up with
- overwork
- upgrade
- vary*

Adjectives
- enormous*
- flexible*
- leisure
- passionate
- rigid*
- secure*
- temporary*
- worldwide
- traditionally*

Expression
- on the move

* These words are from the Academic Word List. For more information on this list, see www.victoria.ac.nz/lals/resources/academicwordlist/.

Answer to the Culture Note question on page 84:
#5: Switzerland; #4: Sweden; #3: the Netherlands; #2: Austria; #1: Belgium

5 Lifestyles Around the World

"Learn to be happy with what you have while you pursue all that you want."

Jim Rohn
American entrepreneur, author, and motivational speaker.

In this
CHAPTER

In Part 1, you will read about the science of happiness and learn about how happiness might be measured. In the rest of this chapter, you will read about, discuss, and explore the topics of happiness and home.

Connecting to the Topic

1. What do you see in the photo? What are these people doing? Where are they?

2. What are some adjectives that describe how the people feel? Do you sometimes feel like this? In what situations?

3. What are some things that make you happy?

The Science of Happiness

Before You Read

1 **Previewing the Topic** Look at the map. Discuss the questions.

1. Which of these countries are probably the richest? In which countries are people probably the happiest? Why do you think this?

2. What causes some countries to be happier than others?

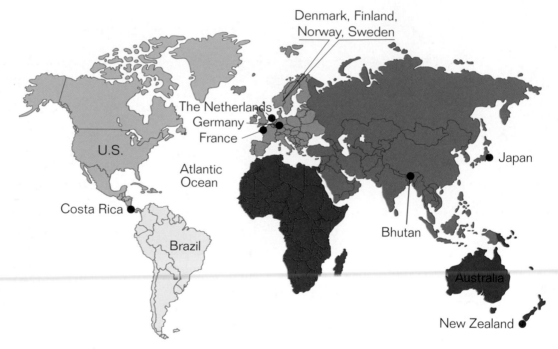

Denmark, Finland, Norway, Sweden

The Netherlands
Germany
France

U.S.

Atlantic Ocean

Japan

Costa Rica

Bhutan

Brazil

Australia

New Zealand

2 **Previewing Vocabulary** Read the words and phrases below. Listen to the pronunciation of each word. Put a check mark (✓) next to the words you don't know. Don't use a dictionary.

Nouns
- balance
- components
- concept
- essence
- findings
- gap

- life expectancy
- polls
- solidarity
- sum total
- trend
- well-being

Verbs
- catch on
- measure

Adjectives
- complex
- reasonable

Adverbs
- actually
- enthusiastically

3 Previewing the Reading Look over the reading on pages 95-97. Discuss these questions with a partner.

1. What is the topic of the whole reading? (Look at the title of the reading.)
2. What are the seven subtopics? (Look at the heading of each paragraph.)
3. Look at the photos. What do you think the reading will include?

Read

4 Reading an Article As you read the following selection, think about the answer to this question: *How is the happiness of a nation measured?* Read the selection. Do not use a dictionary. Then do the exercises that follow the reading.

The Science of Happiness

A How can we **measure** the happiness of a nation? What causes one nation to have greater **well-being**—more prosperity or happiness—than another? Most economists use the **GDP** to compare various countries. The GDP, or Gross Domestic Product, is the value 5 of all goods and services from a nation in one year. If we look at GDP, the top five countries (in this order) are: the United States, China, Japan, Germany, and France. However, in recent years, there has been growing dissatisfaction with this measure. One drawback of 10 using GDP is that disasters such as storms and fires and social ills such as sickness and crime **actually*** *improve* a country's GDP because they cause an increase in economic activity. Also, GDP doesn't tell us if there is a big **gap** between the rich and poor in a country. And it certainly doesn't tell us if the people are *happy*. Increasingly, there is understanding that GDP is 15 not enough of a measure of a nation's well-being.

▲ Can national happiness be measured?

Reading Tip

*****actually** =
"in fact," but it has additional meanings. It also suggests that the writer **1.** thinks the information is surprising; **2.** is correcting a mistake; or **3.** is changing his/her mind. What do you think it means in Paragraph A?

Human Development Index

B Since 1993, the United Nations has used the **HDI**, or Human Development Index, to measure the well-being of a nation. Many people 20 see the HDI as an improvement over the rigid GDP because it has three **components** instead of just one. The HDI measures income, average years of education, and **life expectancy**, or 25 how long people can expect to live. (Life expectancy is a good way to measure both people's basic health

▲ The U.S.: High GDP

and the healthcare system in the country.) According to the HDI, the top five countries (in this order) are: Norway, Australia, the Netherlands, the United States, and New Zealand—quite different from the GDP rankings. 30

C What's Missing from the HDI?

Not everyone **enthusiastically** accepts the HDI, however. The National Bureau of Economic Research points out that the HDI does not include a measure of *mental* well-being—in other words, happiness. Two researchers, Blanchflower and Oswald, point out that many areas of everyday life 35 can influence a person's happiness: "unemployment, the divorce rate, real income, friendship, traffic jams, crime, health, and much else." The HDI does not reflect most of these areas.

D Happiness and Bhutan

▲ Bhutan: Low GDP, High GNH

Back in 1972, an interesting idea came out of the tiny Himalayan country of Bhutan. Bhutan's king began 40 to refer to the country's **"GNH"**—or Gross National Happiness. The idea is that happiness is far more **complex** than economic growth. This **concept** is now part of the constitution of Bhutan, and 45 there are regular **polls** where people answer questions about their satisfaction in *nine* areas of life, including a good **balance** of time at work and in leisure, psychological well-being, and a clean 50 environment. The government makes decisions based on the results of these questionnaires.

E The Spread of This Concept

This concept of measuring GNH is **catching on** worldwide. In many countries, the use of "happiness polls" has become a **trend**—a general 55 direction of change that is becoming common. In 2009, the 5th International

▲ Costa Rica: Low Income, High Education and Health Care, High GNH

Gross National Happiness Conference was held in Brazil. At such conferences, people discuss the various polls and their results. According to John de Graaf in *Yes!* magazine online, year 60 after year, such polls find that the countries with "the highest levels of satisfaction" are Denmark, Finland, the Netherlands, and Sweden. What do these countries have in common? They all have a good work–life 65 balance, a small gap in income between the rich and the poor, strong social **solidarity** (agreement among people), and strong social **safety nets** (ways to help people in difficult situations). These countries all have high taxes, too. Although

these four countries have high income, the "happiness polls" also show that 70
many *poor* countries (ones with a low GDP) have high life satisfaction. One
of these is Costa Rica, where the average income is low but where there is
a high level of education and health care—and where there is passionate
solidarity about the importance of the environment.

F **A New Measure**

As this concept of GNH becomes more popular, there is an effort to find 75
a new, *global*, measure for well-being. Various organizations have suggested
ways to measure the well-being of nations instead of using the HDI. The
proposal of the International Institute of Management, for example, is
similar to the GNH poll in Bhutan, but they call it **GNW**, or Gross National
Wellness. It measures seven types of wellness: economic, environmental, 80
physical, mental, workplace, social, and political.

G **What Happiness Is—and Isn't**

We have learned a lot in recent years about what makes a happy person
or a happy nation. According to the National Bureau of Economic Research,
there are several characteristics. First, "money does buy a **reasonable** amount
of happiness." But for most people, having a higher income does not make 85
as much of a difference as other life events, such as marriage. Second,
nations "do not seem to get happier as they get richer." Another **finding** is
that "happiness is U-shaped in age." This means that people are generally
happy when they are young, then become less happy in middle age; but
they become happier again as they get older. Finally, women usually "report 90
higher well-being than men," and "more educated people report higher levels
of happiness" than people with less
education.

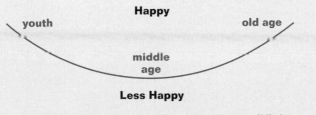
▲ If we measure happiness according to age, we get a "U" shape.

H **Conclusion**

Clearly, some nations are
happier than others. It is possible to 95
measure the happiness of a nation,
but it is challenging. Happiness is
more complex than people used to
think it was. Happiness does not seem to have an **essence**—a central quality.
Instead, it is the **sum total** of many characteristics. One of these is money, 100
but it is certainly not the most important one.

After You Read

5 **Finding the Main Idea** Read the sentences on page 98 and select the main
idea of the article, "The Science of Happiness." Remember, the topic is happiness,
and the main idea is what the author wants to say about it.

(A) The HDI is a better measure of happiness than the GDP because the GDP focuses on only economic activity, while the HDI focuses on three components.

(B) Happiness is a combination of many components, one of which is income.

(C) Measuring the happiness of a nation or person is complex.

(D) People in some countries, such as Bhutan and Costa Rica, have a low average income but a high level of satisfaction with life.

(E) We have learned a lot in recent years about the characteristics of well-being on a national level.

6 **Identifying the Main Idea in Paragraphs** Go back to the passage. Underline one or two sentences in each paragraph that contain the main idea of that paragraph. When you finish, compare the sentences that you marked with those of other students. Did you choose the same sentences? Explain why you chose the sentences that you did.

Strategy

Understanding Acronyms

An **acronym** is an abbreviation of a phrase or expression. We form an acronym with the first letter of each word from the phrase or expression. There are thousands of acronyms in English. Some are very common, and many people use them frequently.

Examples

AC = air-conditioning; air conditioned   Q&A = question and answer

FYI = for your information   VIP = very important person

OJ = orange juice

Don't worry about learning the *less* common acronyms. When you see them in an article, you will always find the full phrase somewhere in the context.

Example

Most economists use the **GDP** to compare various countries. The GDP, or Gross Domestic Product, is the value of all goods and services from a nation in one year.

GDP = Gross Domestic Product

7 **Checking Acronyms** Look quickly through the reading. Find three acronyms and their meanings.

8 **Checking Your Understanding** Turn back to Activity 4 on page 95 and answer the question *How is the happiness of a nation measured?* Discuss your answer with a partner.

9 **Getting Meaning from Context: Vocabulary Check** Scan the reading passage to find the meaning of each of these words. On each line, write a definition or synonym from the reading passage or in your own words. Do this exercise without a dictionary.

1. well-being: _____ *prosperity or happiness* _____

2. components: _____

3. life expectancy: _____

4. concept: _____

5. trend: _____

6. solidarity: _____

7. safety nets: _____

8. proposal: _____

9. finding: _____

10. essence: _____

10 **Finding Details** Go back to Paragraphs A, B, and E in the reading passage to find examples of the terms in the chart.

Drawbacks of GDP	Components of HDI	Countries with "the highest levels of satisfaction"

 11 **Discussing the Reading** In a small group, discuss concepts of happiness from the reading.

1. Did anything surprise you about Paragraph G? If so, what?

2. On the pie chart to the right, write the components of happiness ("seven types of wellness") in the proposal from the International Institute of Management.

3. Discuss a country that you know well. How do you think it ranks in each of the areas on the pie chart (high? medium? low?)?

4. What components would *you* include in a measure of well-being or happiness? Are there components that seem to be missing from the pie chart?

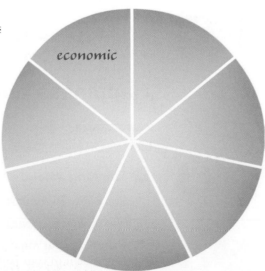

economic

Using the Internet

Interpreting Source Material from the Internet

You frequently do research in college. Sometimes, you want more information than you can find in a chapter or lecture. Often, you need to do research in order to write a report or term paper. Here are some basic guidelines for doing Internet research and interpreting information that you find.

- You should not rely on just one website. Go to a number of websites.
- Notice that sometimes information from two or more websites is **contradictory** (opposite or different).
- You can **trust** (believe) some sources or websites more than others. Look for the name of the organization that hosts the site. Is it well known? Does it have a good reputation? If you aren't sure, ask your instructor.

12 **Searching the Internet** In your group, each person will research answers to these questions. Remember to check if the website seems useful. Each person will probably find different websites. When you finish, share your findings with the group.

1. Find the most recent list of GDP rankings. What are the top ten countries? Where on the list does Bhutan rank? Where does Costa Rica rank?

2. Find the most recent list of HDI rankings. What are the top ten countries? Where on the list does Bhutan rank? Where does Costa Rica rank?

3. Try to find the population of Bhutan for three different years. Note: you will have some difficulty with this. In your research, find out why this statistic is not easy to know for certain.

PART 2 Main Ideas and Details

Happiness and the Home

Before You Read

1 **Thinking Ahead** Discuss your answers to these questions.

1. What do you think is the difference between a house and a home?

2. What comes to your mind when you think of the word *home*?

3. Picture in your mind a traditional house in a country that you know well. Describe it to your partner.

4. What do you think is the most important feature (part or quality) in a home?

Strategy

Marking Text When You Read

Students—especially college students—often need to read so much material that they don't have time to reread it before an important exam. For this reason, it's necessary to learn how to mark a book. If you mark your reading material wisely, you can go back later and look over your markings to study for a test without reading the whole passage again. Try to use different colors for different purposes:

- one color for the topic
- a different color for the main idea(s)
- another color for important details or examples

You can also <u>underline</u> or circle important new vocabulary and phrases. You might add notes or question marks in the margin.

It's important to note that there is no one right way of marking a book. You need to find a style that is comfortable to you. However, if you mark too much, you will probably get confused. Choose carefully what to mark.

2 Reading: Marking Text When You Read Read the paragraphs below. As you read, mark the topic, main idea, and important details of each paragraph. Do not use a dictionary. When you finish, write the topic and the main idea of each paragraph. (The first paragraph is marked for you, as an example.)

Happiness and the Home

Reading Tip

In this paragraph, **green** highlight is the topic; **yellow** highlight is the main idea, and **tan** highlight is important details.

A   Most people would agree that true happiness usually includes a good home. Various languages have proverbs that support this. But what does *home* mean? A home is not only a house, a building. A home is both a physical space *and* all that we associate with it. It is family, security, comfort, beauty, food, and family history. Our personal identity—the qualities that   5 make each person or group different from others—begins in the family home. Our well-being depends on our ability to return home. Today, many people live in modern apartments that are nearly identical, from Singapore to Stockholm. Does this mean that people in various cultures have the same concept of home? What exactly comes to mind when we think of *home*?   10

Topic: _____ *home* _____

Main idea: _*A home is both a physical space and all that we associate with it.*_

_____

B   Our idea of home comes partly from geography because the land determines the building materials and the design. In the forested areas of Europe and North America, traditional houses are built of wood. In central Africa, Pygmies build *lobembe* from plant materials. These temporary structures are appropriate for nomadic people who frequently move from place to place. In Mongolia, which has few trees, the traditional house is the *gher*—wooden poles covered with skins and textiles. The Mongols, too, are nomadic and

▲ Wooden house, Europe

need portable houses, but their *gher* must also protect them from the harsh winter weather. The white color of the *gher* is important to the people because in their language, *tsagaan* means both "white" and "happy." In southern Greece, too, traditional village houses are always white—but built of stone. When Greeks move to cities or other countries, into modern apartment buildings, their idea of "home" is often the traditional village of their grandparents, which they might visit only at holiday time.

▲ Structure made of plant materials, Southwest Central African Republic

▲ A Mongolian *gher*

A village in southern Greece ▶

Topic: _____

Main idea: _____

_____

C   There is an almost universal association of home with the hearth—the fireplace or area in front of the fireplace. Fire is essential in all cultures; it brings security and comfort and allows us to cook our food. On a cold winter night in Japan, a family in a traditional house gathers around the *kotatsu*, a heater under a low table. There is a blanket over the table, and the family sits with the blanket over their legs. Here, they talk, drink tea, read, do homework, and keep warm. However, even in central Africa, where the weather is not so cold, the Pygmy people see fire as essential to their survival. Although they have a deep knowledge of the forest around them, they have a terrible fear of elephants and believe that fire keeps these animals away. In *all* cultures, though, people associate the hearth with food, and this usually means the kitchen. This room is often seen as the emotional center of the house. Is this why, at a party in a New York apartment, people begin in the living room but often end up gathering in the kitchen? Clearly, a hearth is more than it might seem. Interestingly, in English, the word *hearth* has an additional symbolic meaning: "home."

Topic: _____

Main idea: _____

_____

D   Home can also be an expression of personal identity. The choice of colors, furniture, art, photos, carpets, and *chotchkies*—those small items that many of us collect—is unique to each person. These days, the idea of home can even include spaces on the Internet, where people can create a "home" online. This is expanding the concept, making home not just a physical and emotional place but also a virtual one. Wherever it is, whatever it is, home is the place where many people are the most secure, comfortable, relaxed and, possibly, the happiest.

Topic: _____

Main idea: _____

_____

3 Checking Your Answers After you write the topic and main idea of each paragraph, compare your answers with another student's. Are your answers the same? Are your answers the same but perhaps in different words? Do you agree about the main ideas? If you don't agree, give reasons for your answers. Remember, you can change your answers if you wish!

F☉CUS

Understanding Italics

Writers use *italics* (slanted letters) in English for several reasons:

- for emphasis—to stress an important word
- to mean *the word* _____ or *the term* _____
  Example *Red* sounds the same as the past tense verb *read*.
- for words in foreign languages

Sometimes there are two different reasons for the use of italics in the same sentence or paragraph. With your class, find the different reasons for using italics in the example below.

Example

Does *happiness* mean the same thing to people of different cultures? Perhaps not. *Ataraxia*, from ancient Greek, actually translates as "peace of mind." The Chinese word *gaoxing* is often used to mean "happy," but it is closer to "enjoyment." To reach happiness, is it necessary for us to *do* something, or is it enough simply to *be*?

---

4 Understanding Italics Look through the reading on pages 101-103. Highlight every example of italics. In each case, decide why the writer used them. Then compare your answers with those of other students.

Strategy

Studying for Exams: Organizing Information
After you have read and marked material in a textbook, you usually need to study this material for an exam. You can absorb and remember more if you do something active with the material that you have marked. Here's what you can do:

- Open your book to the material that you have marked.
- Have a notebook next to your book.
- In the notebook, create a graphic organizer (see pages 30-31, 55, and 79 for examples of graphic organizers) and write the information you highlighted in it.
- Study your graphic organizer. If you have carefully chosen the information to include, you won't need to read the material again.

5 Studying for Exams: Organizing Information Fill in this chart with the topic, main idea, and important details that you marked in Paragraphs B, C, and D. You can copy directly from the text or put it in your own words—or both. Paragraph A is done as an example

	Topic	Main Idea	Important Details
A	home	A home is both a physical space and all that we associate with it.	· family · security · comfort · beauty · food · family history
B			
C			
D			

6 Discussing the Reading Talk about your answers to these questions.

1. What other types of houses—besides those in the reading—do you know about? Describe them for your group.

2. What do you think of as the "emotional center" of a house?

3. Think about a country you know well. Is there a difference between traditional houses and places where most people now live? If so, explain this to your group.

4. What's important for *you* to make your house into a home? Name five things.

5. Look at the Proverbs from Around the World below. Explain each one.

> **Proverbs from Around the World**
>
> "He who wants to be happy must stay at home." Greek
>
> "Into the house where joy lives, happiness will follow." Japanese
>
> "The sun at home warms better than the sun elsewhere." Albanian
>
> "The wise man and the tortoise travel but never leave their home." Chinese
>
> "Home is where the heart is." English

7 **Summarizing** Read these two summaries of Paragraph A on page 101. Both are good summaries, but they are different. Compare them to the original paragraph. Write the points that are similar and the points that are different in the two paragraphs.

Summary 1

For most people, having a good home is necessary for them to be happy. A home is more than a building. It is everything in the house (or apartment), including the tangible things (such as food and furniture) and intangible things (such as security and family history). Of course, home also includes the people who live there. Home is where people's personal identity comes from.

Summary 2

One of the components of happiness, for most people, is home. There are proverbs about the importance of home in different languages. The difference between a house and a home is that a house is just a place, a building. A home is the physical space together with everything in it, including the family (and their history), sense of security, and even food.

Similarities: _____

_____

Differences: _____

---

8 **Writing Your Own Summary** Choose one of the following paragraphs to summarize. Remember that a summary is shorter than the original text.

- Paragraph A from Part 1, page 95
- Paragraph E from Part 1, pages 96-97
- Paragraph B from Part 2, page 102
- Paragraph C from Part 2, page 103

In order to summarize the paragraph in your own words, read the paragraph again, but *don't look at the original paragraph as you write*. When you finish writing, compare your summary with those of other students who summarized the same paragraph. Note the similarities and differences.

9 **Writing a Response** Choose one of the topics below to write a paragraph about. Write your own thoughts. Try to use vocabulary from this chapter.

- the components of your own happiness
- where your country might rank in a "happiness poll"—and why
- your opinion about what's essential in a good home
- how your home is an expression of your own identity

What is the main idea of your paragraph? Write the main idea below.

_____

_____

PART **3** Building Vocabulary and Study Skills

1 **Focusing on Words from the Academic Word List** Fill in the blanks with words from the Academic Word List in the box.

areas	constitution	income	researchers
complex	Economic	mental	
concept	environment	psychological	

Not everyone enthusiastically accepts the Human Development Index. The National Bureau of _____ Research points out that 1 the HDI does not include a measure of _____ well-being— 2 in other words, happiness. Two _____, Blanchflower and 3 Oswald, point out that many areas of everyday life can influence a person's 5 happiness: "unemployment, the divorce rate, real _____, 4 friendship, traffic jams, crime, health, and much else." The HDI does not reflect most of these _____. 5

Back in 1972, an interesting idea came out of the tiny Himalayan country of Bhutan. Bhutan's king began to refer to the country's "GNH"— 10 or Gross National Happiness. The idea is that happiness is far more

_____ than economic growth. This _____ is
    6   7

now part of the _____ of Bhutan, and there are regular polls
                          8

where people answer questions about their satisfaction in nine areas of life,

including a good balance of time at work and in leisure, _____ 15
                                                                9

well-being, and a clean _____. The government makes
                                 10

decisions based on the results of these questionnaires.

F⊙CUS

Analyzing Suffixes

As you learned in Chapter 3, suffixes such as *-er, -sion, -ment* and *-ive*, often indicate
the part of speech of a word (see the list on page 64). Here are some more suffixes,
listed by the parts of speech that they usually indicate.

Nouns	Verbs	Adverb
-ity	*-ate*	*-ly*
-ship	*-ize*	

2 **Analyzing Suffixes** The words below include suffixes from this chapter and
Chapter 3. Write the part of speech for each word: *n.* for nouns, *v.* for verbs, *adj.*
for adjectives, and *adv.* for adverbs. In some cases, two answers are correct.

1. __*n*__ friendship
2. _____ universal
3. _____ apartment
4. _____ security
5. _____ exactly
6. _____ expression
7. _____ additional
8. _____ balance
9. _____ enthusiastically
10. _____ expensive
11. _____ associate
12. _____ traditional

13. _____ summarize
14. _____ frequently
15. _____ satisfaction
16. _____ physical
17. _____ environment
18. _____ ability
19. _____ organization
20. _____ actually
21. _____ solidarity
22. _____ essence
23. _____ reasonable
24. _____ central

Analyzing Prefixes

The prefix (beginning) of a word sometimes gives a clue to its meaning. Some prefixes create a word with an opposite meaning.

Example

We've <u>dis</u>covered many <u>un</u>usual and interesting houses in our travels.

(*Discover* means to "uncover" information—i.e., to find out something that we didn't know before. *Unusual* means "not usual"—i.e., out of the ordinary.)

The following prefixes can have the meaning "no" or "not."

un-	:	unpopular: not popular	*ir-*	: irresponsible: not responsible
in-	:	inconvenient: not convenient	*dis-*	: disrespect: no respect
im-	:	improbable: not probable		

3 **Analyzing Prefixes** Use one of the prefixes in the Focus Box above to change each word into its opposite as in the examples. Use your dictionary, if necessary. In some cases, two answers are correct.

1. __un__ happy   5. _____ secure   9. _____ comfortable

2. _____ agree   6. _____ able   10. _____ satisfaction

3. _____ ability   7. _____ important   11. _____ possible

4. _____ traditional   8. _____ frequent   12. _____ interesting

More Prefixes

Here are some other prefixes and their usual meanings:

con-/com-	:	with, together	*re-*	: again, back
ex-/e-	:	out of, from	*sur-*	: over, above
inter-		between, among	*trans-*	: across
mis-		wrong	*uni*	: one
pre-		first, before		

4 **Matching Words** The words on the left include prefixes that you've learned. Use your understanding of the meaning of prefixes to match each word with its definition. Write the letters of the definitions on the lines.

1. __e__ reflect   a. among other countries
2. _____ survive   b. get knowledge from life (not books)
3. _____ expand   c. a meeting where people come together
4. _____ conference   d. stop something before it happens
5. _____ international   e. throw back; give back an image of
6. _____ experience   f. joining together of two or more things
7. _____ component   g. special; one of a kind
8. _____ prevent   h. one of several parts of something bigger
9. _____ combination   i. continue to live or exist
10. _____ unique   j. become or make larger; move outward

FOCUS

Understanding Dictionary Entries: Single and Multiple Meanings

Some words have only one meaning. You can find the meaning in a dictionary entry (print or online).

Examples coffee, elephant, lamp, recent

Most words, however, have more than one meaning. Often the same word can be more than one part of speech, and each part of speech can have different meanings.

Examples cry, home, support, watch

---

5 **Understanding Dictionary Entries: Single Meanings** Read these two dictionary entries and answer the questions about them.

> **el·e·phant** *noun* a tall, heavy, plant-eating mammal of tropical Africa and south central Asia, with a long, flexible prehensile trunk, ivory tusks, and large ears

> **re·cent** *adj.* happening, appearing, or being made not long ago; new, modern

1. What part of speech is *elephant*? _____

2. What is the dictionary definition of the word? _____

   _____

3. What part of speech is *recent*? _____

4. What is the dictionary definition of the word? _____

   _____

6 **Understanding Dictionary Entries: Multiple Meanings** Refer to the dictionary entries below to answer these questions. The word *support* is both a noun (with several meanings) and a verb (with several more).

sup·port *noun* **1.** the act of helping by giving encouragement, love, etc. **2.** an object that bears the weight or part of the weight of a structure **3.** a person or thing that gives aid **4.** the means of income of a person or family **5.** evidence for a story, statement, or idea

sup·port *verb* **1.** to bear the weight or part of the weight of a structure **2.** to endure bravely or quietly : BEAR **3.** to give approval to a decision, idea, or cause **4.** to give evidence for a story, statement, or idea **5.** to keep strong; to strengthen **6.** to maintain financially

1. What part of speech is the word *support* when it means "the act of helping by giving encouragement, love, etc."? _____ Look online for an example of the word *support* in a phrase when it means "encouragement." Write the example here.

    _____

2. How many meanings does the word *support* have as a noun? _____

    As a verb? _____

3. Write the part of speech of the word *support* in each of these sentences.

    a. He <u>supports</u> three children and his wife on a small salary. _____

    b. You need more <u>support</u> for the main idea in your paragraph. _____

    c. I called tech <u>support</u> with a question about my computer. _____

    d. She doesn't <u>support</u> your decision. _____

4. Write the dictionary definition of the word *support* in each of these sentences.

    a. He <u>supports</u> three children and his wife on a small salary.

    _____

    b. You need more <u>support</u> for the main idea in your paragraph.

    _____

    c. I called tech <u>support</u> with a question about my computer.

    _____

    d. She doesn't <u>support</u> your decision.

    _____

7 Dictionary Practice Read the example sentences 1-6 and the dictionary definitions to the right. Then write the part of speech and the meaning of the underlined word in each sentence.

1. I need to find a <u>home</u> for these kittens.

   _____

   _____

2. We should go to the game to support the <u>home</u> team.

   _____

   _____

3. Thick clouds <u>blanketed</u> the mountains.

   _____

   _____

4. It's really cold tonight. You'll need an extra <u>blanket</u>.

   _____

   _____

5. His story <u>moved</u> me deeply.

   _____

   _____

6. That was a smart <u>move</u> to take that job.

   _____

   _____

home *noun*
1. one's place to live; residence; domicile
2. an environment of comfort, security, and happiness

home *adj.* relating to a place of origin or residence

blan·ket *noun* a large piece of textile usually found on a bed

blan·ket *vt* to cover with in the same way as a blanket

move *noun* an action or act in a game or in life

move *vi* **1.** to change position or place **2.** to go forward
vt **1.** to cause to change position or place **2.** to provoke emotions of sadness, joy, or connection

8 Searching the Internet Search the Internet for unusual home architecture. Type a key term like *unusual houses* or *unusual residences* in a search engine. Find one that interests you. Show your group a picture of it and answer these questions:

1. Where is this building? _____

2. What kind of building is it? _____

3. Why does it interest you?_____

4. Does this make a good home? Why or why not?_____

FOCUS

Vocabulary Questions on the TOEFL® iBT

The TOEFL® iBT asks vocabulary questions only about items that appear in a reading. None of the vocabulary questions targets an item by itself, without any context.

Because context is so important, many questions ask about items that could have several meanings in other contexts. Your task is to look at four multiple-choice options and choose the one that best matches the vocabulary item in its context. Be careful. At least one of the incorrect choices will be a meaning that the target item could have in a different context.

1 **Practice** Look again at the reading, "Happiness and the Home" on pages 101-103. Read it again if necessary. Then answer the vocabulary questions below. Try to answer all the questions in ten minutes.

1. Which of the following is closest in meaning to *space*, as it is used in Paragraph A?

    (A) period of time

    (B) empty area

    (C) place

    (D) region with stars and planets

2. Which of the following is closest in meaning to *structures*, as it is used in Paragraph B?

    (A) plants

    (B) ways that people are organized

    (C) materials

    (D) buildings

3. Which of the following is closest in meaning to *universal*, as it is used in Paragraph C?

    (A) including all members of a group

    (B) single; only one

    (C) occurring everywhere

    (D) certain

4. Which of the following is closest in meaning to *fire*, as it is used in Paragraph C?

  (A) shooting of a gun

  (B) light and heat from burning

  (C) strong emotion such as love

  (D) kitchen stove

5. Which of the following is closest in meaning to *allows*, as it is used in Paragraph C?

  (A) makes it possible for

  (B) permits

  (C) fails to prevent

  (D) accepts

6. Which of the following is closest in meaning to *gathers*, as it is used in Paragraph C?

  (A) brings together

  (B) collects

  (C) increases

  (D) comes together

7. Which of the following is closest in meaning to *deep*, as it is used in Paragraph C?

  (A) large

  (B) serious and bad

  (C) full and complete

  (D) with a great distance to the bottom

8. Which of the following is closest in meaning to *end up*, as it is used in Paragraph C?

  (A) finish

  (B) come to an unplanned situation

  (C) be the final part of something

  (D) stop

Self-Assessment Log

Read the lists below. Check (✓) the strategies and vocabulary that you learned in this chapter. Look through the chapter or ask your instructor about the strategies and words that you do not understand.

Reading and Vocabulary-Building Strategies

- ☐ Previewing the reading
- ☐ Finding the main ideas
- ☐ Expressing an opinion
- ☐ Getting meaning from context
- ☐ Finding details
- ☐ Understanding acronyms
- ☐ Interpreting source material from the Internet
- ☐ Marking text when you read
- ☐ Understanding italics
- ☐ Organizing information
- ☐ Analyzing suffixes
- ☐ Analyzing prefixes
- ☐ Understanding dictionary entries

Target Vocabulary

Nouns

- areas*
- balance
- concept*
- components*
- constitution*
- environment*
- essence
- findings
- gap
- income*
- life expectancy
- polls
- researchers*
- solidarity
- sum total
- trend*
- well-being

Verbs

- catch on
- measure

Adjectives

- complex*
- economic*
- mental*
- psychological*
- reasonable

Adverbs

- actually
- enthusiastically

* These words are from the Academic Word List. For more information on this list, see www.victoria.ac.nz/lals/resources/academicwordlist/.

6 Global Connections

INTERNATIONAL COOKING CONTEST

ONLY on the World Food Network

"We… have a cultural phenomenon: the emergence of a global culture, or of cultural globalization."

Peter L. Berger
Austrian-American sociologist

Who in the world is the best chef?

Famous chefs from 15 countries will come together, seeking the title of

WORLD'S BEST CHEF."

Using the freshest ingredients, these chefs and their assistants will compete to assemble the most creative, surprising, and delicious dish. Who will win?

Be watching on Channel 7, April 23-25!

In this **CHAPTER**

In Part 1, you will read about changes in the global food supply that influence what we eat. In the rest of the chapter, you will read about, discuss, and explore globalization—the spreading and mixing of the world's cultures due to travel, trade, and technology.

Connecting to the Topic

1 What foods do you see in this brochure? Who do you think these people are?

2 What foods do you eat that come from other countries? Do you sometimes watch cooking shows on TV?

3 In what ways does the world now have a "global culture?" In what ways do you have access to other cultures? For example, do you know of any TV shows that come from other countries?

Globalization and Food

Before You Read

1 **Previewing the Topic** In small groups, discuss the questions.

1. What are some differences between the foods that you eat and foods that your great-great grandparents probably ate?

2. What foods can you find at a food court*? Which ones are from other countries? Make a list. What are your favorite international foods?

3. Do you think that people today have access to a greater or smaller variety of foods than in the past? Why?

2 **Previewing Vocabulary** Read the words and phrases below. Listen to the pronunciation of each word. Put a check mark (✓) next to the words you don't know. Don't use a dictionary.

Nouns		**Verbs**	**Adverb**
▨ benefit	▨ nutrients	▨ contribute	▨ approximately
▨ consumer	▨ obstacle	▨ shift	
▨ extinction	▨ shift		**Expression**
▨ fuel	▨ staples	**Adjectives**	▨ in turn
▨ livestock		▨ endangered	
		▨ processed	

3 **Previewing the Reading** Look over the reading on pages 119–121. Discuss these questions with a partner.

1. What is the topic of the whole reading? (Look at the title of the reading.)

2. What are the five subtopics? (Look at the heading of each paragraph B-F.)

3. Which foods in this article does your country import? Which foods does your country export?

Read

4 **Reading an Article** As you read the following article, think about the answer to this question: *How—and why—is our diet changing?*

Read the selection. Do not use a dictionary. Then do the exercises that follow the reading.

*The photo on page 119 shows a food court.

Globalization and Food

A   We often hear about the world's "changing diet," and we think of this as a modern concept, but in a sense, the human diet has *always* been changing. The banana, for example, whose origins appear to be in the region that today is Malaysia, traveled to India, where ⁵ Alexander the Great first tasted it; his soldiers brought it back to Greece in about 350 B.C. The potato had been grown in South America for thousands of years before the Spanish brought it ¹⁰ back to Europe in 1570. Increasing travel and trade, **in turn**, took both the banana and the potato to all corners of the world. It is true, however, that globalization is changing our diet faster than ever before. ¹⁵

▲ An international food court

Our Diet Today

B   In several ways, our modern diet differs from that of our great-great grandparents. Today, we have access to more kinds of foods from other countries. (The favorite food of many people worldwide? Pizza.) These days, we also have more fast foods and more take-out foods than in the past. More people are moving to urban areas, ²⁰ where they spend a lot of time both working and commuting to work, so there is less time to cook. Buying fast food and take-out food saves **consumers** time, and it also saves the cost of cooking **fuel**. Another change in the ²⁵ modern diet is a **shift** from traditional **staples** (basic, important foods) to more **processed** foods, which have chemicals or colorings added to preserve them, improve the taste, or make them look attractive. In many countries, foods ³⁰ that were staples in the past, such as tubers and root vegetables, are often replaced by rice—and rice, in turn, is replaced by wheat products, like ready-made bread, which doesn't have as many **nutrients** as the traditional tubers.

Favorite Cuisines Worldwide	Top Food Commodities
• Italian	• Rice
• Chinese	• Wheat
• Indian	• Maize (corn)
• Mexican	• Bananas

Loss of Variety

C   Visit an international food court in almost any country, and it might *seem* that we have a greater variety of foods than in the past. You'll find ³⁵ foods from Mexico, Thailand, Japan, Italy, India, Korea, China, the United States, and so on. Our great-great grandparents did not have access to so many cuisines. Surprisingly, though, there are far *fewer* varieties of many foods than in the past. Imagine—our great-great grandparents may have tasted types of rice, corn, potatoes or bananas that we will never experience. ⁴⁰

For example, according to primalseeds.org, there were 8,000 traditional varieties of rice in China in 1949. By 1970, there were only 50. In the Philippines, too, thousands of kinds of rice have been lost. Mexico has lost approximately 80% of its varieties of maize. There are also *thousands* of other food crops—fruits, vegetables, nuts, and honey—and varieties of **livestock** (such as sheep and chickens) that are on the path to **extinction**. Unlike our ancestors, we might never have the opportunity to taste Melipona bee honey from Argentina, a Masakari pumpkin from Japan, a Ribera vanilla orange from Italy, or Dominique chicken from the United States. As Jeff Bentley, of the BBC, puts it, "Our generation" is killing ancient crops "which fed the Incas, the Mayans, the Sumerians, and the Tang dynasty."

Causes of Disappearing Varieties

Why are varieties of so many foods disappearing worldwide? The key reason is that farmers are replacing traditional varieties with modern ones—partly because these modern varieties are popular and partly because they are easy to ship to distant countries. Big industrial agriculture **contributes to** the problem: huge international companies are buying small family farms and **shifting** to newer—and fewer—crops but in great quantities. According to the Rainforest Conservation Fund, in the past, agriculture in different regions of the world was "independent and local. Now, however, much of it has become part of the global exchange economy." The seed industry contributes to the problem, too. Much of the seed that farmers plant is now produced by only three huge companies, and they sell only a few varieties. The difficulty of finding a variety of seeds is an **obstacle** to farmers who want to plant traditional crops.

The Story of Two Crops

Why should we be concerned? Two crops—the potato and the banana—illustrate the root of the problem. In the 19th century, much of Europe—especially poor people—became dependent on potatoes as their main food source. However, only a few of the thousands of varieties of potato in the Americas had been introduced in Europe. When a terrible plant disease swept through western Ireland in 1845, the potato crop failed. There was no other, healthy variety to replace it. Over the next seven years, **approximately** one million people died of starvation. Hunger drove over one million more to emigrate from Ireland. Today, industrial agriculture might be causing a similar problem with the banana. There are about 300 varieties of banana, but in much of the world, people have access to exactly one—the Cavendish. If disease sweeps through the Cavendish crop, people in many countries will no longer have bananas on their breakfast table.

Original crop   Disease hits   After disease

Diverse potatoes

Single variety of potatoes

= susceptible potato   = potato with disease

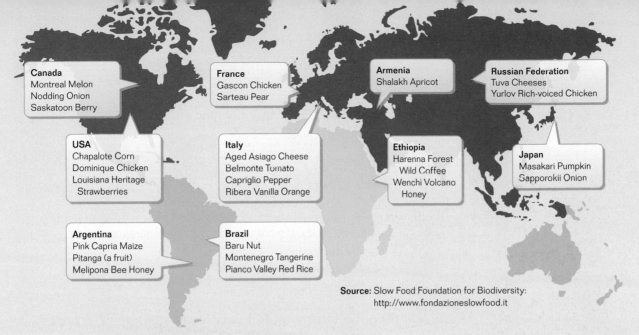

▲ A Sample of Endangered Foods from the Ark of Taste

Source: Slow Food Foundation for Biodiversity:
http://www.fondazioneslowfood.it

Localization—The Solution

F   It's not too late, however, to save some of these **endangered** crops. The "Buy Local" movement is encouraging people to support farmers near their home. These are farmers who often grow less common varieties of food. An additional **benefit** for consumers at farmers' markets is that the food is fresh and full of nutrients because it hasn't been shipped around the world. Also, a **priority** of several organizations, such as the Slow Food Foundation, is to collect seeds of endangered varieties and encourage local farmers to plant them. If they are successful, we have hope that one day we will be able to taste "forgotten flavors" such as a Shalakh apricot or a Saskatoon berry.

85

90

After You Read

5 Finding the Main Idea Write *T* on the lines before the statements that are true, according to the reading. Write *F* before the statements that are false.

1. _____ The human diet has always been changing, but now it's happening faster than ever.

2. _____ Our modern diet is very different from the diet of our great-great grandparents.

3. _____ There are far more varieties of many foods than in the past.

4. _____ Farmers are replacing traditional varieties of many food crops with modern ones.

5. _____ The situation of the banana today is very different from the situation of the potato in the 19th century.

6. _____ Local farmers and several organizations are working to save food crops from disappearing.

Strategy

Understanding the Literal and Figurative Meanings of Words
Many words with one basic *literal* meaning have other *figurative* meanings.

Example

The diseased **seeds** in the farmer's hand planted a **seed** of worry in his mind.

The first usage of the noun *seeds* is literal and means "small objects from which plants grow." However, the second usage of the noun *seed* is figurative and means "the beginning of something that continues to develop."

6 **Understanding the Literal and Figurative Meanings of Words** The underlined words in the sentences below are used figuratively. For each sentence, choose the appropriate meaning for the underlined word in that context.

1. The Spanish brought the potato to Europe. Travel and trade, in turn, took it to all <u>corners</u> of the world.
   - (A) points where two walls meet
   - (B) points where two roads meet
   - (C) distant places
   - (D) difficult positions from which there is no escape
   - (E) edges

2. Thousands of food crops are on the <u>path</u> to extinction.
   - (A) track that people walk or run on
   - (B) area in front of a moving thing or person
   - (C) field in which a farmer grows plants
   - (D) way, direction, movement toward
   - (E) line that something (e.g. an arrow) moves along

3. This is the <u>key</u> reason that varieties of many foods are disappearing.
   - (A) metal instrument that opens a door
   - (B) main, primary, most important
   - (C) something that helps to find an answer
   - (D) part of a piano or a computer
   - (E) list of answers to exercises in a textbook

4. Two crops <u>illustrate</u> why we should worry.
   - (A) decorate with pictures
   - (B) have no equal
   - (C) are photographs
   - (D) are examples of
   - (E) make diagrams or drawings

5. The possibility of crop failure is the <u>root</u> of the problem.

    Ⓐ part of a plant that grows in the soil

    Ⓑ cause or source

    Ⓒ solution

    Ⓓ feeling of belonging to one place

    Ⓔ part of a tooth or hair that holds it to the rest of the body

6. A terrible plant disease <u>swept</u> through Ireland in 1845.

    Ⓐ removed dirt or dust with a broom

    Ⓑ became suddenly popular

    Ⓒ pushed or carried with great force or power

    Ⓓ was felt suddenly

    Ⓔ moved or passed quickly

7. Hunger <u>drove</u> one million people to emigrate from Ireland.

    Ⓐ caused

    Ⓑ took (someone) in a car

    Ⓒ made (something) work

    Ⓓ directed the movement of a car, truck, bus, etc.

    Ⓔ owned and used a car, truck, bus, etc.

7 **Checking Vocabulary** Find the words and expressions in the reading selection "Globalization and Food" that have the following meanings and write the words on the lines.

1. advantage = _____ benefit _____

2. change = _____

3. helps to cause something to happen = _____

4. something that produces heat or power = _____

5. after that = _____

6. something that prevents success = _____

7. people who buy things = _____

8. substances (such as vitamins) in foods = _____

9. the situation when something such as a plant or animal dies out completely =

_____

10. something that is more important than other things =

_____

11. animals used for food = _____

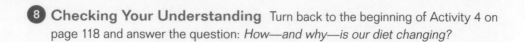

8 Checking Your Understanding Turn back to the beginning of Activity 4 on page 118 and answer the question: *How—and why—is our diet changing?*

Strategy

Understanding Outlines

Many reading selections follow an outline. The outline is the plan, or the organization, of the material. It shows the relationship of the topics, main ideas, supporting details, and examples. Outlining reading material after you read can help you see clearly the relationships between and among ideas. You can also write an outline to organize your ideas when you are preparing to write an essay.

In an outline, the general ideas are labeled with Roman numerals such as I, II, III. The more specific ideas are labeled with capital letters (A, B, C) and are written below the general ideas. If there are more details or examples, they are labeled with numbers (1, 2, 3) and written below the specific idea. More specific ideas are indented to the right.

Example

The outline below is of the reading on pages 119-121.

Globalization and Food

I. Introduction: The World's Changing Diet

  A. Always changing

    1. Banana from India to Greece, about 350 B.C.

    2. Potato from South America to Europe, 1570

    3. From there to the rest of the world

  B. Globalization changing our diet faster now

II. Our Diet Today—how it differs from our great-great grandparents'

  A. Foods from other countries

  B. Fast foods, take-out foods

  C. A shift from traditional staples to more processed foods

III. Loss of Variety

  A. An *apparent* greater variety of foods today (international foods)

  B. But fewer *varieties* of many foods than in the past

    1. Rice, corn, potatoes, bananas

      a. e.g., 8,000 varieties of rice in China in 1949 vs. 50 in 1970

      b. e.g., loss of 80% of varieties of maize in Mexico

    2. Other food crops and livestock

IV. Causes of Disappearing Varieties

  A. Farmers replacing traditional varieties (key reason)

  B. Big industrial agriculture

  C. Seed industry

V. The Story of Two Crops

  A. Potato—in the past

   1. 1845 in Ireland, potato crop failed

   2. No other, healthy variety to replace it

   3. One million people died of hunger

  B. Banana—today

   1. 300 varieties

   2. But only *one* variety in much of the world

VI. Localization—the Solution

  A. The "Buy Local" movement

  B. Organizations collecting seeds of endangered varieties

9 **Understanding Outlines** Answer these questions about the outline.

1. What is the topic of the whole outline?

_____

2. What are two examples of foods that moved from one part of the world to another?

_____

3. What are three reasons that food varieties are disappearing?

_____

4. What are two foods that illustrate why we should be concerned?

_____

5. What are two solutions to the problem of disappearing food varieties?

_____

10 **Finding the Main Idea** What is the one main idea of the reading selection, "Globalization and Food"?

  (A) Today, we have access to international foods, fast foods, and take-out foods that our great-great grandparents did not.

  (B) Worldwide, there are fewer varieties of many foods than in the past.

  (C) One problematic change in our diets is loss of food varieties worldwide, but there are attempts to save endangered crops.

  (D) The history of the potato illustrates why loss of variety is a problem, and we might have the same problem with the banana.

  (E) Organizations such as the Slow Food Foundation are collecting seeds of endangered varieties and encouraging local farmers to plant them.

11 Discussing the Reading Talk about your answers to these questions.

1. Think of a country that you know well. What international foods and cuisines are available there?

2. Go to the Ark of Taste on the Slow Food Foundation for Biodiversity website: http://www.slowfoodfoundation.org/pagine/eng/arca/cerca.lasso?-id_pg=36. Find your country or a country you know. List the endangered foods in this country.

3. Are most of the fruits and vegetables that you buy *local*—or *from other countries*? In your city, do you go to farmers' markets to buy local produce? Why or why not? Where do you buy produce?

4. What are ways in which the human diet is changing worldwide, according to "Globalization and Food"? In your opinion, does the writer think that these changes are more beneficial (good) or more harmful (bad)? Why do you think this?

PART 2 Main Ideas and Details

Life in a Fishbowl: Globalization and Reality TV

Before You Read

1 Thinking Ahead Discuss your answers to these questions.

1. What are your favorite TV programs? Why?
2. What are some examples of reality TV? What are characteristics of reality TV?
3. Why do you think these programs are popular in so many countries?
4. How is YouTube similar to reality TV?

Read

2 Skimming for Main Ideas Read the following paragraphs quickly, without using a dictionary. After each paragraph, choose the sentence that best expresses the main idea.

Life in a Fishbowl: Globalization and Reality TV

A   Increasingly, we have a rich global culture in which countries influence each other's food, music, education, technology, fashion, and entertainment.

One popular form of entertainment that has spread to all corners of the world is reality TV. It's not clear when and where reality TV actually began. Perhaps its roots are in a 1970s TV series called *An American Family*, which followed a real California family through several years of daily life and explored topics that had been taboo before then, such as divorce. For the family members, it was life in a fishbowl: they gave up their privacy. Anyone with a TV in the U.S. could watch the smallest details of their lives—details that were often embarrassing and sometimes tragic. However, the concept of reality TV as we know it today probably began in the 1990s with several European TV shows. These shows took real people and put them in difficult situations to see what would happen—and this is the essence of reality TV.

▲ Life in a fishbowl: no privacy

What is the main idea of Paragraph A?

(A) Countries influence each other's culture in various ways.

(B) It's not clear for certain where and when reality TV actually began.

(C) In one TV series from the 1970s, an American family agreed to give up their privacy and allow TV viewers to follow the details of their daily life.

(D) Reality TV probably began in the 1990s, in Europe.

(E) Reality TV, which probably began in Europe in the 1990s and has spread worldwide, involves real people in difficult situations.

B   The most typical reality TV shows are competitions. They combine elements of several kinds of TV programs: game shows, talent shows, and drama. *Idol*, originally from Britain, is a combination of a talent show and a singing competition. There are elements of drama, too, as the audience learns about the life stories of the contestants. Some of these stories are real tearjerkers! Judges select the contestants, and audience members at home choose the

◄ *Puerto Rico Idol:* Drama, talent, and competition

winner. *Survivor*, from Sweden, where it was called *Expedition Robinson*, sends teams of contestants ("tribes") to rough it in out-of-the-way tropical locations. It tests their ability to survive with very few—or no—tools and almost no food. Contestants vote each week to decide who gets kicked out. On *Fear Factor*, which began in the Netherlands, contestants battle each other by doing extremely dangerous stunts such as you see in movies. Other stunts don't involve danger but do involve something disgusting or painful: swallowing live insects, sitting in a tub of snakes, walking on broken glass with bare feet, and so on. It goes without saying that there is a good deal of drama on this program!

What is the main idea of Paragraph B?

(A) There is danger for contestants on most reality TV shows.

(B) Reality TV shows began in three European countries: Britain, Sweden, and the Netherlands.

(C) Reality TV shows are competitions that combine elements of other types of TV programs.

(D) Three examples of reality TV shows are *Idol*, *Survivor*, and *Fear Factor*.

(E) Reality TV involves discomfort, pain, and danger.

C   Have you ever seen a reality TV program? Chances are you have. If you haven't, at least you've heard about such shows because they're spreading like wildfire. Versions of the original shows now exist in many countries, on all continents. For example, you can see *Canadian Idol*, *Malaysian Idol*, *Vietnam Idol*, *Nouvelle Star* (France), *Super Idol* (in the Arab world), or *World Idol* (well, everywhere). In an attempt to localize the concept, some countries have created programs that follow the same format (contestants who overcome difficulties in competing for a prize) but are specific to that culture. There was *Australian Princess*, for example, which trained twelve young Australian women to handle themselves in the highest of society (if they were ever to become a royal). There was *Space Korea*, which chose the first Korean astronaut. And in the United States, there was *The Biggest Loser*, which taught overweight people about healthy diets and put them through hours of daily exercise. Some programs that were aimed at local audiences, though, quickly became popular in other countries, too. For example, *The Biggest Loser* now has versions in the Arab world, Asia, and Scandinavia, among other areas. It seems that "local" can become "global" very quickly in today's world! Will we soon see *Brazilian Princess* or *Space Norway*?

■ These countries take part in a series with other countries.
■ These countries film their own version of *Idol*.

▲ Countries that show a version of *Idol*

What is the main idea of Paragraph C?

Ⓐ The concept of reality shows has spread worldwide.

Ⓑ Versions of *Idol* now exist in many countries.

Ⓒ The basic format of reality TV shows is that contestants overcome difficulties in competing for a prize.

Ⓓ Some reality TV shows were aimed at a local audience but have now become global.

Ⓔ Some reality shows are popular in only certain countries; others are popular worldwide.

D   Back in the 1970s, you could follow the intimate details in the life of one California family, but only for one hour each week, and you had to be sitting in front of a TV in the United States. Today, in Canada, Global Reality Channel provides round-the-clock programming of many popular reality TV shows. And anywhere in the world, if you have access to the Internet, 65 you can watch almost anything. For example, *Ultimate Cheapsters* was an Internet series for college students in the difficult economic times of 2011-2012. Contestants were challenged to see how little money they could spend on food, clothing, and rent. They fought tooth and nail to be the "ultimate cheapster"—the person who spent the least money. Another trend in reality 70 shows is toward 24/7, live broadcasts. No series does this better than *Big Brother*, in which a group of people lives for several months in a house with cameras following their every action and every word. There are versions of

Big Brother in 81 countries. Viewers who want more than an hour a week—or an hour each evening—can now subscribe monthly and watch anytime, day or night, on their TV, computer, or cell phone. (Even as the participants in the house are sleeping, the cameras are not!) Today, the Internet and social media make it possible for just about anyone to be a "producer" of a sort of reality show. Anyone can post a video on YouTube. Anyone can create a blog. Sometimes, these catch on and go viral—become wildly popular.

What is the main idea of Paragraph D?

Ⓐ Watching a reality show forty years ago was very different from watching one today.

Ⓑ *Big Brother* is the reality show that best provides access to viewers any time of the day or night, but they must subscribe monthly.

Ⓒ These days, almost anyone can create a "reality show" in which they participate and which they put online.

Ⓓ There is a TV channel in Canada on which viewers can watch many different reality shows at any time.

Ⓔ Today, the Internet and social media make it possible both to view live broadcasts of reality TV shows and to produce one's own reality show.

▲ *Survivor:* Who will hold on the longest?

E   What explains the huge popularity of reality TV? On the surface, it might seem that it allows viewers an escape into fantasy, drama, and rags-to-riches stories. It also gives people something to talk about with their friends or co-workers. If we dig deeper, though, psychological research suggests darker reasons. It appears that many viewers of reality shows are competitive, with a desire for high status. Is it possible that they confuse status with fame? After all, contestants on reality programs are ordinary people who become suddenly famous. Perhaps many viewers imagine that they, too, could become celebrities if they were on such a show. Other research suggests that people who watch reality TV place a high value on revenge—punishment for doing harm. Do they enjoy watching the failure of a contestant whom they greatly dislike? It's quite possible. When a contestant's character flaws—faults or imperfections in their basic nature—lead to their failure (e.g., they are "voted off the island" and lose the competition), it is the essence of drama and of tragedy. The desire to see the "good guy" win and the "bad guy" lose seems to reflect universal human values.

What is the main idea of Paragraph E?

(A) Reality TV gives viewers an escape into fantasy.

(B) Most people enjoy reality TV because it gives them a topic of conversation.

(C) Psychology suggests two, darker, reasons for the popularity of reality TV.

(D) Viewers of reality TV shows have a desire to have high status or be famous.

(E) The character flaws of contestants usually lead to their failure.

After You Read

FOCUS

Understanding Idioms

An idiom is a word or phrase that means something different from the individual words in it. Idioms are most common in informal English but are found everywhere. The reading selections in this chapter contain several. Some phrases have both a literal meaning and an idiomatic (figurative) meaning.

Example

For the family on a reality TV show, it was life in a fishbowl.

In this case, *in a fishbowl* is an idiom that means "without any privacy." The context usually helps you figure out if the expression has a literal meaning or is an idiom, and you can often guess the meaning of an idiom from the context. Sometimes, as in the preceding example, it helps to visualize ("see" in your mind) the literal meaning of the idiom.

---

3 **Understanding Idioms and Figurative Language** For each of the following items, find an idiom or word used figuratively in the reading selection "Life in a Fishbowl: Globalization and Reality TV" that has a similar meaning and write it on the line. The letters in parentheses indicate the paragraphs where the idioms appear.

1. stories that are sad and make people cry (B) = _____ *tearjerkers* _____

2. live in a simple, uncomfortable way (B)= _____

3. far away and difficult to reach (B) = _____

4. is eliminated, removed (B) = _____

5. compete with each other (B) = _____

6. It's obvious/It's unnecessary to say, but... (B) = _____

7. a lot (B) = _____

8. probably (C) = _____

9. fast (C) = _____

10. competed with great energy (D) = _____

11. become wildly popular, especially online (D) = _____

12. situations where people move fast from poor to rich (E) = _____

4 **Summarizing** Choose one of the following paragraphs to summarize. Remember that a summary is shorter than the original.

- Any one of the paragraphs from Part 1, pages 119-121
- Any one of the paragraphs from Part 2, pages 126-130

In order to summarize this in your own words, make sure that you read and understand the paragraph. Then write the summary, but *don't look at the original paragraph as you write*. When you finish writing, compare your summary with those of other students who summarized the same paragraph.

5 **Writing Your Own Ideas** Choose *one* of the two topics below. Write two paragraphs about it. Each paragraph should answer one of the questions. In the second paragraph, try to convince the reader of your opinion.

Topic 1: Food

Questions:

1. Where in your city do people buy different kinds of food?
2. What's your favorite place to buy food (a specific store, restaurant, farmers' market, etc.)? Why?

Topic 2: Reality TV

Questions:

1. Describe one reality TV show. What happens on it?
2. What's your opinion of this show? Why?

 6 **Discussing the Reading** Talk about your answers to these questions.

1. What kinds of TV programs are most interesting to you? Why?
2. Think of a country that you know well. Are reality shows popular? If so, which ones? Why do you think people like them?
3. Would you ever like to be a contestant on a reality show? Why or why not?

 7 **Searching the Internet** Search the Internet to find either:

- an unusual reality program in another country
- an article about the psychology of people who watch or are contestants on reality programs.

Tell your group what you learn. Then each group chooses the most interesting information to share with the whole class.

1 Focusing on Words from the Academic Word List Fill in the blanks with words from the Academic Word List in the box. (You'll use one word twice.)

access	chemicals	consumers	processed	shift
areas	concept	globalization	region	traditional

We often hear about the world's "changing diet," and we think of this as a modern _____, but in a sense, the human diet has *always*
    1
been changing. The banana, for example, whose origins appear to be in

the _____ that today is Malaysia, traveled to India, where   5
         2

Alexander the Great first tasted it; his soldiers brought it back to Greece in

about 350 B.C. The potato had been grown in South America for thousands

of years before the Spanish brought it back to Europe in 1570. Increasing

travel and trade, in turn, took both the banana and the potato to all corners

of the world. It is true, however, that _____ is changing our   10
                       3

diet faster than ever before.

In several ways, our modern diet differs from that of our great-great

grandparents. Today, we have _____ to more kinds of foods
             4

from other countries. (The favorite food of many people worldwide? Pizza.)

These days, we also have more fast foods and more take-out foods than in   15

the past. More people are moving to urban _____, where they
                 5

spend a lot of time both working and commuting to work, so there is less

time to cook. Buying fast food and take-out food saves _____
                            6

time, and it also saves the cost of cooking fuel. Another change in the

modern diet is a _____ from _____ staples   20
         7   8

(basic, important foods) to more _____ foods, which have
                  9

_____ or colorings added to preserve them, improve the taste,
10

or make them look attractive. In many countries, foods that were staples in

the past, such as tubers and root vegetables, are often replaced by rice—and

rice, in turn, is replaced by wheat products, like ready-made bread, which   25

doesn't have as many nutrients as the _____ tubers.
11

2 **Expressions and Idioms** Complete each sentence with the missing words. Choose from the expressions and idioms in the box. You will use only eight of them.

a good deal	tearjerkers	went viral
spread like wildfire	all corners of the world	fight tooth and nail
out-of-the-way	round-the-clock	Chances are
It goes without saying	roughing it	rags-to-riches

1. I don't like to go camping because I don't like

   _____. I prefer to stay in a

   comfortable hotel.

2. The news _____. Within minutes, people

   everywhere knew about it. (two possible answers)

3. People in _____–from Alaska to

   Zamboanga–seem to enjoy one reality show or another.

4. _____ you have seen at least one reality

   show at some time because they are so popular in so many places.

5. _____ that many people would not want

   to be contestants on *Fear Factor*, where they would need to do such things as

   sitting in a tub of snakes or walking on broken glass. (two possible answers)

6. It's a real _____ story: she's from a poor

   family, but then she won $1,000,000 on a reality show.

7. For our next vacation, we want to find a(n)

   _____ place, not some crowded

   tourist resort.

8. The contestants on that show _____ to

   win the final prize.

Using Participles as Adjectives

Some adjectives come from verbs:

interest ➔ *interesting/interested*   *bore* ➔ *boring/bored*   *tire* ➔ *tiring/tired.*

Present participles (*-ing*) are used for the cause of an emotion. (The book is *interesting*.)
Past participles (*-ed*) are used for the result or effect. (I'm *interested* in that book.)

Examples

Contestants on *Fear Factor* have to complete many **frightening** tasks.

I have no desire to be on *Fear Factor*. I'd be too **frightened** to do most of those things.

(These participles come from the verb *frighten*.)

---

3 **Using Participles as Adjectives** Read the verbs in the box and the sentences below it. Fill in the blanks with the present or past participles of the verbs in the box. (Use a dictionary if necessary.) You will have opinions on which words to choose, but each word must fit the context of the sentence(s).

challenge	embarrass	entertain	horrify
disgust	encourage	excite	interest

1. A lot of viewers seem to be _____ by *Fear Factor*. They enjoy watching contestants do things like eat live insects. But I don't think that's _____ at all! I think it's just _____! Yuck!

2. The death of one million Irish because of the failure of the potato crop was truly _____. It's important to prevent something similar from happening today, with other crops. It's _____ that some organizations are working to collect and save seeds of many endangered varieties.

3. I'm _____ in trying different kinds of food from different countries, but sometimes it's _____ for me to find unusual foods because I live in a small city without a great variety of restaurants.

4. I guess some people think that a chance to be a contestant on a reality show would be _____. They would do almost anything for such an opportunity. But other people couldn't get _____ about being on one of these shows. They don't want to live in a fishbowl. They'd be _____ if millions of people watched them do stupid things.

FOCUS

Understanding Inferences

In previous chapters you learned about and practiced making inferences. This skill is important to help you understand the meaning of reading passages. It is also important for test taking because questions about implied meaning are common on tests. In this section there are three exercises—two from the first reading in this chapter and one from the second—which will help you practice your inferencing skills.

1 **Practice** Complete each sentence by choosing the answers that the reading selection "Globalization and Food" on pages 119-121 either states or implies. Note: each item has more than one answer.

1. The human diet _____.
   - (A) has changed only in modern times
   - (B) has always been changing
   - (C) is influenced by travelers
   - (D) is better than it was in the past
   - (E) is changing faster than before because of globalization

2. Today, our diet _____.
   - (A) is different from the diet in the past
   - (B) includes more international food, fast foods, and take-out foods than in the past
   - (C) is healthier than it was in the past
   - (D) has more tubers and root vegetables than in the past
   - (E) might not be as healthful as in the past because of ready-made bread

3. Varieties of many foods are disappearing because _____.
   - (A) farmers want to plant popular varieties and varieties that are easy to ship
   - (B) small family farms are disappearing
   - (C) agriculture these days is mostly independent and local
   - (D) big international companies are buying small farms and planting fewer varieties
   - (E) seed companies don't sell many varieties of seeds

4. The potato _____.
   - (A) is an example of a food with many nutrients
   - (B) was introduced to Europe from the Americas
   - (C) was an inexpensive food source in Europe in the 19th century
   - (D) is an example of the problem of lack of variety
   - (E) illustrates what might happen with other crops today, such as the banana

2 **Distinguishing Stated from Inferred Information** Look back at the answers you chose in Activity 1. Which of this information was clearly stated in the reading? Which was inferred? Discuss this with a partner.

3 **Critical Thinking: Identifying Inferences** Read the statements below about the article "Life in a Fishbowl: Globalization and Reality TV" on pages 126-130. Put a check mark (✓) by the statements that you can infer from the reading selection. Do not check the other statements, even if you think they are true. Then, on the line after each inference, write the phrases from which you inferred the information. Leave the other statements blank.

Paragraph A

1. _____ Global culture these days does not have much variety.

_____

_____

2. __✓__ Countries influence each others' cultures in several ways.

countries influence each others' food, music, education, technology, fashion,

and entertainment

3. _____ Reality TV can be found everywhere in the world. _____

_____

4. _____ The people in the series called *An American Family* did not enjoy being famous. _____

_____

Paragraph B

1. _____ All reality TV shows are talent shows. _____

_____

2. _____ Competition is usually part of a reality TV show.

_____

_____

3. _____ Viewers don't know anything about the personal lives of contestants on reality TV. _____

_____

4. _____ The writer of this paragraph probably doesn't want to be a contestant on *Fear Factor*. _____

_____

Paragraph C

1. _____ Most people have probably not seen or heard of reality TV shows.

_____

_____

2. _____ Versions of *Idol* are better in some countries than in others.

_____

_____

3. _____ A reality TV show is a good way to choose astronauts.

_____

_____

4. _____ Ideas for a program in one country can spread fast to other countries.

_____

_____

Paragraph D

1. _____ People who enjoyed watching a TV program about a California family in the 1970s probably needed to have some patience.

_____

_____

2. _____ These days, viewers of many reality shows don't need much patience.

_____

_____

3. _____ Every reality program is now on the Internet. _____

_____

4. _____ Today, you can probably watch a reality program at almost any time, in almost any place. _____

_____

Paragraph E

1. _____ All contestants on reality TV are poor, but many become rich because of the program.

_____

_____

2. _____ All viewers of reality programs would like to become famous.

_____

_____

3. _____ Viewers of reality TV like to watch unpleasant contestants lose.

_____

_____

4. _____ People in all cultures seem to want good to win over evil.

_____

_____

Self-Assessment Log

Read the lists below. Check (✓) the strategies and vocabulary that you learned in this chapter. Look through the chapter or ask your instructor about the strategies and words that you do not understand.

Reading and Vocabulary-Building Strategies

☐ Finding the main idea
☐ Understanding the literal and figurative meanings of words
☐ Understanding outlines
☐ Understanding idioms and figurative language
☐ Using participles as adjectives
☐ Understanding inferences

Target Vocabulary

Nouns

access*	globalization*
areas*	livestock
benefit*	nutrients
chemicals*	obstacle
concept*	region*
consumer*	shift*
extinction	staples
fuel	

Verbs

contribute*
shift*

Adjectives

endangered
processed*
traditional*

Adverbs

approximately*

Expression

in turn

7 Language and Communication

"Language shapes the way we think and determines what we can think about."

Benjamin Lee Whorf
American linguistr

In this **CHAPTER**

In Part 1, you will read about research on how animals communicate. In the rest of the chapter, you will read about, explore, and discuss both animal and human communication.

 Connecting to the Topic

1. What two species do you see in the photo?

2. How does each species communicate?

3. What do you think they are "saying" to each other?

If We Could Talk with Animals...

Before You Read

1 **Previewing the Topic** Look at the photos and discuss the questions.

1. What might be some ways in which these animals communicate?

2. In your opinion, what is the difference between communication and language?

3. Do you think animals can learn language? Can they learn grammar?

▲ Primatologist Jane Goodall with chimps in the wild   ▲ Working with dolphins

▲ A whale in the ocean

ultrasonic wave
超音

▲ How do ants communicate?

2 Previewing Vocabulary Read the words and phrases below. Listen to the pronunciation of each word. Put a check mark (✓) next to the words you don't know. Don't use a dictionary.

Nouns		Verbs	Adverb
▦ brain	▦ mammals	▦ acquire	▦ upright
▦ chatter	▦ organs	▦ claims	
▦ creatures	▦ pod	▦ coin	**Idioms and**
▦ degree	▦ prey	▦ echoes	**Expressions**
▦ echo	▦ primates	▦ feeds	▦ head (of
▦ gender	▦ species	▦ reassure	something)
▦ gestures	▦ subjects	▦ vocalize	▦ head back
▦ grin	▦ swagger	▦ wagging	▦ picked up
▦ lexigrams			▦ shedding
			light on

3 Previewing the Reading Look over the reading on pages 143–147. Answer these questions with a partner.

1. What is the topic of the reading? (Look at the title.)

2. What are the seven subtopics? (Look at the heading of each paragraph.)

3. What do the pictures in the article lead you to expect?

4. What are at least three questions you have about the reading after previewing it?

Read

4 Reading an Article As you read the following article, think about the answer to these questions. *How do animals communicate? Do animals have the capacity to learn language?* Do not use a dictionary. Then do the exercises that follow the reading.

If We Could Talk with Animals...

A   In a famous children's story, Dr. Doolittle is able to talk to—and understand—animals. This has long been a dream of many people—to be able to communicate with animals and know what they're thinking. For almost as long, scientists have wondered if animals actually have language. It seems clear to anyone who has a dog or cat or who closely   5 observes animals that there is certainly communication going on. But how do animals communicate? What do they "say"? And is it truly language? Recent research into everything from ants to chimpanzees is **shedding light on** animal communication.

The "Language" of Smell

B Many animals produce chemicals called pheromones, which send "smell-messages" to other animals of the same species. These odors have different meanings. One odor attracts a mate. Another sends a warning. Another marks a territory. A honeybee, for example, makes over thirty-six different pheromones to communicate such information as where to find good flowers. An ant that has found food will take a bit of it and then **head back** "home" to the anthill. As it carries the food, it wipes its stomach on the ground. This leaves a chemical trail or path so that other ants will know where to go for more food.

10

15

Body Language

C Just as humans do, animals communicate with body language and sometimes **gestures.** In addition to using odors, for example, a honeybee uses its entire body in a complex "dance" to give other bees exact directions to flowers. A dog expresses happiness by **wagging** his tail, as most people know. But what is the dog in the photo "saying"? His stomach is on the ground; his rear end is up in the air, and his tail is **wagging.** This means "I want to play." Chimpanzees in the wild communicate a wide variety of gestures and facial expressions, as we learn from the research of primatologist Jane Goodall. To express anger, for example, a chimp stands **upright** on two legs, moves with a **swagger**—a proud walk, swinging from side to side—and waves her arms or throws branches. A nervous chimp who is afraid of a more powerful chimp will lower himself to the ground. Then he either holds out his hand or shows his rear end to the other chimp. Interestingly, when a chimp "smiles," it is not a smile of happiness. Instead, it is an expression similar to the nervous, fearful **grin** that a human makes in a tense or stressful situation. A powerful chimp will **reassure** a nervous, fearful chimp by touching, hugging, or kissing him.

20

25

30

35

40

▲ What is this dog "saying"?

Vocalizations

D Like humans, many animals **vocalize,** but we are only beginning to understand the meaning of these sounds. As they move through the ocean, some whales make use of echolocation: first they make clicking noises that travel through the water as sound waves. When these sound waves encounter an object such as a boat or **prey** such as fish, they rebound

45

or **echo**. The whales use these **echoes** to locate and identify the objects the echoes are bouncing from, even in cloudy water, where it's difficult to see. Some whales also produce mysterious "songs." These are probably calls to communicate with other members of their **pod**, or group, and to know where each member is. So far, we don't know much more than that. Research into whale communication is especially difficult because different populations of whales have different songs—even if those whales are of the same **species**.

▲ What might this gesture mean?

E   We have a better understanding of the **chatter** of prairie dogs. A professor at Northern Arizona University, Con Slobodchikoff, has spent over ten years studying one colony of prairie dogs in the wild. He records their sounds. He also carefully observes their actions and all events that happen at the same time as the sounds. He then **feeds** the data into a computer. The computer puts together the chatter—the "talking"—and the actions. By utilizing the computer in this way, Slobodchikoff **claims** that he has identified about 50 words. So what are these prairie dogs talking about? They often alert each other when they spot danger from such **creatures** as a human, dog, or coyote. Surprisingly, in their chatter, they can apparently distinguish shapes, colors, and sizes. They might "say," for example, "There's a tall blue human coming from the north" about a person wearing blue clothes. Slobodchikoff believes that they can distinguish **gender** (a man from a woman) and a dog from a coyote. Their chatter also varies

▲ Can prairie dogs really communicate?

according to the **degree** of danger: Is this creature very dangerous or just something to be careful about?

The Use of Symbols by Dolphins

F   Many scientists wonder about animals' capacity to understand a system of symbols, such as language. At the University of Hawaii, studies with dolphins have been going on since 1979. Researchers are teaching these ocean **mammals** a language of hand signals that includes nouns *(ball, basket, pipe)*, adjectives *(big, small, red)*, directions *(left, right)*, verbs *(go, take)*, and prepositions *(in, under)*. The dolphins prove that they understand

50
55
60
65
70
75
80
85
90

by following commands such as "Go to the ball on your right and take it to the basket." There is even clear evidence that dolphins understand the grammatical difference between subjects and objects. The **head** of the research program, Dr. Louis Herman, says that with a vocabulary of about 50 words, the dolphins demonstrate their intelligence by following new commands that they have never before experienced or practiced.

The Use of Symbols by Primates

G Since the 1970s, other researchers have been studying the capacity for language among **primates**—especially among chimpanzees. Because chimps don't have vocal **organs** that allow them to form spoken words, researchers decided to teach them other types of language. One of the earliest **subjects**, a chimp named Washoe, began to learn ASL (American Sign Language, the hand signals of deaf Americans) when she was less than a year old. By age four, she understood and used 132 ASL signs. In other studies, researchers have been communicating with chimps by using a keyboard with special symbols called **lexigrams**. One chimp named Kanzi **picked up** this language naturally; in other words, he watched as people tried (unsuccessfully) to teach this language to his mother.

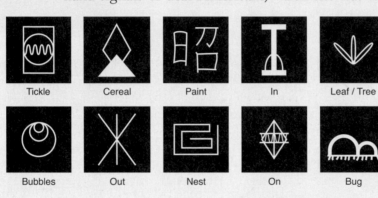

| Tickle | Cereal | Paint | In | Leaf / Tree |
| Bubbles | Out | Nest | On | Bug |

▲ Lexigrams

II How much can chimps understand? And what can they do with these words? They understand the difference between "take the potato outdoors" and "go outdoors and get the potato." They understand adjectives such as *good, funny, hungry,* and *stupid.* They can combine words into short sentences: "You me out"; or "Me banana you banana me you give." Perhaps most interestingly, they can **coin** new words or phrases when they don't know a word—for example, "water bird" for a swan and "green banana" for a cucumber. And they can express emotion: "Me sad."

Language?

  But is this language? What distinguishes communication from true language? Do chimps actually

▲ What kind of birds are these?

have the capacity for language? (There is much disagreement about this.) Some people argue that chimps can **acquire** the vocabulary of only a 2 ½-year-old human. They also point out that a sentence such as "Lana tomorrow scare snake river monster" is not exactly Shakespearean English. It goes without saying that there is a gap between the language ability of chimps and humans. But clearly, this gap is not as wide as we used to think it was. Recent research is now focusing on the structures and activity of the brain. Biologists have looked at one small area of the **brain**, the *planum temporale*, which humans use to understand and produce language. In chimps, this is larger on the left side of the brain than on the right. In the journal *Science*, researchers tell us that this is "essentially identical" to the *planum temporale* in humans. This is not surprising to people who believe that chimps do have the capacity for language. After all, they say 99 percent of the genetic material in chimps and humans is identical, making chimps our closest relative.

135

140

145

Conclusions

J   (It is clear, then, that animals certainly communicate in various ways.) However, the question "Is it language?" is still open. The famous linguist Noam Chomsky believed that what distinguishes communication from true language is *syntax*—that is, the use of grammar and word order, so he believed that only humans can have language. However, now we know that some animals (dolphins, chimps) have at least simple syntax. Louis Herman suggests, "Some people think of language like pregnancy—you either have it or you don't." But he and other researchers prefer to see language as "a continuum of skills." In other words, some animals simply have more than others.

150

155

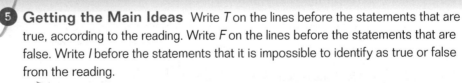

After You Read

5 **Getting the Main Ideas** Write *T* on the lines before the statements that are true, according to the reading. Write *F* on the lines before the statements that are false. Write *I* before the statements that it is impossible to identify as true or false from the reading.

1. __T__ Some animals communicate by producing odors for other animals to smell.
2. __F__ Chimpanzees, like humans, smile when they are happy.
3. __F__ We know a lot about the communication of whales.
4. __I__ With their vocalizations, prairie dogs can warn each other of specific dangers.
5. __F__ **X** Dolphins can understand only sentences that they have memorized.
6. __I__ **X** Chimps can understand much more vocabulary and grammar than researchers previously thought they could.
7. __F__ Researchers agree that all animals communicate but that only humans have a capacity for language.

6 Checking Your Understanding What did you learn from the reading? Answer these questions with a group.

1. What are ways in which animals communicate in the wild (that is, in their natural environment)? List them.

2. What are ways in which dolphins and chimps have been taught by humans to communicate? List them.

3. What are examples of the body language of dogs and chimps, and what do these specific movements mean?

4. What is evidence that indicates the similarity of chimpanzees to humans?

Language Tip

The **context** of a reading can give clues to the meaning of vocabulary words. Use information between commas, dashes, or parentheses, or after connecting expressions such as **in other words** or **that is** (**i.e.**). Also, use information in another sentence or sentence part and your own logic.

7 Getting Meaning from Context Read the definitions below and write the correct words and expressions from the reading "If We Could Talk with Animals…" that fit the definitions.

1. making (something) clear = _____ *shedding light on* _____

2. moving a tail = _____ wagging _____

3. movements that communicate meaning = _____ gesture _____

4. return (verb) = _____ head back _____

5. straight up; standing on two feet = _____ upright _____

6. group of whales = _____ pod _____

7. a smile = _____ grin _____

8. make someone feel better = _____ reassure _____

9. make sounds = _____ vocalize _____

10. an animal that another animal hunts = _____ prey _____

11. a proud walk, from side to side = _____ swagger _____

12. animals of the same type = _____ same specie _____

13. the part of the body with which we think = _____ brain _____

14. says; expresses an opinion = _____ claim _____

15. male or female = _____ gender _____

16. animals with warm blood = _____ mammals _____

17. get; obtain; learn = _____ acquire _____

18. rapid "talk" = _____ chatter _____

8 Categorizing On each line, write the category that the items are examples of. The letters in parentheses refer to the paragraphs in the reading.

1. humans, dogs, coyotes (E) = _____

2. chimpanzees (G) = _____

Understanding Words with Multiple Meanings

As you saw in Chapter 5, many words have more than one meaning. Be aware of this as you read. If you think you understand a word but something seems strange about its use, it is possible that in *that* context, the word might have a different meaning.

Example

I was feeling **blue**, so I called my friend.

(In this context, *blue* does not refer to a color. If you can't guess its meaning from the context, check a dictionary. You will see that *blue* can mean "sad, depressed.")

9 **Understanding Words with Multiple Meanings** Write a word from the reading that fits both definitions. The letters in parentheses refer to the paragraph in the reading.

1. gives food to; puts (information) into (E) = ___*feeds*___

2. amount; title that a university gives students who have completed their studies (E) = ___*degree*___

3. part of the body; director or leader (F) = ___*head*___

4. musical instruments in churches; parts of the body (G) = ___*organs*___

5. topic; person or animal in an experiment (G) = ___*subjects*___

6. lifted from a lower place; learned (G) = ___*pick up*___

7. piece of metal money; create a word or term (H) = ___*coin*___

Understanding Italics and Quotation Marks (Quotes)

Writers use *italics* (slanted letters) in English for several reasons:

- for emphasis—to stress an important word
- to mean *the word* _____, *or the term* _____ (Example: *Red* sounds the same as the past tense verb *read*.)
- for the title of a magazine, newspaper, or book
- for words in foreign languages

Writers use quotation marks for two main reasons:

- to quote direct speech—someone's exact words
- to show that the meaning of the word in quotes is not literal

Examples

There is certainly communication going on. But *how* do animals communicate? What do they "say"?
(The word *how* is in italics for emphasis. The word *say* is in quotation marks because the writer believes that animals don't really say anything.)

10 **Understanding Italics and Quotations** Look through the reading on pages 143–147 beginning with Paragraph B. Highlight every example of italics and quotation marks. In each case, decide why the writer used them. Then compare your answers with those of other students.

11 **Finding Details** Read the types of communication in the chart below. Go back to the article and find examples of each type. Fill in this information to complete the chart.

Types of Communication	Examples
smell	Smells have different meanings: to attract a mate, send a warning, mark a territory, or communicate where to find food.
gestures	direct location express emotion and willing happiness, anger, nevous, afraid, want to play
vocalizations	whales use ~~echo~~ echo to locate and identify object or other number
chatter (by prairie dogs)	alert others the danger creatures can distingush color shapes size gender
symbols (used by dolphins)	can be taught several kinds of words understand the grammar
symbols (used by primates)	can learn Asl than understand and use special symbols keyboard

12 **Checking Your Vocabulary** Turn back to Previewing Vocabulary on page 143. How many words do you know now? Work with a small group. Go through the list and briefly explain each word in one of these possible ways:

- Give a synonym or definition.
- Use gestures or body language.
- Give an example.
- Point to a picture in this chapter.

13 **Discussing the Reading** Discuss your answers to the question in the last paragraph of the reading: *Is it language?* Specifically, discuss the following: *What is the difference between communication and language?*

1. Brainstorm possible kinds of communication. Then brainstorm the characteristics of language. List them in the T-chart on the next page.

Communication	Language
body gesture facial emotion sign sound wave	grammer used

2. Now discuss three species. Complete the chart below.

Species	Do they have capacity for language? (yes/no/not sure)	Evidence
prairie dogs	Not sure	
dolphins	Not sure	
chimps	Yes	they can coin the new words

Culture Note

Animal Sounds

In every language, we imagine that animals make certain sounds. We create words for these sounds. These are words that you often see in children's books. Below are some in English.

Animal	What This Animal "Says" in English	What This Animal "Says" in Another Language
cat	meow	
dog	bow-wow (or woof-woof)	
pig	oink	
small bird	cheep! cheep! (or tweet! tweet!)	
duck	quack	
owl	whoo (or hoot)	
rooster	cock-a-doodle-doo	

It's sometimes fun to compare these in different languages. What do animals "say" in another language you know? Write these sounds in the chart.

"Parentese"

Before You Read

1 **Previewing the Topic** Discuss your answers to these questions.

1. In your opinion, who talks more—men or women?

2. In school, who is better at language skills—boys or girls?

3. Do parents talk differently with their sons than they do with their daughters? Do mothers talk differently to their children than fathers do? If so, how?

4. What kinds of toys do parents usually give to their sons? What kinds of toys do parents usually give to their daughters?

5. In your opinion, what is more important in determining what we are—genetics (biology) or our education and environment?

2 **Identifying the Main Ideas** The following paragraphs are about the language that parents use with their young children—what some people call "parentese." Read these paragraphs without using a dictionary. After each paragraph, choose the sentence that best expresses the main idea.

"Parentese"

A   Who talks more—men or women? Most people believe that women talk more. However, linguist Deborah Tannen, who has studied the communication style of men and women, says that this is a stereotype. According to Tannen, women *are* more verbal, or talk more, in private situations, where they use conversation as the "glue" to hold relationships together. But, she says, *men* 5 talk more in public situations, where they use conversation to exchange information and gain status. Tannen points out that we can see these differences even in children. Little girls often play with one "best friend"; their play includes a lot of conversation. Little boys often play games in groups; their play usually involves more *doing* than talking. In school, girls are often 10 better at verbal skills; boys are often better at mathematics.

What is the main idea of Paragraph A?

(A) Women talk more than men.

(B) Women talk more in private, and men talk more in public.

(C) Little girls and little boys have different ways of playing.

(D) Men and women have different styles of talking, which may begin in childhood.

B   A recent study at Emory University helps to shed light on the roots of this difference. Researchers studied conversation between children age 3–6 and their parents. They found evidence that parents talk very differently to their sons than they do to their daughters. The startling conclusion was that parents use far more language with their girls. Specifically, when parents talk with their daughters, they use more descriptive language and more details. There is also far more talk about emotions, especially sadness, with daughters than with sons.

15

What is the main idea of Paragraph B?

(A) Researchers have studied the conversations of children and their parents.

✓ (B) A research study found that parents talk differently to their sons and daughters.

(C) An Emory University study found that parents talk more with their daughters than with their sons.

(D) Parents don't talk about emotions with their sons.

C   Most parents would be surprised to learn this. They certainly don't plan to talk more with one child than with another. They don't even realize that this is happening. So why do they do it? Interestingly, it begins when the children are newborn babies. It is a known fact that at birth, males are a little less developed than females are. They don't vocalize, or make noises, as much as girls do, and they don't have as much eye contact. Female babies vocalize, look at their parents, and remain alert longer. The result? Parents respond by talking more to the baby girls, who seem to be paying attention and "talking" back to them. Apparently, then, biology determines the amount of language that parents use.

20

25

What is the main idea of Paragraph C?

✓ (A) Parents who talk more to their baby girls are responding to the fact that girls are a little more developed at birth than boys are.

(B) Most parents don't know that they talk more with their girls and would be surprised to learn this.

(C) Baby girls make noises and make more eye contact than baby boys do.

(D) Baby boys don't remain alert as long as baby girls do.

D   There is always this question: What determines our character, personality, and behavior—nature (biology) or nurture (environment and education)? The research with babies seems to suggest that *nature* causes the amount and quality of language use. However, a study from the University of California at Santa Cruz provides evidence that the *situation* or *context* also influences the conversation. For example, parents usually give gender-stereotyped toys to their children. A boy gets a car that he can take apart and put back together, for instance. A girl gets a toy grocery store. The type of talk depends on the toy the child is playing with. A toy grocery store naturally involves more conversation than a take-apart car does. If we consider this, we might decide that *nurture* determines language ability because we *choose* which toys to give our children.

What is the main idea of Paragraph D?

(A) The toys that parents give their son or daughter may influence the child's language ability.

(B) From research with babies, we know that biology determines language use.

(C) Parents usually give gender-stereotyped toys to their children.

(D) Education determines language ability.

E   Campbell Leaper, a researcher at the University of California, believes that the choice of toys is important. Both boys and girls, he says, need "task oriented" toys such as take-apart cars. With these toys, they practice the language that they will need, as adults, in work situations. Both boys and girls also need "social, interactive" toys such as a grocery store. With these toys, they practice the kind of conversation that is necessary in relationships with friends and family. The data suggest that biology does not have to be a self-fulfilling prophecy. Leaper concludes that verbal ability is the result of both nature and nurture. Parents might naturally respond to their baby's biology, but they can choose a variety of toys and can choose how to talk with this child.

What is the main idea of Paragraph E?

(A) Boys usually receive toys with which they practice language that they will use in work situations.

(B) Girls usually receive toys with which they practice language that is necessary in relationships.

(C) Biology is not a self-fulfilling prophecy.

(D) Biology influences language ability, but environment also does, so parents need to give both their boys and girls a variety of types of toys.

3 Getting Meaning from Context For each definition, find a word in the reading that has a similar meaning and write it on the line.

Paragraph A

1. connected with the use of spoken language = _Verbal_

2. sticky liquid that joins things together = _glue_

Paragraph B

3. feelings = _emotions_

Paragraph C

4. understand and believe = _realize_

5. to act in return or in answer = _respond_

6. it seems that = _apparhently_

Paragraph D

7. biology = _nature_

8. environment and education = _nurture_

9. proof; support for a belief = _evidence_

4 Critical Thinking: Identifying Inferences Read the statements below about the article "Parentese" on pages 152–154. Put a check mark (✓) by the statements that you can infer from the reading. Do not check the other statements, even if you think they are true. Then, on the line after each inference, write the phrases from which you inferred the information. Leave the other statements blank. The first one has been done for you as an example.

Paragraph A

1. __✓__ According to Deborah Tannen, the belief that women talk more is partly right but mostly wrong and oversimplified.

Most people believe that women talk more... but this is a stereotype.

2. __✓__ Women talk more in some situations; men talk more in others.

Line 5

Paragraph B

3. _____ Parents enjoy talking more with their daughters than with their sons.

4. __✓__ Girls have more practice discussing sadness than boys do.

Paragraph C

5. _✓_ Vocalization and eye contact are evidence of development in babies.

_____

6. _____ Little girls, like baby girls, are more alert than little boys.

_____

Paragraph D

7. _✓_ People naturally talk more in some situations than in others.

_____

8. _✓_ A toy car probably doesn't involve boys in much conversation.

_____

Paragraph E

9. _✓_ According to Campbell Leaper, we should prepare both boys and girls for the adult world of work and relationships.

_____

10. _✗_ If parents choose their child's toys carefully, biology won't influence the child's verbal ability.

_____

_____

Strategy

Distinguishing Facts from Assumptions

In reading textbooks, students need to be able to determine the difference between a fact (information that has been proven to be accurate) and an assumption (an idea that might or might not be true but whose accuracy has not been proven). One way to do this is to be aware of certain "signal words."

Some words and expressions that indicate a **fact** are:

    found proof   a known fact   evidence

Some words that indicate an **assumption** are these:

    believe   suggest

← apparently   may/might

    seem

adv. 显然的，似乎

5 **Distinguishing Facts from Assumptions** For each statement below, write *fact* or *assumption*, according to the presentation of information in the reading "Parentese." (Look back at the reading for words that indicate a fact or an assumption.)

1. _____ A _____ Women talk more than men.

2. _____ F _____ Parents talk very differently to their sons and daughters.

3. _____ F _____ At birth, males are a little less developed than females are.

4. _____ ~~A~~ F _____ The situation in which conversation takes place—in addition to a child's gender—influences the amount of talk.

5. _____ ~~A~~ A _____ The choice of toys that parents give their children is important. *might, believe*

6. _____ A _____ Biology does not have to be a self-fulfilling prophecy.

6 **Discussing the Reading** Talk about your answers to these questions.

1. According to the reading, what might cause some schoolchildren to be better at language skills than other children?

2. Did anything in the reading "Parentese" surprise you? If so, what?

3. Complete this diagram with information from both the reading and your own experience. What makes us the people we are? In other words, which of our characteristics come from nature? Which come from nurture? Which come from both?

Nature   **Both**   **Nurture**

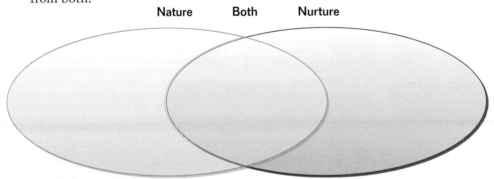

7 **Summarizing** Choose one paragraph from "Parentese" on pages 152–154. Write a short summary of it (two or three sentences). Follow these steps:

• Make sure that you understand the paragraph well.
• Identify the topic, main idea, and supporting details.
• Find the most important details.

In order to summarize it in your own words, *don't look at the original paragraph as you write*. When you finish writing, compare your summary with those of other students who summarized the same paragraph.

8 Writing Your Own Ideas Choose one of these topics to write about.

- animal communication
- "parentese"
- the influence of toys on children

What did you learn about this topic from Part 1 or 2? Write two paragraphs. In the first, tell what you learned about your topic. In the second paragraph, write about one of the following:

- something that especially interested you or surprised you about this topic (and why)
- an experience in your own life that is related to your topic

What is the main idea of each paragraph? _____

_____

_____

Talk it Over

9 Toys Make a list of the toys that you played with most often as a child. What were they? What kind of conversations did they involve you in? (Task-oriented? Social and interactive?) Do you think these toys influenced your language ability? Discuss your answers with a small group.

PART 3 | Building Vocabulary and Study Skills

1 Focusing on Words from the Academic Word List Fill in the blanks with words from the Academic Word List in the box. You will use one word twice.

> √acquire 獲得
> √capacity 容量
> √communication
>
> √focusing
> identical 相同
> √journal 日誌
>
> √percent
> √research
> √structures 結構

But is this language? What distinguishes ___communication___ from true
                                              1
language? Do chimps actually have the ___capacity___ for language?
                                            2
There is much disagreement about this. Some people argue that chimps

can ___acquire___ the vocabulary of only a 2 ½-year-old human.
They also point out that a sentence such as "Lana tomorrow scare snake
river monster" is not exactly Shakespearean English. It goes without saying
that there is a gap between the language ability of chimps and humans.
But clearly, this gap is not as wide as we used to think it was. Recent
___research___ is now ___focusing___ on the ___structures___
and activity of the brain. Biologists have looked at one small area of the
brain, the *planum temporale*, which humans use to understand and produce
language. In chimps, this is larger on the left side of the brain than on
the right. In the ___Journal___ *Science,* researchers tell us that this
is "essentially" ___identical___ to the *planum temporale* in humans.
This is not surprising to people who believe that chimps do have the
___capacity___ for language. After all, they say 99 ___percent___
of the genetic material in chimps and humans is identical, making chimps
our closest relative.

FOCUS

Prefixes and Suffixes

Below is a partial list of word **prefixes** and their approximate meanings. On the next
page are **suffixes**. These were all introduced in previous chapters.

Prefix	Meaning
com-/con-	together; with
im-/in-/un-/dis-	not
inter-	between; among
mis-	wrong
pre-	before; first
re-	again; back

Suffix	Part of Speech	Meaning
-al	adjective	having the quality of
-ar	adjective	of or relating to; resembling
-i(an)	noun	belonging to; characteristic of
-ed	adjective	passive participle
-en	verb	to make; to become
-ence/-ance	noun	state; quality
-ent/-ant	adjective	having the quality of
-er	adjective	comparative form
-er/-or/-ist	noun	a person who
-ess	noun	a person (female)
-est	adjective	superlative form
-ful	adjective	full of
-ible/-able	adjective	having the quality of; able to be
-ic	adjective	having the quality of; affected by
-ing	noun, adjective	active participle; gerund
-ion	noun	state; condition
-ive	adjective	having the quality of; relating to
-less	adjective	without
-ly	adverb	manner (how)
-ment/-ness/-ship	noun	state; condition; quality
-(i)ous	adjective	full of
-ure	noun	state; result
-y	adjective	having the quality of; full of

---

2 **Working with Prefixes and Suffixes** In the parentheses after each word, write the word's part of speech (n. = noun; v. = verb; adj. = adjective; adv. = adverb). Then complete the sentences that follow with the appropriate words.

1. converse (*v.*), conversation (*n.*), conversational (*adj.*) Recent studies show that there is more ___conversation___ between parents and their daughters than with their sons. This begins at birth, when parents ___converse___ more with baby girls, who tend to have more eye contact and make more noises than baby boys do. It continues in childhood, when girls' play is more ___conversational___ than boys' is.

2. linguist (*n.*), linguistic (*adj.*), linguistics (*n.*) The field of ___linguist___ has several branches. In one of these, ___linguist___s study how children acquire language. In another branch, they work to discover if some animals have ___linguistics___ ability.

3. reassurance (*n.*), reassure (*v.*), reassuringly (*adv.*) The mother chimp hugged her frightened baby to ___reassure___ him. Then she kissed him to give him further ___reassurance___. These actions are similar to those of a human, who, in addition, speaks ___reassuringly___ to a fearful child.

4. able (*adj.*), ability (*n.*), ably (*adv.*)
Many people wonder if animals have the _____*ability*_____ to learn language.
Studies with dolphins and chimps indicate that they are _____*able*_____ to
learn a certain amount of vocabulary. They also _____*ably*_____ follow a
number of directions.

5. appear (*adj.*), apparent (*adj.*), apparently (*adv.*)
_____*Apparently*_____, both nature and nurture decide a child's linguistic ability.
It is _____*apparent*_____ that boys and girls vocalize to a different degree from
birth. However, it also _____*appear*_____ s that parents can influence the
amount and type of conversation that their children have.

6. simple (*n.*), simplify (*v.*), simplified (*adj.*)
When humans _____*simplify*_____ their language, chimps are able to
understand a certain amount. The chimps can also use _____*simple*_____
grammar to put together _____*simplified*_____ sentences.

7. vocal (*adj.*), vocalize (*v.*), vocalization (*n.*)
Members of a pod of whales frequently _____*vocalize*_____ with each other.
We believe they are _____*vocal*_____ in this way to make sure where each
member is, but we really don't know much, yet, about their _____*vocalization*_____ s.

3 **Understanding Words in Phrases** As you read, it's important to notice
words that often go together. Go back to the reading on pages 152–154.
Find words to complete the following phrases.

Paragraph A
1. hold relationships _____*together*_____
2. _____*gain*_____ status
3. points _____*out*_____ that
4. are often better _____*at*_____ (mathematics)

Paragraph B
5. shed _____*light*_____ _____*on*_____

Paragraph C
6. a _____*known*_____ fact
7. _____*eye*_____ contact
8. _____*paying*_____ attention

Paragraph D
9. _____*provides*_____ evidence
10. take _____*apart*_____ and put _____*back*_____
_____*together*_____
11. depends _____*on*_____

Paragraph E
12. a _____*self*_____ - _____*fulfilling*_____ prophecy

Strategy

Learning New Vocabulary: Making a Vocabulary Log

While you are reading, you need to understand vocabulary, but you do not need to learn it actively. Sometimes, however, you may want to remember new vocabulary for use in conversation and writing. A vocabulary log may prove useful. Follow these steps to create one:

1. Divide a sheet of paper into three columns. (This will become your Vocabulary Log.) Write these headings at the top of the three columns: Word, Definition, Example. Write the new word or expression and its pronunciation in the first column. In the middle column, write the definition and the part of speech. In the third column, write a sentence that illustrates the meaning of the item. (You can find these sample sentences in the readings in this book.)

2. Look up the words in a dictionary and write related words on the same piece of paper.

3. Pronounce the words to yourself. Try to "see" their spelling in your mind as you learn them. Repeat examples to yourself and make up other examples.

4. Cover the words and examples and try to remember them when you read the definitions.

5. Review your list regularly.

Pay special attention to *how* the word is used. For example, if the word is a verb, is it transitive? (Does it need an object?) Is a preposition used after the word? If it is a noun, is it a count noun (like *teacher*) or a noncount noun (like *water*)?

Example

Word	Definition	Examples
respond (rĭ-spŏnd')	(v.) answer	Parents **respond** to their baby's vocalizations.
response (rĭ-spŏns')	(n.) answer	Her **response** was immediate.
responsive (rĭ-spŏn'sĭv)	(adj.) answering willingly with words or actions	They were **responsive** to their child's needs.

4 Making a Vocabulary Log Choose a few words from Chapters 1 to 7 in this book. Follow the directions in the Strategy box on page 162 to make your own Vocabulary Log. Focus on the words that you had a hard time learning or are having a hard time remembering. Each day, as part of your homework, spend a few minutes adding new words to your Vocabulary Log.

5 Searching the Internet Search the Internet for information about one of the topics below. Share the information you find with a small group.

- Communication among animals and people
  How do they communicate? What words do they know?
  (Tip: You can look up Jane Goodall, chimps in the wild; Con Slobodchikoff, prairie dog communication; Louis Herman, dolphin communication; or Deborah Tannen, human male-female communication.)
- Popular toys
  Find out what the five most popular toys are these days. Which of these toys are task-oriented? Which are social or interactive?

PART 4 Focus on Testing

FOCUS

Comprehension Questions About Details

Standardized tests often give a reading passage followed by questions about it. Many of these questions are about details. You'll be able to answer some from memory, after one quick reading. You'll need to look back and scan for the answers to others.

Hints

- You can usually find the items in the same order in which they appear in the selection, so look for the answer to number 1 near the beginning.
- It usually helps to quickly look over the questions before reading, if possible.

1 Practice First, read the questions that follow the article. Then read the article. Try to keep some of the questions in mind as you read and highlight the answers. Don't worry if you don't understand every word. When you finish reading, answer the questions. Work as quickly as possible, as you would on a test. Your teacher may give you a time limit.

As English Spreads, Speakers Morph It into World Tongue

"English is probably changing faster than any other language," says Alan Firth, a linguist at the University of Aalborg in Denmark, "because so many people are using it."

More than 2 billion people are believed to speak some form of English. For every native speaker, there are three nonnative speakers. Three-quarters of the world's mail is in English and four-fifths of electronic information is stored in English.

As more nonnative speakers converse with each other, hundreds of varieties of English are taking on lives of their own around the world.

But the uncontrolled, global germination of so many "Englishes" has some worried. English purists, led by Britain's Prince Charles, bemoan the degradation of the language as they see it.

Multiculturalists, meanwhile, say the spread of English effectively commits "linguistic genocide" by killing off dozens of other languages.

These differing views lead to the question: Is the world taking English by storm or is English taking the world by storm?

Tom McArthur, editor of the *Oxford Companion to the English Language*, says that in 20 to 30 countries around the world, English is merging with native languages to create hybrid Englishes.

"The tensions between standard English and hybrid Englishes are going to become very, very great," says Mr. McArthur, who calls the process neither good nor bad. "We are going to have to keep on our toes. Some standard form of English [should be maintained]… as a tool of communication."

Prince Charles recently warned of a creeping degradation of the English language, lashing out at Americans for cheapening it with bad grammar.

"People tend to invent all sorts of nouns and verbs and make words that shouldn't be," said Prince Charles at the March launching of a five-year British effort to preserve "English English."

"I think we have to be a bit careful, otherwise the whole thing can get rather a mess," he added.

Danish Professor Firth, who studies conversations between nonnative speakers when they conduct business, says businessmen tend to… use simplified grammar and develop and use their own English terms to cut a deal.

"People develop their own ways of doing business with each other, of talking and even writing ... that native speakers might not understand," Firth says. "And native speakers join in and start to speak that way also." 35

But those who seek to preserve native cultures warn that in many parts of the world, English is taking more than it is giving. Some linguists attending a global Cultural Diversity Conference held in Sydney warned of accelerating global "linguicide." 40

Schools in former European colonies still use English or French to assimilate ethnic populations, eradicating dozens of native languages, they warn.

Oxford Companion editor McArthur says the spread of English can't be halted. The globalization of the world, mostly driven by economics, is inevitable. 45

"It's the [world's] need for a unified language of trade, politics, and culture," he says. "We're going to lose a lot of languages around the world, but if it's not English, it would be something else." 50

Source: Adapted from "As English Spreads, Speakers Morph It into World Tongue" from David Rohde, *The Christian Science Monitor.*

1. According to the article, how many people probably speak English?
   - (A) three-fourths of the world
   - (B) four-fifths of the world
   - (C) more than 2 billion people
   - (D) one in three people

2. Two groups of people with differing views are _____.
   - (A) purists and multiculturalists
   - (B) native speakers and nonnative speakers
   - (C) businessmen and linguists
   - (D) linguists and multiculturalists

3. People who believe that the spread of English is harming (hurting) English

are _____.

   Ⓐ linguists

   Ⓑ multiculturalists

   Ⓒ purists

   Ⓓ editors

4. The article indicates that Prince Charles _____.

   Ⓐ leads the English purists

   Ⓑ does not like the changes in the English language

   Ⓒ does not appear to like American English

   Ⓓ all of the above

5. *Linguicide* (line 41) probably means _____.

   Ⓐ the teaching of languages

   Ⓑ the preservation of languages

   Ⓒ the killing of languages

   Ⓓ the teaching of linguistics

6. Tom McArthur, editor of the *Oxford Companion to the English Language*,

believes that _____.

   Ⓐ English is joining with other languages to create something new

   Ⓑ it's not necessary to have a standard form of English

   Ⓒ the spread of English is unavoidable

   Ⓓ a and b

Beyond the Reading

2 **Interviewing** Choose one of these projects. When you finish, report your findings to the class.

- Interview ten people who are not native speakers of English. Ask them if the spread of English is having any effect on their culture or language, and if so, *what* effect?
- Interview ten native speakers of English. Ask them if they notice any recent changes in the English language (vocabulary, grammar, etc.) due to the influence of other languages, and if so, *what* changes?

Self-Assessment Log

Read the lists below. Check (✓) the strategies and vocabulary that you learned in this chapter. Look through the chapter or ask your instructor about the strategies and words that you do not understand.

Reading and Vocabulary-Building Strategies

☐ Getting the main ideas
☐ Getting meaning from context
☐ Understanding words with multiple meanings
☐ Understanding italics and quotation marks
☐ Finding details
☐ Identifying the main ideas
☐ Identifying inferences
☐ Distinguishing fact from assumption
☐ Working with prefixes and suffixes
☐ Understanding words in phrases
☐ Making a vocabulary log

Target Vocabulary

Nouns

- brain
- capacity*
- chatter
- communication*
- creatures
- degree
- echoes
- gender*
- gestures
- glue
- grin
- journal*

- lexigrams
- mammals
- organs
- percent*
- pod
- prey
- primates
- research*
- species
- structures*
- subjects
- swagger

Verbs

- acquire*
- claims
- coin
- echo
- feeds
- focusing*
- reassure
- vocalize
- wagging

Adjective

- identical*

Adverb

- upright

Idioms and Expressions

- head (of something)
- head back
- picked up
- shedding light on

* These words are from the Academic Word List. For more information on this list, see www.victoria.ac.nz/lals/resources/academicwordlist/.

8 Tastes and Preferences

> Science and art belong to the whole world, and before them vanish the barriers of nationality.
>
> Johann Wolfgang von Goethe
> German philosopher and writer

In this
CHAPTER

In Part 1, you will read about the Silk Road and how trade affects world cultures. In the rest of this chapter, you will read about, explore, and discuss how people (including you) have viewed and view beauty.

 Connecting to the Topic

1. Describe what you see in the photo. What kind of collection is this?

2. Do you collect anything? Clothes, objects, photos, technology, books, etc.? Why or why not?

3. What types of art and products do you like to look at? To buy?

The Silk Road: Art and Archaeology

1 Previewing the Topic Look at the photos and discuss the questions.

1. Compare the map of the ancient Silk Road to the modern map of the same area. What countries exist in this region today?

2. What was the purpose of caravans? Do people still have caravans today? Why or why not?

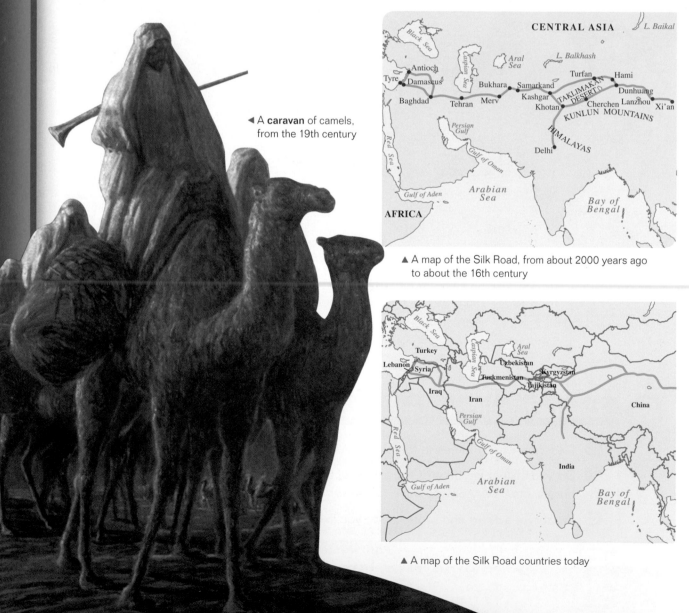

◀ A **caravan** of camels, from the 19th century

▲ A map of the Silk Road, from about 2000 years ago to about the 16th century

▲ A map of the Silk Road countries today

2 **Previewing Vocabulary** Read the words and phrases below. Listen to the pronunciation of each word. Put a check mark (✓) next to the words you don't know. Don't use a dictionary.

Nouns		Verbs	Adjectives
▢ archaeologists	▢ merchants	▢ decorated	▢ exquisite
▢ architecture	▢ mosques	▢ depict	▢ fertility
▢ armor	▢ network	▢ flowered	▢ holy
▢ calligraphy	▢ oasis	▢ spread	▢ significant
▢ caravan	▢ pitcher		▢ vast
▢ caves	▢ silk		
▢ destination	▢ spices		**Expression**
▢ documents	▢ statues		▢ to this end
▢ fabric			
▢ frescoes			
▢ mausoleums			

3 **Previewing the Reading** Look over the reading on pages 171–174.

1. What is the topic of the reading? (Look at the title.)

2. What are the five subtopics? (Look at the heading of each section.)

3. What do the photos in the article lead you to expect?

Read

4 **Reading the Article** As you read the following article, think about the answer to these questions: *What was the Silk Road? What can we learn about ancient life in this region from a study of its art and archaeology?* Read the selection. Do not use a dictionary. Then do the exercises that follow the reading.

The Silk Road: Art and Archaeology

Cross-Cultural Evidence

A
In the ruins of the ancient Roman city of Pompeii, which was destroyed by a volcano in the year 79 c.e.,* a mirror was found. It had an ivory handle in the shape of a female **fertility** goddess. The mirror was from India. In the tomb of Li Xian, a Chinese military official who died in 569 c.e., **archaeologists** found a water **pitcher** in the shape of a vase. The pitcher had a combination of different styles: the shape was from Persia (today's Iran), many details were from Central Asia, and the figures on the side were Greek stories from the Trojan War. In the Japanese city of Nara, the

5

*79 c.e. = the year 79 of our Common Era (79 A.D.)

8th century Shosoin Treasure House holds thousands of **exquisite** objects of great beauty—furniture, musical instruments, weapons, fabric, and military **armor**. These objects come from what is today Vietnam, western China, Iraq, the Roman Empire, and Egypt. Clearly, long before the globalization of our modern world, trade was going on between very distant lands, and the objects tell a story about a place and time.

What Was the Silk Road?

B　　From ancient times, cultures have influenced each other along the famous Silk Road, although it was not truly one continuous road. Instead, it was a 5,000-mile series or **network** of trails that connected East Asia to the Mediterranean. In ancient times, it was never called the "Silk Road." The term *Silk Road* was coined in the 19th century by a German explorer. He was thinking of one of the goods that people in the West found especially desirable—**silk fabric** from China. For centuries, the Chinese kept as a secret the way in which silk is produced. They exchanged this fabric for Mediterranean glass, whose production was also kept secret by the Romans. However, **merchants** also moved many other goods along these trade routes: **spices** (such as cinnamon), musical instruments, tea, valuable stones, wool, linen, and other fabrics. Ideas and knowledge also moved along the Silk Road. Travelers to foreign regions took with them ideas about art, **architecture**, styles of living, and religion.

C　　In a sense, there were *two* Silk Roads—the literal, historical one and the figurative one. The historical network of trails was used from approximately 100 B.C.E.* until the 16th century C.E. Almost nobody actually made a complete trip from one end to the other. Instead, merchants used to carry goods along one section of the road and sell them to other merchants at an **oasis** in the desert or a town in the mountains. These merchants, in turn, took the goods to the next stop, and so on. The figurative Silk Road is a symbol of the cross-cultural exchange of knowledge. This continues even today. In short, the Silk Road was the way that goods and ideas moved across a **vast** area of Asia and southeastern Europe.

▲ A desert oasis

Art, Religion, and the Silk Road

D　　Art and architecture reflect the movement of religion from region to region. At various times, Buddhism, Zoroastrianism, Judaism, Christianity, and Islam, among other religions, **spread** along the Silk Road. Buddhism and Islam were an especially **significant** influence. Buddhism moved north

*100 B.C.E = 100 years before our Common Era (100 B.C.)

and east from India beginning in the 4th century C.E. When Buddhism entered China, the Buddhist love of painting and **statues** moved with it. However, there was at least one change in style: the bare chest of the figure of the Buddha in India was not considered proper by the Chinese, who created figures of the Buddha wearing a robe.

E   As in many religions worldwide, **caves** deep inside mountains seem to have been important **holy** places for Buddhists. For example, in Dunhuang, China, a desert oasis far from towns or cities, Buddhists dug a series of caves and **decorated** them with exquisite **frescoes**—wall paintings—and statues. In these caves, called *Mogaoku* in Chinese, the frescoes are not all religious. Many **depict** scenes of daily life. Also, evidence of some of the many Silk Road cultures

▲ The Mogaoku, "Peerless Caves," in Dunhuang, China

was discovered. In one cave, **documents** were found that were written in five languages: Chinese, Uigur, Sogdian, Tibetan, and Sanskrit.

F   The spread of Islam toward the east in the 7th century C.E. contributed to the disappearance of some art but the creation of other art. Islam played a role in the destruction of many Buddhist statues because the Koran (the book of Islam) taught that images of humans were unholy. However, during this period, Islamic art and architecture **flowered** in many areas along the Silk Road. For example, in Samarkand—in what is Uzbekistan today—the military leader Timur built **mosques** (for Islamic religious worship), **mausoleums** (in which to bury the dead), and palaces. The creators of such

▲ Gur-i Amir Mausoleum in Samarkand, Uzbekistan

buildings followed Islamic law by decorating them with arabesques—exquisite designs of great beauty with images of flowers, geometric forms (such as circles, squares, and triangles), and Arabic **calligraphy**, or writing.

▲ Mummy of a baby from 1000 B.C.E.; the bright colors of the clothing are due to the preserving powers of the very dry, salty land. Blue stones were placed on the eyes.

In brief, it is possible to follow the rise and fall of religions by studying the art and architecture along the Silk Road. 95

A Question of Time: Two Views

Most historians have dated the Silk Road from about 100 B.C.E., when the Chinese 100 emperor Wu Di first sent a representative, General Zhang Qian, with a **caravan** of 100 men on a long, dangerous trip. His **destination** was the Western 105 Territories. Zhang returned 13 years later, with only one of his men but with much information. Recent discoveries, however, shed light on a period long *before* 110 this. These discoveries suggest that people were on the move and trading goods as early as 1000 B.C.E. Archaeologists have found tombs of people in the Takla Makan Desert, in Central Asia, in what is today the northwestern region of China. The dry, salty earth preserved the people's bodies and the goods that were buried with them in these tombs. We have learned that 115 these people had horses and sheep. They ate bread, although wheat did not grow in this area. They had cowry shells from the ocean, although the region is landlocked. They wore brightly colored clothing. They wore leather boots and wool pants. Some were tall: a woman was 6 feet tall (1.83 meters), and a man 6 feet 6 inches (1.98 meters). Perhaps most astonishing, they had long 120 noses and reddish hair, and the men wore beards. Thus, archaeologists are beginning to ask: Were people moving along the Silk Road long before we thought they were?

The Silk Road Today

Today, there is new interest in the history and culture of the Silk Road, which the famous Chinese-American musician Yo-Yo Ma has called "the 125 Internet of antiquity." New technology is helping us to learn more about this ancient "Internet." Special radar on the space shuttle allows archaeologists to "see" objects and ruined cities 1–2 meters under the dry desert sand, for example. Tourists now come from all over the world to follow the old trade routes. And people with a love of art and culture want to make sure that the 130 customs in the vast region do not die out as the world modernizes. **To this end**, Yo-Yo Ma has founded the Silk Road Project, which encourages the living arts of these traditional lands. The result is that the people along the ancient Silk Road continue to learn from each other.

After You Read

5 **Checking Your Understanding** What did you learn from the reading? Answer these questions with a group.

1. Where are three pieces of evidence that indicate trade between distant lands was occurring before the 9th century?

2. Where were the two opposite ends of the Silk Road?

3. What were two goods whose method of production was kept a secret?

4. What was moved along the Silk Road?

5. How did merchants move goods along the Silk Road?

6. What is evidence of the movement of Buddhism to China?

7. What is evidence of the spread of Islam to the east?

8. What was found in tombs of people in the Takla Makan Desert in Central Asia?

9. What does Yo-Yo Ma's Silk Road Project encourage?

6 **Getting Meaning from Context** Read the sentences below. Answer the questions and write a definition for each underlined vocabulary word. When you finish, check your definitions in a dictionary.

1. Many of the wall paintings <u>depict</u> scenes of everyday life.

What part of speech is *depict* (noun, verb, adjective)? _____

In this example, what *depicts* these scenes? _____

_____

What does *depict* mean? _____

_____

2. Timur built <u>mosques</u> for Islamic religious worship.

What part of speech is *mosques*? _____

What did Timur do? _____

_____

What happens in *mosques*? _____

_____

What does *mosques* mean? _____

_____

Strategy

Getting Meaning from Context
Sometimes you need to see a word in several different forms or contexts before you can guess the meaning.

Example
It was found in the **tomb** of Li Xian, who died in the year 569.

Archaeologists have found **tombs** of people in the desert. The dry, salty earth preserved the people's bodies.

(You can guess that **tombs** are places for dead people.)

7 **Getting Meaning from Context** Read the sentences below. Highlight the words that give clues to the meanings of the underlined words. Then write a definition of the underlined word. When you finish, check your definitions in a dictionary.

1. As in many religions worldwide, <u>caves</u> deep inside mountains seem to have been important holy places for Buddhists.

   People dug a series of <u>caves</u> and decorated them with exquisite wall paintings.

   What are *caves*? _____

2. They were important <u>holy</u> places for Buddhists.

   The Koran (the book of Islam) taught that images of humans were <u>unholy</u>, so many statues were destroyed.

   What does *holy* mean? _____

3. In the Japanese city of Nara, the 8th century Shosoin Treasure House holds thousands of <u>exquisite</u> objects of great beauty.

   The creators of such buildings followed Islamic law by decorating them with arabesques—<u>exquisite</u> designs of astonishing beauty with images of flowers and geometric forms.

   What does *exquisite* mean? _____

8 **Checking Your Vocabulary** Read the definitions below and write the correct words and expressions from the reading. The first one has been done for you as an example.

1. people who study ancient cultures = _____*archaeologists*_____

2. something that a soldier wears to protect the body in a battle = _____

3. any material (including silk) for clothing = _____

4. writing as an art form = _____

5. a place with water and trees in the desert = _____

6. in order to do this = _____

7. official papers with written information = _____

8. a place that someone is trying to reach = _____

9. buildings where dead people are buried = _____

10. beautiful decoration with images of flowers and geometric forms = _____

11. people who sell things = _____

12. grew and spread = _____

13. important = _____

Strategy

Recognizing Summaries in a Reading

Below are some common connecting words that indicate a summary will follow.

in short	in conclusion	to sum up
in brief	in summary	as we've seen
the result is	thus/therefore	clearly

9 **Recognizing Summaries** Copy or paraphrase the sentences from the reading that begin with the connecting words below. Then circle the number of the sentence below that best expresses the main idea of the entire reading.

1. Clearly, _____

_____

2. In short, _____

_____

3. In brief, _____

_____

4. Thus, _____

_____

5. The result is _____

_____

10 **Understanding Outlines** Complete the outline below of the reading selection "The Silk Road: Art and Archaeology." The five general topics are filled in, but the reading also contains many subtopics that serve as supporting material. Write these specific topics in the correct places. Some are done for you. Use the list of subtopics on page 179. You will need to look back at the reading to see where they belong.

The Silk Road: Art and Archaeology

I. Introduction: Cross-Cultural Evidence

    A. _____

    B. _____

    C. _____

    D. _____trade between distant lands long before today's globalization_____

II. What Was the Silk Road?

    A. _____

        1. _____

        2. _____exchange of ideas and knowledge_____

    B. _____

        1. _____

        2. _____figurative_____

III. Art, Religion, and the Silk Road

    A. _____

    B. _____the spread of Islam toward the east_____

IV. A Question of Time: Two Views

    A. _____

        1. _____100 B.C.E_____

        2. _____

    B. _____archaeological view_____

        1. _____

        2. _____

V. The Silk Road Today

    A. _____

    B. _____

    C. _____

1. the spread of Buddhism north and east from India

2. two Silk Roads

3. new technology

4. example: Indian mirror in Roman Pompeii

5. historical view

6. series or network of trails that connect East Asia to the Mediterranean

7. example: pitcher with styles from three cultures in a Chinese tomb

8. exchange of goods (silk, glass, spices, etc.)

9. 1000 B.C.E

10. tourism

11. example: the Shosoin Treasure House in Japan

12. literal

13. General Zhang Qian, sent by emperor

14. encouragement of living arts

15. tombs in the Takla Makan Desert

11 **Checking Your Understanding** Turn back to the beginning of Activity 4 on page 171 and answer the two questions in the instructions.

12 **Making Inferences** Look at Paragraph G on page 174 to answer these questions.

1. What were the physical characteristics of the people buried in the Takla Makan Desert?

2. What inference can you make about this? In other words, what does the reading not say directly but instead *imply*?

13 **Discussing the Reading** Talk about your answers to these questions.

1. Have you been to any places along the Silk Road? If so, tell your group about them.

2. Do you know of any other long road that connected distant places in ancient times? If so, tell your group about it.

3. What is one type of art from ancient times in your country? Tell your group about it.

4. What kinds of art do you like? Why?

Fashion: The Art of the Body

Strategy

Identifying Main Ideas by Analyzing Details
The main idea is not always clearly expressed in a paragraph. Instead, the details may *imply* the main idea, which sums up all the information in the paragraph.

Example
For various reasons, clothing of some type has been worn by human beings since the beginning of time. The Inuit (Eskimos) wear animal fur to protect them against the cold winter weather. Nomadic desert people wear long, loose clothing for protection against the sun and wind of the Sahara. But is clothing really essential for protection? Perhaps not. Scientists point out the absence of clothing among certain Indians of southern Chile, where the temperature is usually 43°F (7°C) and often colder. Similarly, the tribal people of Australia, where the weather is like that of the Sahara Desert, wear almost no clothing.

(The topic of the paragraph is clothing. The important details are that some groups wear clothing for protection against the weather, while others do not. Thus, the main idea of the paragraph is that protection is one function of clothing, but not an essential one.)

1 Identifying the Topic and Main Idea Read each paragraph. Then to help you figure out the main idea, answer the three questions that follow each paragraph.

Fashion: The Art of the Body

A   The enormous and fascinating variety of clothing may express a person's status or social position. Several hundred years ago in Europe, Japan, and China, there were many highly detailed sumptuary laws—that is, strict regulations concerning how each social class could dress. In Europe, for example, only royal families could wear fur, purple silk, or gold cloth. In Japan, a farmer could breed silkworms, but he couldn't wear silk. In many societies, a lack of clothing indicated an absence of status. In ancient Egypt, 5

▲ A street in Paris

for instance, children—who had no social status—wore no clothes until they were about twelve. These days, in most societies (especially in the West), rank or status is exhibited through regulation of dress only in the military, where the appearance or absence of certain metal buttons or stars signifies the dividing line between ranks. With the exception of the military, the divisions between different classes of society are becoming less clear. The clientele of a Paris café, for example, might include both working-class people and members of the highest society, but how can one tell the difference when everyone is wearing denim jeans?

10

15

20

1. What is the topic of Paragraph A?

    (A) the military

    (B) sumptuary laws

    (C) uniforms

    (D) status

2. What details about the topic does the paragraph provide? (Choose more than one answer.)

    (A) Strict laws in some countries used to regulate what people of each social class could wear.

    (B) Rich people wear more beautiful clothing than poor people do.

    (C) In many societies, the absence of clothing indicated an absence of status.

    (D) Today, the divisions between social classes are becoming less clear from the clothing that people wear.

3. What do the answers to numbers 1 and 2 have in common? That is, what is the main idea of Paragraph A?

    (A) Today, the differences between various social classes can be seen only in military uniforms.

    (B) Laws used to regulate how people could dress.

    (C) Clothing (or its absence) has usually indicated status or rank, but this is less true in today's world.

    (D) Clothing has been worn for different reasons since the beginning of history.

B   Three common types of body decoration are *mehndi*, tattooing, and 25
scarification. *Mehndi* is the art of applying dye (usually dark orange or dark
brown) to the skin of women in Hindu and Islamic cultures in southern
Asia and in Africa. The dye comes from the henna plant and is applied in
a beautiful design that varies from culture to culture—fine, thin lines in
India and large flower patterns in the Arab world, for example. A tattoo is 30
also a design or mark made with a kind of dye (usually dark blue); however,
unlike henna, it is put into a *cut* in
the skin. In scarification—found
mainly in Africa—dirt or ashes
are put into the cuts instead of 35
dye; the result is a design that
is unique to the person's tribe.
Three lines on each side of a
man's face identify him as a
member of the Yoruba tribe of 40
Nigeria, for example. A complex
geometric design on a woman's
back identifies her as Nuba
(from Sudan) and also makes her
more beautiful in the eyes of her 45
people. In the 1990s, tattooing
became popular among youth in
urban Western societies. Unlike
people in tribal cultures, these
young people had no tradition 50
of tattooing, except among
sailors and criminals. To these
young people, the tattoos were
beautiful and were sometimes also
a sign of rebellion against older, 55
more conservative, people in the
culture. These days, tattooing has
become common and is usually
not symbolic of rebellion.

▲ Modern tattooing

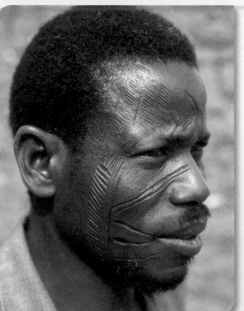
◄ Scarification

1. What is the topic of Paragraph B?
   - (A) the Yoruba people
   - (B) geometric designs
   - (C) dirt and ashes
   - (D) body decoration

2. What details about the topic does the paragraph provide? (Choose more than one answer.)
   - (A) *Mehndi*, tattooing, and scarification are types of body decoration.
   - (B) Tattoos and scarification indicate a person's tribe or social group, although youth in Western societies sometimes use tattoos as a form of rebellion.
   - (C) Scarification is very painful and is symbolic of strength.
   - (D) Designs on a person's face or body are considered beautiful.

3. Which idea below includes all the details that you chose in number 2? In other words, what is the main idea of the paragraph?
   - (A) Everyone who wants to be beautiful should get a tattoo.
   - (B) People decorate their bodies for the purposes of identification, beauty, and sometimes rebellion.
   - (C) *Mehndi* and tattoos are designs made by putting dye on or in the skin.
   - (D) Men more often decorate their faces; women often decorate their backs.

C   In some societies, women overeat to become plump because large women are considered beautiful, while skinny women are regarded as unattractive. A woman's plumpness is also an indication of her family's wealth. In other 70 societies, by contrast, a fat person is considered unattractive, so men and women eat little and try to remain slim. In many parts of the world, people lie in the sun for hours to darken their skin, while in other places light, soft skin is seen as attractive. People with gray hair often dye it black, whereas those with naturally dark hair often change its color to blond or green or purple. 75

1. What is the topic of Paragraph C?
   - (A) hair
   - (B) skin
   - (C) body shape
   - (D) body changes

2. What details about the topic does the paragraph provide? (Choose more than one answer.)
   - (A) It is unhealthy to lose or gain too much weight.
   - (B) Some societies consider large people attractive; others, slim ones.
   - (C) Some people prefer dark hair or skin; others, light.
   - (D) Most wealthy people try to stay thin.

3. What is the main idea of Paragraph C?

    (A) Individuals and groups of people have different ideas about physical attractiveness.

    (B) Lying in the sun darkens the skin.

    (C) In some societies, thinness is an indication that a family is poor.

    (D) Dark-skinned people usually have dark hair.

D   In most modern cultures, many people visit a dentist regularly for both hygiene and beauty. They use toothpaste and dental floss daily to keep their teeth clean. They have their teeth straightened, whitened, and crowned to make them more attractive to others in their culture. However, *attractive* has had quite a different meaning in the past and in some cultures today. In the past, in Japan, it was the custom for women to blacken, not whiten, the teeth. People in some areas of Africa and central Australia have the custom of filing the teeth to sharp points. And among the Makololo people of Malawi, the women wear a very large ring—a *pelele*—in their upper lip. As their chief once explained about *peleles*: "They are the only beautiful things women have. Men have beards. Women have none. What kind of person would she be without the *pelele*? She would not be a woman at all." While some people in modern urban societies think of tribal lip rings as unattractive and even "disgusting," other people—in Tokyo or New York or Rome—might choose to wear a small lip ring or to pierce their tongue and wear a ring through the hole.

1. What is the topic of Paragraph D?

    (A) dentistry

    (B) blackening or whitening the teeth

    (C) changes to the human mouth

    (D) peleles and beards

2. What details about the topic does the paragraph provide? (Choose more than one answer.)

    (A) White teeth are attractive to all cultures.

    (B) In the West, people visit dentists and have their teeth straightened, whitened, and crowned.

    (C) In some cultures, people blacken their teeth or file them to sharp points, and in other cultures young people wear lip rings or tongue rings.

    (D) Makololo women wear a large ring in their upper lip.

3. What is the main idea of Paragraph D?

    (A) People can easily change the color or shape of their teeth.

    (B) What is *attractive* has different interpretations.

    (C) The human mouth suffers change and abuse in many societies.

    (D) Some methods of changing the appearance of the mouth are dangerous, but others are safe.

▲ Papua New Guinean man wearing tribal face paint

▲ Woman wearing modern "face paint"

E Body paint or face paint is used mostly by *men* in preliterate societies in order to attract good health or to ward off disease. Anthropologists explain that it is a form of magic protection against the dangers of 95 the world outside the village, where men have to go for the hunt or for war. When it is used as warpaint, it also serves to frighten the enemy, distinguish members of one's own group from the enemy, 100 and give the men a sense of identity, of belonging to the group. *Women* in these societies have less need of body or face paint because they usually stay in the safety of the village. Women in Victorian 105 society in England and the United States were expected to wear little or no makeup. They were excluded from public life and therefore didn't need protection from the outside world. In modern societies, 110 however, cosmetics are used mostly by women, who often feel naked, unclothed, without makeup when out in public—like a tribal hunter without his warpaint.

1. What is the topic of Paragraph E?
   - (A) body and face paint
   - (B) men's warpaint
   - (C) modern women's cosmetics
   - (D) magic protection

2. What details about the topic does the paragraph provide? (Choose more than one answer.)
   - (A) Body or face paint is usually worn by men in tribal societies.
   - (B) People wear body or face paint to make them more attractive.
   - (C) Makeup ("face paint") is usually worn by women in modern societies.
   - (D) When women are excluded from public life, they wear little or no makeup.

3. What is the main idea of Paragraph E?
   - (A) Body paint gives men a sense of identity.
   - (B) Women in modern times wear makeup to be more beautiful.
   - (C) In the past, men wore face paint, but in modern times, women wear it.
   - (D) Body or face paint may be worn as a sort of protection by people who leave the home or village.

2 Critical Thinking: Identifying Inferences Read the statements below about the article "Fashion: The Art of the Body." Put a check mark (✓) by the statements that you can infer from the reading. Put an ✗ by the other statements, even if you think they are true. Then, on the line after each inference, write the phrases from which you inferred the information. Leave the other statements blank. The first two are done for you as examples.

1. __✗__ All people wear clothing to keep warm.

   _____

   _____

2. __✓__ Fur provides warmth, while long, loose clothing is useful in hot weather.
   The Inuit (Eskimos) wear animal fur to protect them against
   the cold winter weather. Nomadic desert people wear long, loose
   clothing for protection against the sun and wind of the Sahara.

3. _____ Rich people wear more clothing than poor people do.

   _____

   _____

4. _____ Social status might be less important now than it was in the past.

   _____

   _____

5. _____ Some methods of body beautification may be uncomfortable or painful.

   _____

   _____

6. _____ Body or face paint may make people feel protected.

   _____

   _____

7. _____ Women are more interested in looking good than men are.

   _____

   _____

8. _____ There are some similarities between tribal people and modern urban people in their views of body decoration.

   _____

   _____

3 **Discussing the Reading** Talk about your answers to these questions.

1. Why are people often unhappy with their bodies? What are their reasons for changing their appearance?

2. What do you think of the methods of body beautification that are described in the reading? Why?

3. What methods of "body art" are common in your culture (makeup? tattoos? ear piercing? hair dyeing? etc.)? What do you think of them?

Responding in Writing

4 **Summarizing** Choose one paragraph—B, F, or G—from the reading "The Silk Road: Art and Archaeology" on pages 171–174. Write a short summary of it (two or three sentences). To write this summary, follow these steps:

- Make sure that you understand the paragraph well.
- Choose the main idea.
- Find the most important details.

In order to summarize this in your own words, *don't look at the original paragraph as you write*. When you finish writing, compare your summary with those of other students who summarized the same paragraph.

5 **Writing Your Own Ideas** Choose one of these topics to write about:

- clothing and status
- your society's views on weight
- tattooing
- *mehndi* designs
- body piercing

What is your opinion about the topic you chose? Write a one-paragraph letter to your teacher in which you explain your opinion.

What's the main idea of your paragraph? _____

_____

_____

_____

Beauty and the Past

In ancient Egypt, both rich and poor people used many kinds of scented oils to protect their skin from the sun and wind and to keep it soft. These oils were a mixture of plants and the fat of crocodile, hippo, or cat. Many people shaved their heads and wore wigs. Other people dyed their hair black when it began to turn gray. Men, women, and children all wore **kohl**—black eye liner—both for beauty and to protect their eyes from disease. On special occasions, people wore exquisite jewelry, especially necklaces and earrings, and on top of their wigs wore a white cone made of sweetly scented ox fat. As the evening went on, the cone melted, and the fragrance dripped down over their wigs, faces, and clothes.

◄ Egyptians on a special occasion: notice the white cones on their heads.

Talk it Over

6 **Art and Beauty** Below are some quotations about art and beauty. Read them and discuss your answers to each of the questions that follow.

Quotations

"Beauty is in the eye of the beholder."   Margaret Hungerford

"Alas, after a certain age, every man is responsible for his own face."   Albert Camus

"Remember that the most beautiful things in the world are the most useless: peacocks and lilies, for instance."   John Ruskin

"I'm tired of all this nonsense about beauty being only skin-deep. That's deep enough. What do you want, an adorable pancreas?"   Jean Kerr

"Form follows function."   motto of the Bauhaus (a German school of design)

"Great artists have no country."   Alfred de Musset

Questions

1. What does each quotation mean? (You might need to use a dictionary.)

2. Do you agree with any of them? Explain why you do or do not agree.

3. What are some proverbs or quotations about art or beauty in your language? Translate them into English and explain them.

7 **Analyzing Advertisements** Go online to find advertisements about beauty treatments and methods (hairstyling salons, makeup, plastic surgery, etc.). Discuss the new vocabulary you find in the advertisements. Tell the class about the most interesting ads and your opinions of them.

PART 3 Building Vocabulary and Study Skills

Strategy

Recognizing Words with Similar Meanings
Although words with similar meanings can often be substituted for one another, they may have somewhat different definitions.

Example
I'm taking a geography **course**. The **class** meets twice a week and there is a different **lesson** at each meeting.

(*course* = series of lessons on a subject; *class* = a meeting of a course or the students who are taking a course; *lesson* = a separate piece of material on a subject or the amount of teaching at one time)

1 **Recognizing Words with Similar Meanings** The words in each of the following groups have similar meanings, but they are not exactly the same. Match the words with their definitions by writing the letters on the lines as in the examples. If necessary, check your answers in a dictionary.

1. __b__ study
    _____ memorize
    _____ learn

    a. gain knowledge or skill in a subject
    b. make an effort to learn
    c. to know something exactly from memory

2. _____ depict
    _____ indicate
    _____ express

    a. show in the form of a picture
    b. point out; make known
    c. put (thoughts, feelings) into words

3. _____ target   **a.** objective; purpose

_____ goal   **b.** the place where someone is going

_____ destination   **c.** an object or mark someone tries to reach or hit

Strategy

Understanding General and Specific Words
The meaning of one word can *include* the meanings of many others.

Example
Beautiful art can be found in different kinds of **structures**: churches, mosques, and palaces.

(Churches and mosques are religious buildings, and palaces are buildings for royalty. The word *structures* can mean "buildings," so it includes the meanings of the three other words.)

2 **Understanding General and Specific Words** In each of the following items, circle the one word that includes the meanings of the others. The first one is done for you as an example.

1. (art)   statue   painting   **5.** bus   subway   transportation

2. script   calligraphy   writing   **6.** cosmetics   lipstick   dye

3. architecture   house   building   **7.** hard rock   music   jazz

4. traveler   tourist   passenger   **8.** murder   crime   theft

Strategy

Understanding Connotations
Sometimes words with similar meanings have different connotations (implied meanings, "feelings"). Some of the meanings can be positive; some can be negative.

Example
In some societies, women overeat to become **plump** because **large** women are considered beautiful. In other cultures, a **fat** person is considered unattractive.

(The words *plump, large,* and *fat* all mean "over normal weight." However, to say someone is *fat* is an insult, while *plump* and *large* are more polite ways of referring to the same characteristic.)

Some dictionaries provide information on the usage of words in different situations and on connotations of words with similar meanings.

3 **Understanding Connotations** Read the dictionary entries below and complete the following activities.

---

thin¹ /θɪn/ *adj.* comparative **thinner**, superlative **thinnest 1** something that is thin is not very wide or thick [≠ **thick**]: *a thin slice of cheese* | *The walls here are* **paper-thin** (=very thin). **2** having little fat on your body [≠ **fat**]: *He's tall, very thin, and has dark hair.*

THESAURUS
slim and **slender** – used about someone who is thin in an attractive way
skinny – used about someone who is very thin in a way that is not attractive
lean – used about someone who is thin in a healthy way: *He has a runner's physique: long legs and a lean body.*
underweight – used, especially by doctors, about someone who is too thin, in a way that is not healthy
emaciated – used about someone who is extremely thin and weak because of illness or not eating

3 if someone has thin hair, they do not have very much hair [≠ **thick**] **4** air that is thin is difficult to breathe because there is not much OXYGEN in it **5** a substance that is thin has a lot of water in it [≠ **thick**]: *thin broth* —**thinness** n. [U]

beau·ti·ful /ˈbyutəfəl/ *adj.* **1** extremely attractive to look at: *She was the most beautiful woman I've ever seen.* |*a beautiful baby* | *The views from the mountaintop were beautiful.*

THESAURUS
attractive, good-looking, pretty, handsome, gorgeous, stunning, nice-looking, cute
→see Thesaurus box at ATTRACTIVE

2 very good or giving you great pleasure: *beautiful music* | *The weather was beautiful.*

Write a plus sign (+) before the words with positive connotations and a negative sign (−) before the words with negative ones.

1. _____ slim   **3.** _____ skinny   **5.** _____ fat

2. _____ emaciated   **4.** _____ slender   **6.** _____ overweight

Next, circle the words that have a polite connotation.

1. underweight   **3.** plump   **5.** obese

2. emaciated   **4.** chubby   **6.** heavy

For each pair of words, circle the one with the stronger meaning. The first one is done for you as an example.

1. (beautiful)/pretty   **4.** ugly/plain

2. ugly/hideous   **5.** beautiful/good-looking

3. attractive/gorgeous   **6.** unattractive/ugly

4 **Choosing the Appropriate Words** Choose all of the possible polite answers for each blank to complete each sentence.

1. He's a very _____ man.

    Ⓐ skinny

    Ⓑ handsome

    Ⓒ attractive

    Ⓓ ugly

2. What a _____ baby!

    Ⓐ beautiful

    Ⓑ handsome

    Ⓒ fat

    Ⓓ good-looking

3. This is a very _____ garden.

    Ⓐ exquisite

    Ⓑ plain

    Ⓒ pretty

    Ⓓ attractive

5 **Writing Words with Similar Meanings** On a separate piece of paper, write words with meanings similar to the following words. Use your dictionary for help. Then write the lists of similar words on the board and discuss with your classmates differences in meanings, connotation, and usage.

1. woman

2. thief

3. talk

4. believe

5. old

6. small

6 **Recognizing Words in Phrases** As you read, it's important to notice words that often go together. Go back to the paragraphs on pages 171–174. Find words to complete the following phrases.

Paragraph A

_____ the shape _____ a female fertility goddess

Paragraph B

a network _____ trails

Paragraph C

was used _____ approximately 100 B.C.E.

_____ the 16th century

Paragraph D

_____ region _____ region

Paragraph F

1. contributed _____ the disappearance of some art

2. _____ brief

Paragraph H

_____ _____ end

7 Focusing on Words from the Academic Word List Fill in the blanks with words from the Academic Word List in the box. You will use one word twice.

continue	founded	region	technology
culture	Project	routes	traditional

Today, there is new interest in the history and _____ of
1
the Silk Road, which the famous Chinese-American musician Yo-Yo Ma
has called "the Internet of antiquity." New _____ is helping
2
us to learn more about this ancient "Internet." Special radar on the space
shuttle allows archaeologists to "see" objects and ruined cities 1–2 meters
under the dry desert sand, for example. Tourists now come from all over the
world to follow the old trade _____. And people with a love of
3
art and _____ want to make sure that the customs in the vast
4
_____ do not die out as the world modernizes. To this this
5
end, Yo-Yo Ma has _____ the Silk Road _____,
6   7
which encourages the living arts of these _____ lands. The
8
result is that the people along the ancient Silk Road _____ to
9
learn from each other.

8 Searching the Internet Search the Internet for one of the topics below.
Explore one website and find something that interests you. Share what you find with
a small group. Choose from these topics:

- tours of the Silk Road
- the meaning of tattooing or scarification among tribal peoples
- *mehndi* designs in different cultures
- the latest fashions in "body art"

FOCUS

Questions About Basic Comprehension

In the Focus on Testing section of Chapter 1, the three types of reading questions on the TOEFL® Internet-Based Test (iBT) are listed. One type is the *basic comprehension question*, which focuses on the understanding of facts, what facts mean, and how language ties one fact to others. You must understand not only words and phrases but entire groups of sentences. You must also be able to find main ideas and recognize how they are supported in the reading.

Vocabulary questions make up 20 to 25 percent of all TOEFL® iBT reading questions. These are considered *basic comprehension questions*. To answer them, you have to understand the context, not just the words themselves.

1 **Practice** Reread the Focus on Testing reading in Chapter 7, "As English Spreads, Speakers Morph It into World Tongue," on pages 164–165. Answer the basic-comprehension questions below. You may refer to the reading as often as you want. Try to answer all five questions in five minutes or less.

1. According to the article, which pair of groups both dislike the spread of "Englishes" around the world?

    A purists and multiculturalists

    B native speakers and nonnative speakers

    C businesspersons and linguists

    D linguists and multiculturalists

2. According to the article, which of the following statements would Tom McArthur, editor of the *Oxford Companion to the English Language*, agree with?

    A People invent too many new words.

    B Hybrid Englishes are not really English.

    C The spread of English is unstoppable.

    D The British should stop the degradation of English.

3. Professor Firth's comments indicate that people involved in international business often think which of the following?

    A Any communication strategy is good if it helps business get done.

    B Nonnative speakers of English invent terms so that native speakers won't understand them.

    C Nonnative speakers of English should let native speakers cut most deals.

    D English is changing too fast for businesses.

4. Which of the following is closest in meaning to *hybrid*, as it is used in this reading?

    (A) foreign   (C) incorrect

    (B) mixed   (D) grammatical

5. Which of these other terms from the reading is closest in meaning to *linguistic genocide*?

    (A) creeping degradation   (C) linguicide

    (B) tension   (D) global germination

Self-Assessment Log

Read the lists below. Check (✓) the strategies and vocabulary that you learned in this chapter. Look through the chapter or ask your instructor about the strategies and words that you do not understand.

Reading and Vocabulary-Building Strategies

- ☐ Getting meaning from context
- ☐ Recognizing summaries in a reading
- ☐ Identifying main ideas by analyzing details
- ☐ Critical thinking: identifying inferences
- ☐ Recognizing words with similar meanings
- ☐ Understanding general and specific words
- ☐ Understanding connotations

Target Vocabulary

Nouns

- archaeologists
- architecture
- armor
- calligraphy
- caravan
- caves
- culture*
- destination
- documents*
- fabric
- frescoes
- mausoleums
- merchants
- mosques
- network
- oasis
- pitcher
- project*
- region*
- routes*
- silk
- spices
- statues
- technology*

Verbs

- called*
- decorated
- depict
- flower
- found*
- spread

Adjectives

- exquisite
- fertility
- holy
- significant*

- traditional*
- vast

Expression

- to this end

* These words are from the Academic Word List. For more information on this list, see www.victoria.ac.nz/lals/resources/academicwordlist/.

9 New Frontiers

"If the brain were so simple [that] we could understand it, we would be so simple [that] we couldn't."

Lyall Watson
African biologist and author

In this
CHAPTER

In Part 1, you will read about the human brain and recent research on the mind. In the rest of this chapter, you will read about, explore, and discuss how genetics, parents, family, and society influence personality.

Connecting to the Topic

1. Describe what you see in the photo.
2. How are computers and brains similar? How are they different?
3. What kind of research do you think is important? Why?

The Human Brain—New Discoveries

Before You Read

1 Getting Started Look at the diagram of the human brain and the photos on the next page. Discuss these questions.

1. Which areas of the brain might a person use to compose music? To throw a ball? To paint a picture?

2. If you feel cold and want to put on a sweater, which area of the brain is probably active?

3. Which area(s) of your brain might you be using when you have a memory of a beautiful sunset? Of a tennis game that you played last week?

4. Look at the diagram and at Photo A on page 199. Which areas of the brain is this artist probably using? What other activities require creative thinking? Do you think people can learn to be more creative?

5. Look at Photo B on page 199. Do you think that teenagers' brains are more similar to the brains of children or of adults? What might be some differences between the brains (and way of thinking) of males and females?

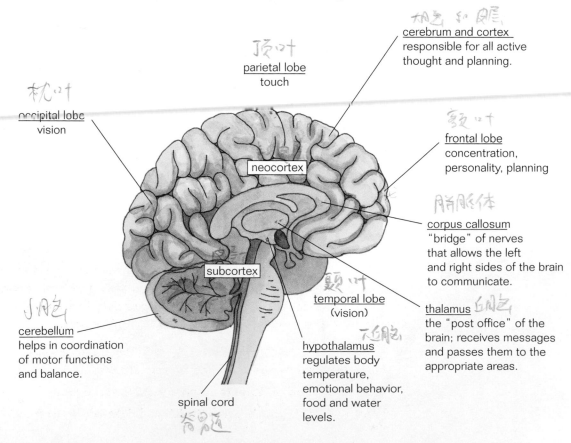

顶叶
parietal lobe
touch

拥包 和 皮层
cerebrum and cortex
responsible for all active
thought and planning.

枕叶
occipital lobe
vision

额叶
frontal lobe
concentration,
personality, planning

neocortex

脑胼胝体
corpus callosum
"bridge" of nerves
that allows the left
and right sides of the brain
to communicate.

subcortex

temporal lobe
(vision)

thalamus 丘脑
the "post office" of the
brain; receives messages
and passes them to the
appropriate areas.

小脑
cerebellum
helps in coordination
of motor functions
and balance.

题叶

下丘脑
hypothalamus
regulates body
temperature,
emotional behavior,
food and water
levels.

spinal cord
脊髓道

◄ Photo A

Photo B ▶

2 Previewing the Reading Look over the reading on pages 200–203 and answer these questions with a partner.

1. What is the topic of the reading?
2. What are the eight subtopics?
3. List three things that you expect to learn from the reading.

_____

_____

_____

3 Preparing to Read Asking yourself questions before and during reading often helps you understand and remember the material. Look again at the illustration of the brain on page 198 and at the headings in the following reading. Then check (✓) the questions in the following list that you think the reading might answer.

1. _____ What is the function of different parts of the brain?
2. _____ How are human brains different from animal brains?
3. _____ Why do some people seem to be more creative than others?
4. _____ What is the difference between the left and right side of the brain?

5. _____ Are the happiest memories of most people's lives from their childhood?

6. _____ Is it possible to have a memory of something that never happened?

7. _____ How can we improve our memories?

8. _____ Are teenagers' brains different from adults' brains?

9. _____ How do men and women communicate with each other?

10. _____ What activities may make people less focused intellectually?

11. _____ What activity may make people more relaxed?

 4 **Previewing Vocabulary** Read the words and phrases below. Listen to the pronunciation. Put a check mark (✓) next to the words you don't know. Don't use a dictionary.

Nouns
- blood vessels
- colleagues
- hemispheres
- insights
- intuition
- logic
- maturation
- maturity
- memory
- neuroscientists
- origins
- toxins
- wiring

Verbs
- rotate

Adjectives
- cognitive
- exposed
- logical
- mature

Expression
- precise
- repressed

Expression
- going into training

Read

 5 **Reading an Article** As you read the following article, think about the answers to the questions that you checked in Activity 3. Read the selection. Do not use a dictionary. Then do the exercises that follow the reading.

The Human Brain—New Discoveries

A   Most of us learn basic facts about the human brain in our middle or high school biology classes. We study the <u>subcortex</u>, the "old brain," which is found in the brains of most animals and is responsible for basic functions such as breathing, eating, drinking, and sleeping. We learn about the <u>neocortex</u>, the "new brain," which is unique to humans and is where 5 complex brain activity takes place. We find that the <u>cerebrum</u>, which is responsible for all active thought, is divided into two parts, or **hemispheres**. The left hemisphere, generally, manages the right side of the body; it is responsible for **logical thinking**. The right hemisphere manages the left side of the body; this hemisphere controls emotional, creative, and artistic 10 functions. And we learn that the <u>corpus callosum</u> is the "bridge" that <u>connects the two hemispheres</u>. Memorizing the names for parts of the

brain might not seem thrilling to many students, but new discoveries in
brain function *are* exciting. Recent research is shedding light on creativity,
memory, **maturity**, gender, and the possibility of changing the brain.   15

Left Brain/Right Brain: Creativity

B   Psychologists agree that most of us have creative ability that is greater
than what we use in daily life. In other words, we can be more creative than
we realize! The problem is that we use mainly one hemisphere of our brain—
the left. From childhood, in school, we're taught reading, writing, and
mathematics; we are **exposed** to very little music or art. Therefore, many of   20
us might not "exercise" our right hemisphere much, except through dreams,
symbols, and those wonderful **insights** in which we suddenly find the answer
to a problem that has been bothering us—and do so without the need for
logic. Can we be taught to use our right hemisphere more? Many experts
believe so. Classes at some schools and books (such as *The Inner Game of*   25
Tennis and Drawing on the Right Side of the Brain) claim to help people to
"silence" the left hemisphere and give the right a chance to work.

Memory—True or False?

C   In the 1980s in the United States, there were many cases of adults who
suddenly remembered, with the help of a psychologist, things that had
happened to them in childhood. These memories had been **repressed**—   30
held back—for many years. Some of these newly discovered memories have
sent people to prison. As people remember crimes (such as murder or rape)
that they saw or experienced as children, the police have re-opened and
investigated old criminal cases. In fact, over 700 cases have been filed that
are based on these repressed memories.   35

D   However, studies in the 1990s suggested that many of these might
be *false* memories. At a 1994 conference at Harvard Medical School,
neuroscientists discussed how memory is believed to work. It is known
that small pieces of a memory (sound, sight, feeling, and so on) are kept in
different parts of the brain; the limbic system, in the middle of the brain,   40
pulls these pieces together into one complete memory. But it's certain that
people can "remember" things that have never happened. Even a small
suggestion can leave a piece of memory in the brain. Most frightening,
according to Dr. Michael Nash of the University of Tennessee, is that "there
may be no structural difference" in the brain between a false memory and a   45
true one.

The Teen Brain

E   Parents of teenagers have always known that there is something, well,
different about the teen years. Some parents claim that their teenage
children belong to a different species. Until recently, neuroscience did not
support this belief. The traditional belief was that by the time a child was   50
eight to twelve, the brain was completely **mature**. However, very recent
studies provide evidence that the brain of a teenager differs from that of

both children and adults. According to Jay Giedd of the National Institute of Mental Health, "**Maturation** does not stop at age ten, but continues into the teen years" and beyond. In fact, Giedd and his **colleagues** found that the corpus callosum "continues growing into your 20s." Because, it is believed, the corpus callosum is involved in self-awareness and intelligence, the new studies imply that teens may not be as fully self-aware or as intelligent as they will be later. Other researchers, at McLean Hospital in Massachusetts, have found that teenagers are not as able (as adults are) to "read" emotions on people's faces.

Differences in Male and Female Brains

F   Watch a group of children as they play. You'll probably notice that the boys and girls play differently, speak differently, and are interested in different things. When they grow into men and women, the differences do not disappear. [Many scientists are now studying the **origins** of these gender differences.] Some are searching for an explanation in the human brain. Some of their findings are interesting. For example, they've found that more men than women are left-handed; this reflects the dominance of the brain's right hemisphere. By contrast, more women listen equally with both ears while men listen mainly with the right ear. Men are better at reading a map without having to **rotate** it. Women are better at reading the emotions of people in photographs.

G   One place to look for an explanation of gender differences is in the hypothalamus, just above the brain stem. This controls anger, thirst, hunger, and sexual desire. One recent study shows that there is a region in the hypothalamus that is larger in heterosexual men than it is in women and homosexual men. Another area of study is the corpus callosum, the thick group of nerves that allows the right and left hemispheres of the brain to communicate with each other. The corpus callosum is larger in women than in men. This might explain the mystery of "female **intuition**," which is supposed to give women greater ability to "read" and understand emotional clues.

A Change of Mind?

H   We all know the expression *to change your mind*. But is it possible *literally* to change your mind—or, to be more **precise**, to change your *brain*? Reports from 2005 say yes. First, the bad news, at least for smokers: a study from the University of Aberdeen and the University of Edinburgh, in Scotland, concludes that smoking makes people less intelligent. On **cognitive** tests (that is, tests that involve judgment), smokers did significantly worse than nonsmokers. The theory is that **toxins**—poisons—in the smoke enter the blood and damage **blood vessels** providing the brain with oxygen. And there is more bad news, for most of us: a study from the University of London says that "infomania"—the constant flood of information from cell phones, emails, and text messaging—can reduce intelligence by ten points on an IQ test.

However, there is also good news: meditation seems to change the "**wiring**" 95 in the brain in several positive ways. In a study that compared the brains of eight lifelong Buddhist meditators who work with the Dalai Lama with the brains of beginning meditators, scientists 100 discovered that there were significant differences. The expert meditators had higher levels of gamma brain waves, which improve memory, learning, and concentration. Meditation appears to do 105 for the brain what physical training does for the body. The researcher Richard Davidson said, "The trained mind, or brain, is physically different from the untrained one." Perhaps we should 110 consider **going into training**.

▲ Does meditation change the brain?

After You Read

6 Getting the Main Ideas Read the statements below. Write T on the lines before the statements that are true, according to the reading. Write F on the lines before the statements that are false. Write I on the lines before the statements that are impossible to know from the reading.

1. _____ Different parts of the brain control different activities or parts of the body.

2. _____ Most people probably don't use all their creative ability.

3. _____ Newly discovered memories from childhood are false memories.

4. _____ The human brain is mature by the age of 12.

5. _____ There is no real difference between the brains of males and females.

6. _____ Certain activities might make us more or less intelligent.

7 Vocabulary Check Turn back to the vocabulary preview on page 200. Which words do you now know? Check them off (✓). With a partner, discuss what you think each word means. For words that you aren't sure of, look through the reading to find them in bold and try to guess their meaning.

Strategy

Distinguishing Facts from Assumptions

As you saw in Chapter 7, certain words or expressions in statements usually indicate the existence of facts—that is, information that has been proven accurate. Here are some more words that indicate facts:

certain	objective	scientific
clear	positive	show
know	prove	sure

Other words can indicate assumptions—that is, ideas that are believed by some people but have not been proven to be true. Here are some more words that indicate assumptions:

claim	imply	possibly	theorize
(dis)agree	likely	probably	think
doubt	possible	subjective	

8 **Distinguishing Facts from Assumptions** For each statement below, write *fact* or *assumption*, according to the presentation of information in the reading selection "The Human Brain—New Discoveries" on pages 200–203. (You'll need to look back at the reading for words that indicate fact or assumption.)

B   agree   1. _A____Fact___ Most of us have creative ability that is greater than what we use in daily life.

B   might   2. ____Fact____A__ Many of us don't "exercise" our right hemisphere much.

B   believe   3. _____A____ We can be taught to use our right hemisphere more.

B   claim   4. _____A____ Some books help people "silence" the left hemisphere and use the right hemisphere.

C   In fact   5. _____F____ Over 700 cases have been filed that are based on newly discovered memories.

D   might   6. _____A____ Many newly discovered memories are false.

D   known   7. _____F____ Small pieces of memory are kept in different parts of the brain.

D   certain   8. _____F____ People "remember" things that have never happened.

D   may   9. _____A____ There is no structural difference between a false memory and a true one.

E   provide   10. ____F____A__ The brain of a teenager differs from that of both children and adults.

E   may   11. _____A____ Teens are not as fully self-aware as adults are.

12. _____ There is a region in the hypothalamus that is larger in heterosexual men than in women and homosexual men.

13. _____ Women have a greater ability to understand emotional clues because they have a larger corpus callosum than men do.

14. _____ In smokers, toxins damage the blood vessels that take oxygen to the brain, so the brain doesn't get enough oxygen.

15. _____ Meditation changes the wiring in the brain.

9 **Checking Your Understanding** Turn back to Activity 3 on pages 199–200 and answer the questions that are discussed in the reading.

10 **Critical Thinking: Application** If you want to improve your brain, what can you do? Turn back to the reading and find at least one way. In a small group, discuss what you can or will do to improve your brain.

PART 2 **Main Ideas and Details**

Personality: Nature or Nurture?

Before You Read

1 **Identifying the Main Idea by Analyzing Details** Read each paragraph and answer the questions that follow. Then combine the answers to express the main idea of each paragraph. Answers for Paragraph A are given as examples.

Personality: Nature or Nurture?

A   The nature/nurture question is not a new one. Its roots go back at least several hundred years. In the 1600s, the British philosopher John Locke wrote that a newborn infant was a "blank slate" on which his or her education and experience would be "written." In other words, Locke believed that environment alone determined each person's identity. In the 5 1700s, the French philosopher Jean Jacques Rousseau claimed that "natural" characteristics were more important. Today, we realize that both play a role. The question now is, to what degree? To answer this question, researchers are studying identical twins, especially those who grew up in different environments. 10

1. What is the main topic of Paragraph A?

   (A) John Locke

   (B) Jean Jacques Rousseau

   (C) newborn infants

   (D) the nature/nurture question

   (E) identical twins

2. What details about the topic does the paragraph provide? (Choose more than one answer.)

   (A) People have just recently begun to discuss the nature/nurture question.

   (B) John Locke believed in "nurture."

   (C) Jean Jacques Rousseau believed in "nature."

   (D) Today, we know that both nature and nurture determine a person's identity.

   (E) Researchers are studying identical twins to learn the degree to which nature and nurture determine personal characteristics.

3. The main idea of the paragraph is that _both nature and nurture play a role in determining a person's identity, but the question is to what degree._

B   Jim Lewis and Jim Springer are identical twins who were separated five weeks after birth. They grew up in different families and didn't know about each other's existence. They were reunited at the age of 39. It is not surprising that they were physically alike—the same dark hair, the same height and weight. They both had high blood pressure and very bad headaches. But they also moved in the same way and made the same gestures. They both hated baseball. They both drank the same brand of beer, drove the same make of car, and spent their vacations on the same small beach in Florida. They had both married women named Linda, gotten divorced, and then married women named Betty. Studies of these and other separated twins indicate that genetics (biology) plays a significant role in determining personal characteristics and behavior.

▲ Pairs of identical twins

15

20

25

30

35

1. What is the main topic of Paragraph B?

  (A) a reunion

  (B) twins

  (C) similarities in twins who grew up in different environments

  (D) genetics

  (E) personal characteristics and behavior

2. What details about the topic does the paragraph provide? (Choose more than one answer.)

  (A) Jim Lewis and Jim Springer were identical twins who grew up together.

  (B) Jim Lewis and Jim Springer were identical twins who grew up separately.

  (C) They have similar physical characteristics, interests, and preferences for specific products.

  (D) They married the same woman.

  (E) Their example indicates the significance of genetics in determination of identity.

3. The main idea of the paragraph is that _____

_____

C   Various research centers are studying identical twins in order to discover the "heritability" of behavioral characteristics—that is, the degree to which a trait is due to genes ("nature") instead of environment. They have reached some startling conclusions. One study found, for example, that optimism and pessimism are both very much influenced by genes, but only optimism is affected by environment, too. According to another study, genes influence our coffee consumption, but not consumption of tea. Anxiety (nervousness and worry) seems to be 40 to 50 percent heritable. Another study tells us that happiness does not depend much on money or love or professional success; instead, it is 80 percent heritable! Among the traits that appear to be largely heritable are shyness, attraction to danger (thrill seeking), choice of career, and religious belief.   40   45

1. What is the main topic of Paragraph C?

  (A) research centers

  (B) optimism and pessimism

  (C) behavioral characteristics

  (D) happiness

  (E) heritability of behavioral characteristics

2. What details about the topic does the paragraph provide? (Choose more than one answer.)

- Ⓐ Researchers want to understand "heritability."
- Ⓑ Researchers are studying identical twins.
- Ⓒ Most behavioral characteristics are the result of genes, not environment.
- Ⓓ A person who has money, love, and success will probably be happy.
- Ⓔ Examples of characteristics that are heritable to some degree are optimism, pessimism, happiness, thrill seeking, and choice of career.

3. The main idea of the paragraph is that _____

_____

D   It is not easy to discover the genes that influence personality. The acid that carries genetic information in every human cell, DNA, contains just 50 four chemicals: adenine, cytosine, guanine, and thymine. But a single gene is "spelled out" by perhaps a million combinations. As the Human Genome Project (which provided a "map" of human genes) was nearing completion in the spring of 2000, there were a number of newspaper headlines about specific discoveries: "Gene Linked to Anxiety," "Gay Gene!" and "Thrill 55 Seeking Due to Genetics." The newspaper articles led people to believe that a single gene is responsible for a certain personality trait, in the same way a single gene can be responsible for a physical characteristic or disease. However, one gene alone cannot cause people to become anxious or homosexual or thrill seeking. Instead, many genes work together, and they 60 direct the combination of chemicals in the body. These chemicals, such as dopamine and serotonin (which affect a person's mood), have a significant influence on personality.

1. What is the main topic of Paragraph D?

- Ⓐ the Human Genome Project
- Ⓑ the effect of genes on personality
- Ⓒ chemicals
- Ⓓ DNA
- Ⓔ thrill seeking

2. What details about the topic does the paragraph provide? (Choose more than one answer.)

- Ⓐ It's difficult to find out which genes influence personality.
- Ⓑ A single gene is responsible for each personality trait such as thrill seeking.
- Ⓒ Many genes work together.
- Ⓓ Genes direct the combination of chemicals in the body.
- Ⓔ Chemicals have a significant influence on personality.

3. The main idea of the paragraph is that _____

_____

E   If, indeed, personality traits are, on average, about 50 percent heritable, then environment still plays an important role. Unlike other animals, human beings have choice. If our genes "program" us to be anxious, we can choose a low-stress lifestyle or choose to meditate or do relaxation exercises. But because of the powerful influence of genes, most psychologists believe that there is a limit to what we can choose to do. Thomas Bouchard, a psychologist and the director of one twin study, says that parents should not push children in directions that go against their nature. "The job of a parent," he says, "is to look for a kid's natural talents and then provide the best possible environment for them."

1. What is the main topic of Paragraph E?

   Ⓐ the role of environment

   Ⓑ personality traits

   Ⓒ anxiety

   Ⓓ psychologists

   Ⓔ parenting

2. What details about the topic does the paragraph provide? (Choose more than one answer.)

   Ⓐ Environment still plays an important role.

   Ⓑ Human beings have choice.

   Ⓒ Human beings can choose to do anything they want.

   Ⓓ Psychologists say that parents should not push children against their nature.

   Ⓔ Parents should provide their child with the best environment for the child's natural talents.

3. The main idea of the paragraph is that _____

_____

After You Read

❷ Critical Thinking: Making Inferences Read the statements below and on the next page about the article "Personality: Nature or Nurture?" Put a check mark (✓) by the statements that you can infer from the reading. Put an ✗ by the other statements, even if you think they are true. Then, on the line after each inference, write the phrases from which you inferred the information. Leave the other lines blank.

1. _____ The philosophical question of nature vs. nurture is an old one.

_____

_____

2. _____ The environments in which Jim Springer and Jim Lewis grew up had no effect on their behaviors or personalities.

_____

_____

3. _____ The goal of twin studies is to identify the amount of influence from genes and the amount from education and experiences that determine our identity.

_____

_____

4. _____ The possibility of being happy is mostly a result of our genes, not our situations in life.

_____

_____

5. _____ A single gene determines each personality characteristic.

_____

_____

6. _____ The genetic contribution to personality is complicated.

_____

_____

7. _____ Human beings are able to change their genetics.

_____

_____

3 Discussing the Reading Talk about your answers to these questions.

1. Do you know any identical twins? If so, how are they similar or different?

2. What characteristics are found in many of your family members or members of other families you know well? Think of characteristics such as the following:

- interests
- health
- optimism or pessimism
- anxiety
- happiness

- shyness
- thrill seeking
- choice of career
- religious belief
- artistic talent

Responding in Writing

4 Summarizing Choose one paragraph from pages 200–203 or one from pages 205–209. Write a short summary of it (two or three sentences). To write this summary, follow these steps:

- Make sure that you understand the paragraph well.
- Choose the main idea.
- Find the most important details.

In order to summarize in your own words, *don't look at the original paragraph as you write*. When you finish writing, compare your summary with those of other students who summarized the same paragraph.

5 **Writing Your Own Ideas** Choose one of these topics to write about:

- a memory you have that is different from a family member's memory of the same event
- what you can do to improve your brain
- how you and your brother or sister are similar (or different)
- how nature has influenced you and/or how your environment has influenced you

Write a one- to two-paragraph letter to one of your family members in which you explore your topic.

What is the main idea of your letter? _____

_____

Talk it Over

6 **Genes for Crime?** It is highly possible that there is a genetic link or contribution to violence or criminality. In other words, our genes may contribute to the possibility of becoming a thief, murderer, or other type of criminal.

Psychologist David Lykken believes that people who want to become parents should be tested and given a license. If both the man and the woman have genes for violence or criminality, they should not be allowed to have a baby. He says that this will reduce crime in society. What do you think? Discuss this with a group.

PART 3 Building Vocabulary and Study Skills

1 **Understanding Words with Similar Meanings** The words in each of the following groups have similar meanings, but they are not exactly the same. Match the words with their definitions by writing the letters on the lines. If necessary, check your answers in a dictionary.

1. _____ brain   **a.** the faculty of thinking, reasoning, or feeling

_____ mind   **b.** the ability to remember

_____ memory   **c.** an organ of the body that controls thought and feeling

2. _____ identity   **a.** the qualities of a person specific to him or her

_____ personality   **b.** the way a person is recognizable as a member of a particular group

_____ behavior

c. the way that someone acts

3. _____ insight

_____ knowledge

_____ logic

a. thinking and reasoning with formal methods

b. understanding that comes from experience and learning

c. the power of using one's mind (especially the right brain) to understand something suddenly

4. _____ colleague

_____ peer

_____ co-worker

a. a person of equal status or age

b. a person who works in the same place as another

c. a person who works in the same profession as another

Strategy

Putting Words in Categories

It often helps to learn words in groups (words with the same stem, words with similar meanings, words with opposite meanings, etc.). One method of grouping words is to put them together in categories, such as people, animals, buildings, and so on. One kind of category is a "content area"—the subject with which all the words are associated.

The following are words associated with the content area of science: _laboratory, neuroscientist, subjects, experiment._

2 **Putting Words in Categories** Cross out the word in each line that does not belong, as in the example. Write the category or content area of the words that belong together.

1. genes   ~~nurture~~   nature   biology
   genetics

2. infant   maturity   baby   newborn

3. doctor   neuroscientist   psychologist   musician

4. creativity   cerebrum   hypothalamus   corpus callosum

5. meditation   disease   insomnia   headache

6. height   eye color   weight   anxiety

7. reading   writing   dreams   mathematics

Analyzing Word Roots and Affixes

It is often possible to guess the meanings of new words from affixes (prefixes and suffixes) and word roots (also called "stems"). There is a list of many affixes in Chapter 7 on pages 159–160. Below are more affixes and word roots and their meanings.

Prefix	Meaning
a-, an-	no, without
ante-	before
micro-	small
poly-	many

Suffix	Meaning
-ism	belief in; act or practice
-ist	a person who believes in or performs a certain action

Word Root	Meaning
anthro, anthropo	man, human
ced	go, move
chrom	color
chron	time
graph	write, writing
hetero	different
homo	same
metr, meter	measure; an instrument for measuring
morph	form
phil	love
psych	mind
somn	sleep
sphere	round; ball-shaped
tele	far
theo, the	god

3 Analyzing Word Roots and Affixes Without using a dictionary, guess the meaning of each underlined word. Use the list of word roots and affixes. (Not all the underlined words are common.)

1. It is believed that an earthquake <u>anteceded</u> the fire.
   a. caused
   b. happened after
   c. happened before
   d. put out; worked against
   e. was caused by

2. There were some <u>amorphous</u> clouds in the sky.
   a. without form or shape
   b. thick and dark
   c. beautiful
   d. related to rain
   e. bright white

3. Movies often <u>anthropomorphize</u> creatures from other planets.
   a. study
   b. give human form or characteristics to
   c. present in a terrible way
   d. depict
   e. try to imagine

4. The actors wore <u>polychromatic</u> body paint.
   a. beautiful
   b. symbolic
   c. complex
   d. made of natural dyes
   e. of many colors

5. My teacher didn't appreciate my <u>heterography</u>.
   a. talking a lot in class
   b. different ideas in the speech that I gave in class
   c. logic
   d. spelling that was different from the rule
   e. answers on my geography examination

6. She sometimes has a problem with <u>somnambulism</u>.
   a. sleepwalking
   b. drinking
   c. lying
   d. breathing
   e. anxiety

7. He used a <u>telemeter</u>.
   a. instrument for seeing something very small
   b. instrument for finding directions
   c. instrument for measuring time
   d. instrument for measuring how far away an object is
   e. instrument for measuring a person's level of anxiety

4 **Focusing on Words from the Academic Word List** Fill in the blanks with words from the Academic Word List in the box.

adults	imply	intelligent	mature	researchers
colleagues	Institute	involved	Mental	traditional
evidence	intelligence	maturation		

Parents of teenagers have always known that there is something, well, *different* about the teen years. Some parents claim that their teenage children belong to a different species. Until recently, neuroscience did not support this belief. The _____ belief was that by the time a child was 8
                        1
to 12, the brain was completely _____. However, very recent
                                          2
studies provide _____ that the brain of a teenager differs from
                       3
that of both children and adults. According to Jay Giedd of the National

_____ of _____ Health, "_____
          4   5   6
does not stop at age 10, but continues into the teen years" and beyond. In

fact, Giedd and his _____ found that the corpus callosum
                              7
"continues growing into your 20s." Because, it is believed, the corpus

callosum is _____ in self-awareness and _____,
                     8   9
the new studies _____ that teens may not be as fully self-aware
                          10
or as _____ as they will be later. Other _____,
           11   12
at McLean Hospital in Massachusetts, have found that teenagers are not as

able (as _____ are) to "read" emotions on people's faces.
                13

5 **Searching the Internet** Choose one of the questions below and search the Internet for the most recent information. Share this information (and any new vocabulary that you learn) with a group of students who chose different questions.

- What are some techniques to improve your memory?
- What are some ways to reduce stress?
- Are there differences between the brain of a musician and a nonmusician?
- What are some other stories of twins who were separated at birth but reunited?
- When a man and woman are in love, do their brains "work" in different ways?

F⊙CUS

Getting Meaning From Context

In the Focus on Testing section of Chapter 2, we saw some vocabulary questions like those on the TOEFL® Internet-Based Test (iBT). Those questions are all related to vocabulary that is defined or explained in a reading passage. Many of the TOEFL® iBT's vocabulary questions will be about words that are not defined or explained for you.

The TOEFL® Internet-Based Test, like many other tests, does not allow you to use a dictionary. If a term without an in-text definition or explanation comes up, you must use the context to figure out its meaning. Often, you need more than the information in one sentence to discover this meaning. You may need several sentences or even paragraphs to figure it out.

1 **Practice** Look again at the reading, "The Human Brain—New Discoveries" on pages 200–203. Answer the following TOEFL® iBT-style questions without using a dictionary.

1. Which of the following is closest in meaning to *shedding light on*, as it is used in Paragraph A?
   - (A) learning about
   - (B) turning on a light
   - (C) making understandable
   - (D) experimenting

2. Which of the following statements is closest in meaning to the sentence in Paragraph B, *We are exposed to very little music or art*?
   - (A) We cannot hear or see truly important music or art.
   - (B) We are taught a little bit about music and art.
   - (C) Music and art are uncovered for everyone to observe.
   - (D) Music and art are not taught very much.

3. Which of the following is closest in meaning to *insights*, as it is used in Paragraph B?
   - (A) the dreams we have while sleeping
   - (B) moments when we suddenly understand something
   - (C) moments when we are very logical
   - (D) the abilities of the human eye

4. Which of the following pairs is closest in meaning to the two uses of *cases* (lines 28 and 34) in Paragraph C?
   - (A) examples and memories
   - (B) memories and crimes
   - (C) examples and events that need police attention
   - (D) crimes and people who belong in prison

5. Which of the following is closest in meaning to *rotate*, as it is used in Paragraph F?

- Ⓐ change jobs
- Ⓑ look at
- Ⓒ understand
- Ⓓ turn around

6. Which of the following is closest in meaning to *intuition*, as it is used in Paragraph G?

- Ⓐ mystery
- Ⓑ the ability to read quickly and accurately
- Ⓒ the ability to understand without using logic
- Ⓓ emotions

7. Which of the following is closest in meaning to *read*, as it is used in Paragraphs E, F, and G?

- Ⓐ understand the meaning of
- Ⓑ understand writings about
- Ⓒ show to someone
- Ⓓ make announcements about

Self-Assessment Log

Read the lists below. Check (✓) the strategies and vocabulary that you learned in this chapter. Look through the chapter or ask your instructor about the strategies and words that you do not understand.

Reading and Vocabulary-Building Strategies

- ☐ Distinguishing facts from assumptions
- ☐ Identifying the main ideas by analyzing details
- ☐ Making inferences
- ☐ Understanding words with similar meanings
- ☐ Putting words in categories
- ☐ Understanding and analyzing word roots and affixes

Target Vocabulary

Nouns

- ▪ adults*
- ▪ blood vessels
- ▪ colleagues*
- ▪ evidence*
- ▪ hemispheres
- ▪ insights*
- ▪ institute*
- ▪ intelligence*
- ▪ intuition
- ▪ logic*
- ▪ maturation*
- ▪ maturity*
- ▪ memory
- ▪ neuroscientists
- ▪ origin
- ▪ researchers*
- ▪ toxins
- ▪ wiring

Verbs

- ▪ imply*
- ▪ rotate

Adjectives

- ▪ cognitive
- ▪ exposed*
- ▪ involved*
- ▪ logical*
- ▪ mature*

- ▪ mental*
- ▪ precise*
- ▪ repressed
- ▪ traditional*

Expression

- ▪ going into training

* These words are from the Academic Word List. For more information on this list, see www.victoria.ac.nz/lals/resources/academicwordlist/.

10 Ceremonies

"When humans participate in ceremony, they enter a sacred space. Everything outside of that space shrivels in importance. Time takes on a different dimension."

Sun Bear
Medicine Chief of the Bear Tribe
Medicine Society

In this
CHAPTER

In Part 1, you will read about rites of passage, rituals such as weddings, funerals, and graduations. In the rest of this chapter, you will read about, explore, and discuss ceremonies from your country and from around the world.

Connecting to the Topic

1 What do you think these people are celebrating? Why?

2 Name ten adjectives to describe this photo.

3 What are some of your favorite ceremonies or celebrations? Describe one of them.

Rites of Passage

1 Getting Started Discuss these questions in small groups.

1. What are some ceremonies or rituals that you are familiar with?

2. What kinds of birthday celebrations have you been a part of? Do you know of any cultures that don't celebrate birthdays?

3. Is there any ceremony or ritual that people perform differently now from the way they performed it in the past? Explain.

2 Previewing the Reading Look over the reading and the photos on pages 221–224. Discuss the questions below with a partner.

1. What is the topic of the reading? What are the five subtopics?

2. Describe the photos. What is new or interesting to you in the photos?

3. Write six questions that you expect the reading to answer.

_____

_____

_____

_____

_____

3 Previewing Vocabulary Read the words and phrases below. Listen to the pronunciation. Put a check mark (✓) next to the words you don't know. Don't use a dictionary.

Nouns

- bride
- coffin
- coming-of-age
- cremation
- deceased
- delivery
- funerals
- groom
- guidance

- incorporation
- monks
- negotiations
- pregnancy
- proposal
- pyre
- rite of passage
- ritual
- scriptures

- taboos
- trousseau
- vision
- vision quest

Verbs

- chant
- regain
- vary

Adjectives

- indigenous
- nomadic
- previous

Expression

- ask for (a woman's) hand

4 Reading an Article As you read the following article, think about the questions that you wrote in Activity 2. Can you find the answers in the reading? Read the selection. Do not use a dictionary. Then do the exercises that follow the article.

Rites of Passage

A   Among many **indigenous** peoples of North America, a 16-year-old boy leaves his family and experiences a ritual in which he spends four days and nights alone in a small cave dug into the side of a mountain. He experiences cold, hunger, thirst, fear, and sleeplessness. He has with him several objects of symbolic value. One of these is a pipe. The belief is that the smoke from   5 the pipe goes up to the spirit world and allows power to come down. His hope is to have a **vision** in which he receives insight and **guidance** for his way in life. At the beginning of the ritual, he is a boy, with a boy's name. At the end, when he comes out of the cave, he is a man, with an adult name, and he knows what his livelihood will be. This ritual, called a **vision quest**,   10 is an example of a rite of passage. Rites of passage are not found only in indigenous cultures. They are universal, found in all cultures, and include certain birthdays, **coming-of-age** rituals, weddings, and **funerals**.

What Are Rites of Passage?

B   Anthropologists use the term *rite of passage* for a ceremony or **ritual** of transition that marks a person's change from one status or social   15 position to another. Although such rites differ in details, they share certain characteristics. All rites of passage include three stages: separation, transition, and **incorporation** of the person back into the society. In the first stage, the person is separated from his or her **previous** status. Sometimes in this stage, as in a vision quest, the person is *literally* and *physically* separated   20 from the community. In the transition stage, the person is in between—not in either status. In the last stage, the person rejoins the society, now with the new status.

Birth Rituals in Korea

C   Many cultures have a rite of passage that marks the birth of a baby. In Korean tradition, the rituals begin during the woman's **pregnancy**. Some   25 of these rituals are still practiced today, but some are not. There are food **taboos**—certain foods that pregnant women are not supposed to eat. These include hot and spicy foods and broken crackers or cookies. In the past, close to the time of birth, there were various symbolic actions that signified an easy **delivery** of the baby. For example, family members left doors open, and   30 did not repair rooms, doors, or fireplaces in the kitchen. Today, as in the past,

▲ The first birthday celebration for a Korean baby

there is special care to keep the mother and baby well after the birth. The mother traditionally eats seaweed soup, full of iron, to **regain** her strength. She is also not supposed to drink cold water for 21 days.

D　At the age of 100 days, there is a special ceremony. Family, friends, and neighbors gather to admire the baby, give thanks for the baby's health, and have a big meal. More important is the first birthday. At this time, the baby, dressed in a traditional outfit, is seated in front of a table with all kinds of objects on it. For example, they may include a bow and arrow (which represents the military), money (wealth), string (a long life), and a pencil and a book (knowledge). These days, people can add any object, such as a baseball, if they want their child to be a great baseball player. The parents encourage the baby to choose something. Everyone is very interested in which object the baby reaches for because the belief is that this object indicates something about the baby's future. Now the baby is truly a person, a member of the family and the community.

Islamic Weddings

E　A wedding in any culture is an important rite of passage. In Islam, the specific stages of a wedding ceremony may **vary** from country to country, but most share certain characteristics. Typical is the traditional wedding of the Bedouin—**nomadic** Arabs who move from place to place (although these days many are settling in urban areas). A Bedouin wedding can last up to a week and reflects the ancient Arab belief that marriage is not just a joining of two people; it is the joining of two families.

F　The first step in a Bedouin wedding is the **proposal**, in which the father of the **groom** (the man) and their close relatives visit the home of the **bride** (the woman) to **ask for**

▲ A Bedouin bride with henna

her hand in marriage. The next step involves **negotiations** between the two families and a marriage contract—a formal, legal agreement. The third step is the henna party, for just the bride and her female friends and relatives. At this party, there is song and dance, and the bride's hands and feet are exquisitely decorated with henna, a dark brown paste. The henna is more than just skin paint. It is associated with health, beauty, and luck. After this, the groom's relatives arrive at the bride's house. Men perform a special dance with swords while women admire the bride's **trousseau**—the personal objects that she will bring to her marriage such as clothing, gifts from the groom's family, and jewelry. The jewelry is usually large, made of silver and expensive stones, and decorated with calligraphy. In the fifth step, the men and women sit separately, and guests bring gifts. In the last step, as the bride enters her new home, she and her new husband meet for the first time. They are officially married. Actually, there is perhaps one more step. One week after the wedding, the bride visits her parents and brings them gifts. This is a symbol of her comfort in her new home.

Funerals in Thailand

G   A person's final passage is death. Every culture has rituals in which the person and his or her family make this transition. In Thailand, a Buddhist country, people believe that after death, the person is born again, in another body. Everything the person did in life—both good and bad—determines whether the next life will be a good one or not. Of course, family members and friends want to achieve a good rebirth for the **deceased**, and this is a major goal of a Thai funeral.

▲ Buddhist monks chanting in front of a funeral pyre

H   As a Thai person is dying, the family members encourage him or her to think about Buddhist **scriptures**—holy writing—or to repeat one of the names of the Buddha. Then, after the person dies, the family takes the deceased to the temple. They lay the body down, cover him or her, and place one hand outside of the blanket. The family and friends show respect by washing the hand of the deceased. Then they put the body in a **coffin**. People burn candles and sweet-smelling incense around the coffin, and Buddhist **monks** come to **chant**—recite prayers. In the next step, perhaps three days, one week, or 100 days later, friends, relatives, and monks take the coffin to the cemetery for the **cremation**, at which there is more chanting. The coffin is placed on a funeral **pyre**. At this point, people come up to

it with white paper flowers, candles, and incense. One by one, they light
the pyre, and the body is burned. It is believed that when the body still   120
exists, the spirit can benefit from the chanting; however, when the body is
cremated, the spirit is cut off from the world. After the cremation, people go
home. The family usually takes some of the ashes home, but some families
keep the ashes at the temple.

The Timelessness of Rites of Passage

The origin of such rites of passage is unclear. However, there is reason   125
to believe that such rites existed long before the beginning of history, before
there was any system of writing to record the rituals. In caves and on rock
walls all over the world, there are paintings from the Paleolithic Era (Old
Stone Age)—exquisite art that may have been part of the people's rituals.
In the graves of even these very ancient people, objects have been carefully   130
placed. Anthropologists believe that this may be evidence of early religion
and of the human need to mark the transitions from one stage to another in
their lives—a universal, timeless need.

After You Read

5 **Getting the Main Ideas** Fill in this chart with information from the reading
about four rites of passage. The first one is done for you as an example.

Rite of Passage	Previous Status	Transition	New Status
vision quest	a boy	4 days isolated in a cave, not a boy or a man	a man with an adult name

6 Checking Vocabulary Turn back to the vocabulary preview on page 220. Which words do you now know? Check them off (✓). With a partner, discuss what you think each word means. For words that you aren't sure of, look through the reading to find them in bold and try to guess their meaning.

7 Making Inferences Put a check mark next to each statement below that you can infer from the reading. Do not check the other statements, even if you think they are true. Then, after the checked statements, write the phrases from which you inferred the information.

1. _____ In a vision quest, a boy finds out about his future career from his vision.

    _____

    _____

2. _____ Korean parents might put a soccer ball in front of their one-year-old if they want him or her to be a great soccer player.

    _____

    _____

3. _____ The Bedouin marriage contract involves money.

    _____

    _____

4. _____ People who put objects in the graves of the dead may have religious beliefs.

    _____

    _____

FOCUS

Understanding Chronology

Time words show the relationship between events and their order in time. Here are just a few examples.

first	beginning	after that	after	last	the next step
second	next	then	at this point	finally	

---

8 Understanding Chronology Look back at Paragraph H on pages 223–224. Quickly look for time words; mark them as you find them. Then use them to help you number these steps in order from first to last.

1. _____ People take the coffin to the cemetery.

2. _____ Friends and family show respect by washing the hand of the dead person.

3. _____ Family members encourage the person to think religious thoughts.

4. _____ People light the funeral pyre, and the body is cremated.

5. _____ Monks and relatives chant at the temple.

9 Understanding Symbols Read the questions below. Turn back to the reading to find the answers. Look for words that indicate symbols.

1. In a vision quest, what does the smoke from the pipe symbolize?

2. In a Korean home, what are some things that people might do as a pregnant woman nears the time of delivery? List them. What do these actions symbolize?

3. In Bedouin culture, what does henna on a woman's hands symbolize?

10 Checking Your Understanding Turn back to Activity 2 on page 220 and answer the questions that you wrote.

11 Applying the Reading Choose one rite of passage from your culture (but not one that was included in the reading). You will tell a group of classmates about this rite. To prepare for this, think about what happens in the rite and fill in information in the graphic organizer below.

The Rite of Passage: _____

Previous Status	Transition	New Status

Are there symbols?   ☐ yes   ☐ no

What are the symbols?

Steps (Details)

_____   _____

_____   _____

_____

_____

New Days, New Ways: Changing Rites of Passage

Before You Read

1 **Identifying the Main Idea and Writing a Summary** For each paragraph that follows, practice what you have learned about finding the main idea and summarizing paragraphs. First, read each paragraph without using a dictionary. Mark the information in any way that helps you to understand it. (For example, you could highlight the main idea with one color and the supporting details with another.) Then write the main idea in one sentence. To summarize the paragraph, write the main idea and add the important details in as few words as possible. (You might need to write more than one sentence.) Paragraph A is done as an example.

New Days, New Ways: Changing Rites of Passage

Vision Quests for Everyone

A   For centuries, Native Americans have gone through vision quests in hopes of gaining guidance and direction. Several companies and organizations are now offering a similar experience for non-Indians. For a fee, anyone who is looking for a new direction in life can go to certain wilderness areas in Canada or the United States and go through such a ritual. The details 5 may vary from one organization to another, but in most cases, experts in psychology or Native American culture help to prepare the person in advance. This preparation usually lasts for several days and includes meditation, natural vegetarian food, lessons in the meaning of a vision quest and perhaps dream groups, in which the seeker of the vision discusses his 10 or her dreams with psychological analysts. As on a traditional vision quest, people on this new-age quest spend one to four days alone in the wilderness. However, a difference is that they might choose to sleep in a tent and to bring drinking water. Some Native Americans are angry that non-Indians are doing this. They see it as a fad and say that the quest is meaningless to a 15 person outside the culture, tradition, and religion.

Main idea: *Anyone can now experience a Native American vision quest, for a fee.*

Summary: *Although some Native Americans do not approve, several companies and organizations are offering non-Indians the opportunity (for a fee) to experience a vision quest that is similar to the traditional one.*

A New Emirati Wedding

B   In the United Arab Emirates, on the Arabian Peninsula, the traditional wedding seems to be changing, at least for some people. A typical Emirati

▲ Grooms at a mass wedding in the United Arab Emirates

wedding is extremely lavish—elegant, expensive, and huge. ²⁰ There might be 1,000 guests at the three-day celebration for the bride and groom. The groom has to pay these bills, and after such a wedding, the ²⁵ couple begins their marriage in terrible debt. Each wedding seems to be bigger than the one before it. Several years ago, the government decided ³⁰ that things were getting out of hand—out of control—so they started a Marriage Fund. This is money for young Emirati men who agree to marry ³⁵ Emirati women, not foreigners.

Many of these men agree to have a group celebration. At one such group celebration, at which the UAE president was the guest of honor, there were several of the components of a traditional wedding: a lavish feast of exquisite food and entertainment by Bedouin dancers waving their swords. ⁴⁰ The difference? There were 650 grooms. It was, one person pointed out, "a symbol of a new spirit of economy."

Main idea: _____

_____

_____

Summary: _____

_____

_____

Getting Married—Japanese Style?

C   In Japan, too, weddings are different these days. A popular wedding is a *seiyaku*, which means "sincere vow or promise." Although less than one percent of all Japanese are Christian, 80 percent choose this Western-style Christian wedding. It certainly *looks* like a Western wedding; the bride wears a white gown, for example, and the groom wears a tuxedo. It also closely follows all the steps in a Christian wedding: there is the processional (in which the bride walks down the center aisle of the church to join the groom at the front), hymns (religious songs), readings of Christian scriptures, the exchange of vows, and of course the wedding kiss. In fact, some people say that this new Japanese-Christian wedding is more traditional than most Christian weddings in the West, except for the fact that the couple is usually careful to choose a "lucky day" for the ceremony. So why do so many Japanese choose this style of wedding when the Japanese culture already has rich, beautiful marriage traditions? One answer may be that this is a trend, and the Japanese are somewhat famous for following new trends. Another reason may be that traditional Japanese weddings are even more expensive than those in the Western style.

▲ A Japanese *seiyaku:* more traditional than a Western wedding?

45

50

55

60

65

Main idea: _____

_____

Summary: _____

_____

_____

Weddings Anywhere, Any Way

D   While most Japanese weddings these days are in a traditional Western style, many couples in Western countries are looking for a *non*-Western wedding experience that expresses something of their personal interests. It is now possible to get married in a helicopter, on a ski slope, in the ocean (with dolphins, in Florida), in a hot-air balloon, or in a drive-through in Las Vegas (in which the couple stays in their car for the ceremony). For couples who

70

75

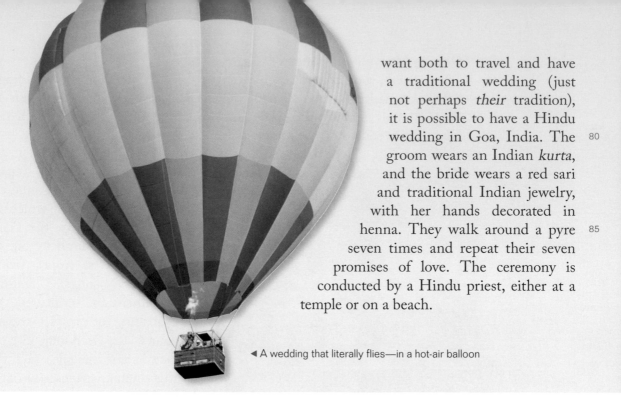

want both to travel and have a traditional wedding (just not perhaps *their* tradition), it is possible to have a Hindu wedding in Goa, India. The groom wears an Indian *kurta*, and the bride wears a red sari and traditional Indian jewelry, with her hands decorated in henna. They walk around a pyre seven times and repeat their seven promises of love. The ceremony is conducted by a Hindu priest, either at a temple or on a beach.

80

85

◀ A wedding that literally flies—in a hot-air balloon

Main idea: _____

_____

_____

Summary: _____

_____

_____

Unique Ways of "Moving On"

E   People are also designing unusual funerals. Several years ago, after the death of an American man who created a popular TV series, his body was cremated, and the ashes from this cremation were sent into space to spend eternity among the stars. In Britain, there are special funerals for people who love motorcycles; one company offers "slow, fast, and very fast funerals." In Malaysia, a group called "33 Taiping Music Band" plays music at funerals. They perform at Buddhist, Christian, or Hindu funerals. The lead singer, Chan Yoke Cheong, speaks fluent English, Cantonese, and Mandarin, so it is not surprising that he also sings in these languages. But what might be surprising is that he also perfectly sings hymns in Tamil—an Indian language he does not speak—at Hindu funerals. The band wears white shirts, black pants, ties, and large leather cowboy hats. Maybe the strangest recent funeral, however, was held in Pennsylvania, in the United States. James Henry Smith had been a huge fan of an American football team, the Pittsburgh Steelers. At his funeral, the guests walked into the funeral home to find Mr. Smith's body not in a coffin but instead in his favorite chair. The

90

95

100

105

deceased was sitting there, wearing the colors of the Steelers. On a small table next to the chair were a pack of cigarettes and a can of beer. In front of him, through the funeral, a TV played a video of a Steelers game. His friends and family knew that he would approve.

Main idea: _____
_____
_____

Summary: _____
_____
_____

Strategy

Identifying Opinions

It's important to be able to recognize the difference between facts and opinions. A fact can be checked and proven, even if you aren't sure if it is true or not. An opinion is an idea that people might disagree about. An opinion expresses a belief, idea, or feeling. One way to distinguish the two is to be aware of words that indicate an *opinion*. Some of these words are modals (*should, shouldn't, ought to*), but most are adjectives or adverbs.

Example

bad (-ly)	exquisite	good (well)	surprising
beautiful	favorite	horrible	too
brilliant	fun	interesting	wonderful (-ly)

Alternatively, instead of looking for specific words when you are trying to recognize opinions, you might try asking yourself, "Would some people disagree with this?" If your answer is *yes*, then it might be an opinion.

2 **Distinguishing Facts from Opinions** On the lines, write fact or opinion, according to what is stated or implied in the sentence.

1. _____ Non-Indians can go through a rite of passage similar to the vision quest of Native Americans.

2. _____ Non-Indians who go through a vision quest are not respectful of Native American culture.

3. _____ The government of the United Arab Emirates is trying to encourage unmarried Emirati men to marry Emirati women.

4. _____ Traditional Emirati weddings are too lavish.

5. _____ Traditional Japanese weddings are more beautiful than the new Western-style ones.

6. _____ A majority of Japanese couples choose a Western-style wedding.

7. _____ Many couples in Western countries are looking for a nontraditional wedding experience.

8. _____ It's very strange to get married in the ocean.

9. _____ Chan Yoke Cheong sings in perfect Tamil.

10. _____ People who don't approve of unusual funerals are too rigid.

 3 Discussing the Reading: Conducting a Survey You are going to interview the students in your class and ask for their opinions on weddings. Then record their answers on another piece of paper.

1. Before you begin, think about your own answers to the questions and write them in the chart below.

> Which do you prefer? (Choose *one*. Then follow the arrow to the next question.)

A. Traditional weddings

B. Nontraditional weddings

Why? What are your favorite parts of a traditional wedding?

What is your idea of a good nontraditional wedding? (What are the elements?)

2. After you have decided on your own answers, pick up your notebook and a pencil. Move around the room. Interview as many people as possible in the time that you have.

- Record how many people answer "traditional" and how many answer "nontraditional."
- For students who answer "traditional," ask them the question under A. Record their answers in note form.
- For students who answer "nontraditional," ask them the question under B. Record their answers in note form.

3. When you finish, come together as a class and discuss your results. Do more people prefer traditional or nontraditional weddings? Did any answers surprise you?

FOCUS

Summarizing a Whole Reading

So far in this book, you've written summaries of single paragraphs. Here are some suggestions for summarizing a longer piece.

- Begin by highlighting key parts of the original piece. Mark the main ideas with one color and important details with another.
- Make sure that you truly understand the original article. It's not possible to write a good summary of something that you don't understand.
- Choose the main idea of each section or paragraph to include in your summary. Also choose a few of the most important details.
- Group some ideas from several sections or paragraphs together in one sentence.
- Remember that *summarizing is not translation*. It's usually easier to write a good summary if you put the original aside and not look at it as you write.
- In writing a summary, use your own words. Do not simply copy from the original. To use your own words, follow these steps:
  - Change sentence structure whenever possible. For example, change the active voice to the passive voice or the passive voice to the active.
  - Use synonyms whenever possible.
  - Do not try to find synonyms for technical terms or for words for which there is no synonym.

4 Discussing the Reading Choose one of the two readings from this chapter: "Rites of Passage" (pages 221–224) or "New Days, New Ways: Changing Rites of Passage" (pages 227–231). Summarize it in one paragraph. When you finish, compare your summary to that of another student who has summarized the same reading.

5 Writing Your Own Ideas Choose one of these topics to write about.

- a traditional rite of passage in your culture
- a new or changing rite of passage in your culture
- your reaction to one of the rituals that you have read about
- your opinion of one of the nontraditional rituals that you have read about
- your idea of the perfect wedding (or funeral)

Write a one-paragraph letter to your teacher in which you explore your topic.

What is the main idea of your paragraph? _____

_____

_____

_____

Building Vocabulary and Study Skills

1 **Determining Categories** Circle the words that typically belong in each underlined category.

1. actions at funerals

   praying   chanting   dancing   smiling

2. people in religion

   priests   colleagues   monks   merchants

3. words that are associated with death

   trousseau   coffin   cremation   deceased

4. groups of people

   organization   tribe   community   society

5. expressions of emotion

   hug   cry   suppress   shout

6. rites of passage

   proposal   wedding   indigenous   coming-of-age

FOCUS

Analyzing Word Roots and Affixes

In Chapters 7 and 9 you learned about word roots and affixes. Here are more word roots, prefixes, and their meanings.

Prefix	Meaning
im-	in; not
pro-	before; forward

Word Root	Meaning
corp	body
dox	opinion, belief
gam	marriage
mort	death
ortho	straight; correct
scribe; script	writing
spir	breathe

2 Analyzing Word Roots and Prefixes Without using a dictionary, guess the meaning of each underlined word. Use the list of word roots and prefixes on the previous page and look back at the list in Chapter 9, page 213, for additional help.

1. The mortality rate is very high in that village.

   (A) birth
   (B) employment
   (C) marriage
   (D) divorce
   (E) death

2. He's in the hospital on a respirator.

   (A) strict diet
   (B) machine that pumps blood (like the heart does)
   (C) machine to help him breathe
   (D) special bed to help his back pain
   (E) machine that checks his temperature regularly

3. The physician studied the corpse.

   (A) dead body
   (B) new medical instrument
   (C) ceremony
   (D) medical text
   (E) evidence

4. People in that society believe in polygamy.

   (A) many gods
   (B) marriage
   (C) marriage to more than one person
   (D) the necessity of marrying someone from a different village
   (E) the economic benefits of globalization

5. Without the wedding ring, the ceremony couldn't proceed.

   (A) end
   (B) begin
   (C) go forward; continue
   (D) occur
   (E) be legal and official

6. It was an unorthodox ceremony.

   (A) not interesting or worth attention
   (B) not religious
   (C) not in a church
   (D) not straight
   (E) not according to accepted opinion

7. Their love was immortal.

   (A) never dying
   (B) beautiful
   (C) pure
   (D) inside marriage
   (E) not accepted by society

8. The ceremony was transcribed.

   (A) postponed
   (B) concluded
   (C) moved to another place
   (D) cancelled
   (E) written down

3 Focusing on Words from the Academic Word List Fill in the blanks with words from the Academic Word List in the box.

community	physically	status	vision
incorporation	previous	transition	

Anthropologists use the term *rite of passage* for a ceremony or ritual of _____ that marks a person's change from one
1
_____ or social position to another. Although such rites
2
differ in details, they share certain characteristics. All rites of passage include three stages: separation, transition, and _____ of
3
the person back into the society. In the first stage, the person is separated from his or her _____ status. Sometimes in this stage, as in
4
a _____ quest, the person is *literally* and _____
5   6
separated from the _____. In the transition stage, the person
7
is in between—not in either status. In the last stage, the person rejoins the society, now with the new status.

4 Searching the Internet Choose one of these rites of passage to research, or select your own. Search the Internet for sites that discuss nontraditional ways to conduct it. Tell your group about either the strangest or the most interesting way that you found.

- a wedding
- a funeral
- an engagement
- a vision quest
- other: _____

FOCUS

Topic-Sentence Patterns on the TOEFL® Internet-Based Test (iBT)

The reading "Rites of Passage" (pages 221–224) shows several interesting main-idea patterns. You can see that the main idea is not always stated in the first sentence of a paragraph.

For example, the main idea of Paragraph A in "Rites of Passage" is expressed at the end. Also, two sentences, not just one, form the main idea. Paragraph B has its main idea in a sentence in a familiar position, at the beginning. The main idea for Paragraph C can be found in the first two sentences of the paragraph.

1 Practice Read the following passage. Pay special attention to the main idea of each paragraph. Then do the exercise that follows.

Learning to Drive:
An American Rite of Passage

A   Every society has rites of passage that fit its culture. In hunter-gatherer societies, passing into adulthood often means going out to a hunting ground to prove one's strength and courage. In societies that value group cooperation over individual glory, the rite of passage may involve joining an organization like the army or a large company and adopting its discipline. American society is perfectly reflected in the rituals of learning to drive and getting one's license.

B   This observation is not just a joke, a way of laughing at America's car culture. Examine driving in relation to other well-known rites of passage. For one thing, most Americans learn how to drive at 15 or 16, about the age for ritually entering adulthood in other cultures. For another, objects that are significant in the culture, such as paperwork and money, are a crucial part of the rite. Other cultures might ritually use rice, water, or clothing instead. Also the values of American culture—such as mobility, independence, and individual responsibility—can be pursued through this rite. The values of other cultures (group loyalty, physical endurance, religious devotion, etc.) are supported by their own rites of passage.

C   Although a few Americans never learn to drive or learn how only in their later years, the vast majority learn in their mid-teens. The timing of the ritual has great significance. Most young Americans have, by this time, gone through puberty (the changes in their body chemistry that make them adults). Most 15-year-olds are tall enough to see clearly from the driver's seat and strong enough to turn a steering wheel. They also typically have enough coordination to operate windshield wipers, headlights, turn signals, and a car radio while safely steering. At earlier ages, they might not have been physically able to handle such tasks.

D   Also at this time, they are ready to move slowly from their homes and schools toward the wider world. Both family and school prepare teenagers for this transition. Many American parents take their children to an empty parking lot between the ages of 12 to 15 in order to let them safely get used to the layout and handling of a car. The parent sits in the passenger seat and tries not to show fear as the child learns how to work the accelerator pedal, the brakes, and other basic controls. The child is then put into the school's hands. Public high schools usually offer "driver's ed" classes to 15-year-olds. The familiar school environment comforts them as they learn about the world and its very serious driving requirements.

E   The ultimate goal for each driving student involves certification from the state that one is qualified to drive. This comes in the form of a temporary driver's permit, then a full driver's license, issued by the state in which the student lives. American society values such state-issued permits and respects the processes for obtaining them. Almost any profession, from hair-dressing to hotel operation to medicine, involves them. Learning to drive is the perfect introduction to this bureaucratic society. Insurance applications, approval slips, score sheets for driving tests—all of these are good preparation for a lifetime of petitioning the state and large companies for permission or fair treatment.

F   America's cultural preoccupation with money is also addressed in the ritual. For perhaps the first time in his or her life, a student faces significant short- and long-term expenses. Most middle-class Americans require a teenager to pay at least part of the cost of driving a car. Parents may help pay for the car itself, or the insurance, but teenagers usually have to buy their own gas and pay their own tickets if they have an encounter with the police. Teenagers who may have thought of money as a toy now see it as necessary to function in their daily lives. Indeed, a teenager may be motivated to get his or her first part-time job in order to pay the costs of driving a car.

G   A diverse place like the United States has several value systems operating alongside each other. It is fair to say, however, that some values are almost universal among Americans. One of these is mobility, the freedom to go where you want, when you want. Another is independence, the freedom to act as you see fit without needing help from any authority. Still another is personal responsibility, the sense that you take the credit or blame for your own successes or your own mistakes. Being a driver brings each of these deep-seated values into play.

H   Nothing promotes mobility like having a car and the fuel to run it. Teenagers who were used to staying within a mile or two of home gain the ability to explore an entire city. They usually want to do so without having to explain themselves to their parents, so they independently learn directions, practice safe-driving techniques, and budget their money for travel. Failure to do so will require them to ask their parents for help, which they do not want to do. And driving is serious, literally a matter of life and death. Even though teenagers are often not as careful as they ought to be, they usually recognize that they are responsible for the lives and safety of themselves and others while they are on the road. This represents a true passage from the world of a child into that of an adult.

2 Identifying the Main Idea For each paragraph, write the main idea on the lines below. If a paragraph does not have its own topic sentence, write the main idea in your own words. Then compare your answers with those of one or two other students. There may be some disagreements about answers because different students will analyze the reading in different ways.

1. Paragraph A _____

_____

2. Paragraph B _____

_____

3. Paragraph C _____

_____

4. Paragraph D _____

_____

5. Paragraph E _____

_____

6. Paragraph F _____

_____

7. Paragraph G _____

_____

8. Paragraph H _____

_____

Self-Assessment Log

Read the lists below. Check (✓) the strategies and vocabulary that you learned in this chapter. Look through the chapter or ask your instructor about the strategies and words that you do not understand.

Reading and Vocabulary-Building Strategies

☐ Getting the main ideas
☐ Making inferences
☐ Understanding chronology
☐ Understanding symbols

☐ Applying the reading
☐ Distinguishing facts from opinions
☐ Summarizing an entire reading
☐ Analyzing word roots and affixes

Target Vocabulary

Nouns

▪ bride
▪ coffin
▪ coming-of-age
▪ community*
▪ cremation
▪ deceased
▪ delivery
▪ funerals
▪ groom
▪ guidance

▪ incorporation*
▪ monks
▪ negotiations
▪ pregnancy
▪ proposal
▪ pyre
▪ rite of passage
▪ ritual
▪ scriptures
▪ status*

▪ taboos
▪ transition*
▪ trousseau
▪ vision*
▪ vision quest

Verbs

▪ chant
▪ regain
▪ vary*

Adjectives

▪ indigenous
▪ nomadic
▪ previous*

Adverb

▪ physically*

Expression

▪ ask for
  (a woman's) hand

* These words are from the Academic Word List. For more information on this list, see www.victoria.ac.nz/lals/resources/academicwordlist/.

Vocabulary Index

Chapter 1

achieve
assignments*
challenging*
compare
competitive
credits*
curriculum
determine
discipline
drawback
effort
entire
exhaustion
finally*
global*
identical*
in contrast to
isolated*
obvious*
one-size-fits-all
on the one hand
on the other hand
rankings
reflect
required*
resources*
schedule*
secondary school
separate
status*
the best and the brightest
track
universal
values

Chapter 2

access*
affluent
agricultural operation
commute
creative*
crops
crowd
cultivate
developing countries
efficiently
environment*
established*

focus*
global*
gridlock
mass transit
pedestrian zone
pollution
predict*
priorities*
produce
recycling plant
residents*
solve
transportation*
trash
urban dwellers
worsening

Chapter 3

access*
anonymous
capacity*
character
collateral
common knowledge
consume*
consumer*
economy*
eradication
fund*
grants*
identical*
items*
invest*
literacy
logic*
microlending
peer pressure
poverty
requirement*
social
subsidiary*
target*
took (take) the initiative
worthless

Chapter 4

areas*
background
benefits*
career counselors
cell phones
computer*
construction
create*
distract
drawback
dream job
economy*
employment agency
enormous*
flexible*
globalization*
identity*
job hopping
job security
keep up with
labor*
leisure
livelihood
manufacturing jobs
on the move
outsourcing
overwork
passionate
pleasure
posts
rigid*
secure*
self-confidence
stress*
telecommuting
temporary*
traditionally*
upgrade
vary*
workaholism
workforce
worldwide

*These words are from the Academic Word List. For more information on this list, see http://www.victoria.ac.nz/lals/resources/academicwordlist/

Chapter 5

actually
areas*
balance
catch on
complex*
components*
concept*
constitution*
economic*
enthusiastically
environment*
essence
findings
gap
income*
life expectancy
measure
mental*
polls
psychological*
reasonable
researchers*
solidarity
sum total
trend*
well-being

Chapter 6

access*
approximately*
areas*
benefit*
chemicals*
concept*
consumer*
contribute*
endangered
extinction
fuel
globalization*
in turn
livestock
nutrients
obstacle
processed*
region*
shift*
staples
traditional*

Chapter 7

acquire*
brain
capacity*
chatter
claims
coin
communication*
creatures
degree
echo/echoes
feeds
focusing*
gender*
gestures
glue
grin
head (of something)
head back
identical*
journal*
lexigrams
mammals
organs
percent*
picked up
pod
prey
primates
reassure
research*
shedding light on
species
structures*
subjects
swagger
upright
vocalize
wagging

*These words are from the Academic Word List. For more information on this list, see http://www.victoria.ac.nz/lals/resources/academicwordlist/

Chapter 8

archaeologists
architecture
armor
called*
calligraphy
caravan
caves
cosmetics
culture*
decorated
depict
destination
documents*
exquisite
fabric
fertility
flower
found*
frescoes
holy
mausoleums
merchants
mosques
network
oasis
pitcher
project*
region*
routes
significant*
silk
spices
spread
statues
technology*
to this end
traditional*
vast

Chapter 9

adults*
blood vessels
cognitive
colleagues*
evidence*
exposed*
going into training
hemispheres
imply*
insights*
institute*
intelligence*
intuition
involved*
logic*
logical*
maturation*
mature*
maturity*
memory
mental*
neuroscientists
origin
precise*
repressed
researchers*
rotate
toxins
traditional*
wiring

Chapter 10

ask for (a woman's hand)
bride
chant
coffin
coming-of-age
community*
cremation
deceased
delivery
funerals
groom
guidance
incorporation*
indigenous
monks
negotiations
nomadic
physically*
pregnancy
previous*
proposal
pyre
regain
rite of passage
ritual
scriptures
status*
taboos
transition*
trousseau
vary*
vision*
vision quest

*These words are from the Academic Word List. For more information on this list, see http://www.victoria.ac.nz/lals/resources/academicwordlist/

Skills Index